THE FOUR SEASONS
A History of America's Premier Restaurant

JOHN MARIANI *with* ALEX VON BIDDER

THE FOUR SEASONS

A History of America's Premier Restaurant

SMITHMARK

With this history I honor the men and
women whose dreams, aspirations, and
dedicated work created The Four
Seasons Restaurant. Forty
years later their dreams live on.

— AVB

For Galina

— JM

Text copyright © 1999 by John Mariani
Recipes copyright © 1999 by The Four Seasons

This edition published in 1999 by SMITHMARK Publishers,
a division of U.S. Media Holdings, Inc.,
115 West 18th Street, New York, NY 10011; 212-519-1300.

SMITHMARK books are available for bulk purchase for sales promotion
and premium use. For details write or call the manager of special sales,
SMITHMARK Publishers, 115 West 18th Street, New York, NY 10011.

ISBN: 0-7651-1709-6

Printed in the U.S.A.

10 9 8 7 6 5 4 3 2 1

Library of Congress Cataloging-in-Publication Data

Mariani, John F.
   The Four Seasons: a history of America's premier restaurant /
John Mariani with Alex Von Bidder. —[Updated ed.]
      p. cm.
   ISBN 0-7651-1709-6
   1 Four Seasons (Restaurant)—History. I. Von Bidder, Alex.
II. Title.
TX945.5.F74M37 1999
647.95747'1—dc21
                                    99-24752
                              CIP

contents

God, it's cold, this Tuesday, January 4, 1994, the first real working day of the new year, and New York City is still snowbound. No one major has died. The Mayor is too new to be criticized, so his precocious young son is the target of choice. The Dow spends all morning pushing just a few points to 3760 and most people do not feel sorry for Disney Chairman's Michael Eisner's forfeiture (due to EuroDisney's woes) of his annual $7 million-plus bonus. But, then again, most people are not lunching at The Four Seasons Grill Room this Tuesday, either.

Inside the Four Seasons restaurant—the Grill Room, not the Pool Room; lunch, not dinner—such things as billion-dollar gambles, takeovers, new alliances, old betrayals, and even the taketh away of a $7 million bonus are not only experienced, but expected, tolerated and mourned. An awesome foursome sits in the middle of the room, made up of QVC's Barry Diller (flushed with a just-bid-for-Paramount glow) and billionaire financier Revlon Chairman Ron Perelman (flushed with a just-divorced glow), flanked by Revlonites Howard Gittis and Donald Drapkin. They are today's stars at the plushest lunch in town—a human centerpiece—and practically everybody manages to say hello, salute them, or at least surreptitiously steal a look.

The Grill Room, a.k.a. the Bar Room, at its classic noon best is not so much a restaurant as it is a community. This huge room, 20 feet high, tucked into the Seagram Building on Park Avenue, holds twenty-one tables on the main floor and eleven on the bal-

The Grill Room's "Power Lunch" in the 1970s.

Notes on Power-Lunching at "The Grill"

by Joni Evans

Joni Evans started her career in book publishing as a manuscript reader at William Morrow. She moved to Simon & Schuster, began eating lunch at The Four Seasons, and rose to the position of publisher of Simon & Schuster's trade division. She subsequently served as publisher of Random House's trade division and of Turtle Bay, her own imprint at Random House. She is now a literary agent at William Morris and she continues to lunch at The Four Seasons.

I once took the president of a fashion company to the Grill Room for lunch. He was obviously impressed but tried to act as if it was not a big deal for him to eat there. As we sat down and had an opening drink he told me how he couldn't understand why people got so "freaked out" about going to the Grill Room and seeing the rich and powerful. After all, he said, it was just lunch.

I said I agreed with him but some people get excited about sitting next to Henry Kissinger, at which point his eyes grew wide as he jumped up and looked around excitedly and exclaimed, "Where is he!?!" I said I was only using that as an example. He sat back down. Just then Henry Kissinger did

cony overlooking it. It is filled to its eighty-five-person capacity. That's the usual part. The unusual part, although much has been written about The Grill's clubby, high-profile guests, is that even the luminaries of The Four Seasons have rarely seen a cast like this one. The assemblage, all decked out sans boots (presumably they either have their own drivers or simply don't care that their Prada shoes are marinating in salted snow), is alive and abuzz. What we have here is a full military alert, a top brass only, an A-List, a never-before-in-the-same-room-at-the-same-time crowd. The sparks, the sheer excitement in the room is so charged you can practically taste it with your crabcakes.

The five main crescent-shaped banquettes (dubbed America's power tables) are fully occupied. Of course, some of the regulars are absent. Simon & Schuster's editor in chief/author Michael Korda—a Grill Room fixture since the day the Forum of the Twelve Caesars closed—is vacationing in his Santa Fe home; Philip Johnson, who designed the restaurant's understatedly spectacular interior (if a restaurant that sports French walnut walls, a Richard Lippold suspended sculpture of anodized metal rods, and aluminum, brass, and copper chains fashioned as window jalousies can be called understated), is somewhere else, perhaps lunching in another architect's dining room. John Loeb Sr., of the fabled "our crowd" and investment banker family (not to be confused with John Loeb Jr., who prefers the more formal Pool Room), is wintering in his Palm Beach home. In their stead—more accurately, in their booths—are Sandy Weill, Chairman and C.E.O. of Primerica Corp., with Frank Zarb, Vice Chairman of the Travelers Inc.; the *New Yorker*'s high priestess Tina Brown with photographer/chronicler Dick Avedon; Dr. Henry Kissinger, whose offices are just across the street in the First Boston Building, with a gentleman who seems unable to get off his cellular phone; the President of Johnnie Agnelli's investment bank, IFINT, Andrea Botta, with Gian Luigi Gabetti, Vice Chairman of Fiat; and communications billionaire Si Newhouse, at his usual corner table with his usual lunching pals, Steve Newhouse, his one-day-to-inherit-some-of-it nephew (who recently married at The Four Seasons in an evening ceremony that closed the restaurant's doors), and current C.E.O. of Random House Alberto Vitale, who has dined at The Four Seasons ever since he was C.E.O. of Doubleday.

The sheer number of Random House power publishers/Condé Nast power editors here today is overwhelming; many have pondered why Mr. Newhouse, C.E.O. of both enterprises, hasn't just bought the place to cut down on his lunch bills. There is Betty Prashker, editor in chief of Crown, a Four Seasoner for some twenty years, sitting at her usual table with a Crown author. *Parade* editor James Brady (his editor in chief, Walter Anderson, is also lunching here) sits in his favorite side booth. Random House publisher Harry Evans, cellular phone in hand, is with Alan Brien, British critic and novelist; Sandy Golinkin, publisher of *Allure* magazine, is lunching with Joe Armstrong, ex-publisher of *New York* magazine and adviser to the great. Shirley Lord, beauty director at *Vogue,* lunches with Deborah Santemma of Clairol. Ann Fuchs, publisher of *Vogue,* sits with Sherry Wilson Grey, head of marketing for Saks Fifth Avenue.

The megamix is complicated. The tycoons come in many shades: litigators, advertising executives, politicians, public relations spin masters, stock market gurus, editors in chief, fashion designers. Real estate mogul Bernie Mendek lunches with Warner LeRoy, the originator of Maxwell's Plum and reinventor of Tavern on the Green. These are big men: Mendek is huge in real estate and LeRoy is just big. While Mort Zuckerman is absent (Aspening? East Hamptoning?) and Lew and Jack and Billy Rudin are probably out buying the small part of Manhattan they don't already own (the Rudin real estate clan spans two generations that usually expands to two tables per lunch), other barons take up the slack. Most notably, David Solomon, the '80s developer who, with his wife, Jean, built a real estate empire, lunches this day with Eric Levin, the attorney to Sir James Goldsmith. Over in the corner Arne Glimcher, the art dealer, and Jerry Speyer, the real estate developer, are lunching with attorney and deal-maker Joel Ehrenkranz.

Perhaps the key to the Grill Room's soul is its mix of tycoons and moguls with artists and writers, both treated with equal appreciation by the management. The key here is that they *are* equal. Pulitzer Prize-winning playwright Wendy Wasserstein, who set a scene in her play *Isn't It Romantic?* in The Four Seasons, is lunching with her brother, Bruce, the financial takeover whiz from Wasserstein-Parella (having recently lost Parella) and is joined by Michiko Kakutani, senior reviewer for the book section of the *New York Times.*

Incestuous? In addition to the Siblings Wasserstein and the Newhouse uncle-nephew team, here is Pete Peterson, chairman of the prestigious Blackstone investment firm, with his daughter, Holly, of TV's *Prime Time Live.* It is not unusual to find husband-and-wife power couples eating together, or, at least at different tables at the same time. Here is advertising

indeed walk in and sit down. I said, "I hate to tell you this, but Henry Kissinger really is here now." He looked at me and said, "Nice try!" He spent the rest of the lunch peeking over his shoulder while continuing to act as casual as possible.

—Jack Kliger, Publisher, *Glamour* magazine

Critics of my writing on the problem of America's deficit spending have found the Achilles' heel of my argument: When asked how I, a constant critic of America's excessive consumption spending, can eat at The Four Seasons so regularly, I can make no rational answer other than "it feels so good."

—Peter G. Peterson, Chairman, The Blackstone Group

Tom Margittai (left) and Paul Kovi, owners of The Four Seasons.

whiz/author/restaurateur/merchant Jerry Della Femina with his well-known wife, Judith Licht. Harry Evans is sitting just across the room from wifey, Tina Brown. Bill Steinberg (owner of Tradewell, the barter company) dines with his wife, Gracie.

Perhaps the majority of the lunch crowd first came to the restaurant because of its two maverick Hungarian owners: Tom Margittai (off to a three-month vacation in Costa Rica) and Paul Kovi, his turn at home, hosting the elegant Pool Room. It is these two sophisticated talents who first knew to provide the loving care that set this restaurant apart and makes it the club that it is. They have been known to check newspapers for mention of their clients each morning; they are familiar with which guest prefers gravlax or is restricted from salt, they know the names of secretaries, families, even lovers, and are ultimately discreet. They would no sooner seat divorcing couples near each other than they would put their respective lawyers on the same side of the room.

Not so discreet, but equally charming, is the new guard. There is Julian, the Lucca-born Giuliano Niccolini, who after running the Grill Room for ten years is now the restaurant's manager, as well as overseer of its impressive wine cellar. Julian's casual-to-the-point-of-danger manner, smooth on-the-cusp-of-cunning intelligence, and total competence keep this high-powered crowd fueled with food and gossip. Just a few days ago, he handed the cellular phone to Nick Dunne, with the words: "The Menendez brothers are on the line for you." Alex von Bidder, Zurich-born of a Prussian family, is the tamer and more levelheaded general manager. He has an "I've seen it all and don't worry, I know just how to handle it" look about him. To appreciate the difference between these two heirs apparent, when Julian is asked about two Scarsdale-ish ladies—the only civilians in the room—occupying a smoking table (in fact, it is *GQ* magazine's editor Art Cooper's usual smoking-permitted table), he answers that this is Ruth Reichl, the new and terrifying restaurant critic for the *New York Times,* with a guest. Alex is the one who assures us that these two ladies are from Dubuque, not the *New York Times.* They happened to be turned away from the booked Pool Room only to walk into the Grill at the right time.

Taking this all in, Trideep Bose, the new Grill Room manager, smiles

Restaurant managers Julian Niccolini (left) and Alex von Bidder.

enigmatically. Trideep, a native of India who came to The Four Seasons by way of New Delhi's Hotel Maurya Sheraton and New York's Arcadia Restaurant and Safari Grill, exudes an effortless, and much appreciated, calm over the proceedings.

And everyone here seems to know everyone here. While table hopping is not tolerated (except on the route out or in, one must follow a straight path), a nod across the room can mean "Congratulations on the deal" or "Why haven't you called me?" or "Do you have the information I need? I'll call you later." Here just being seen is its own reward. Who is lunching with whom is as meaningful as an entire Liz Smith column (a job hire, an impending merger, a love affair). Everything is displayed, nothing is overlooked, all digested with as much ease as the appallingly expensive baked potato with Tuscan olive oil.

There are those moguls who prefer the balcony and rumor has it that to these upstairs perches, where the view is better, the conversations drift up like Sandy Weill's cigar smoke. Edgar Bronfman Jr. has his usual table on the balcony under the theory that the power is where he sits. Period. Today, his table is occupied by President Jack Cooper and a fellow Seagramite, and speculation runs amok as the room wonders if they—eyeing the antics of Mr. Diller below—are plotting their own full Time-Warner takeover. While entertainment lawyer Robert Montgomery is missing from his usual upstairs perch, Paul Weiss/Rifkin/Garrison's chief litigator, Arthur Liman, is the guest of the corporate takeover spinmaster Gershon Kekst. John Mack Carter, king of *Good Housekeeping,* lunches with Annemarie Iverson. Advertising mogul Charlie Goldschmidt, head of Lawrence, Charles and Free, is up there, too. If this is Siberia, who wouldn't enjoy the exile?

Perhaps the largest table in the house is presided over by Jimmy Finklestein, publisher of the *New York Law Journal.* He is hosting five advertisers, regaling them with stories about Revlon's legendary founder Charlie (Fire and Ice) Revson. Jimmy's family are also Four Seasons regulars. While his father, Jerry Finklestein, enjoys the Pool Room, his brother, former Borough President of Manhattan and candidate for mayor Andrew What-ever-happened-to-the-Finkle?-Stein is a frequent Griller.

Investment bankers are well represented. Steve Schwartzmann of the Blackstone Group, Steve Neren of the private investment firm of SRG, and Paul Schiverick with Mike Messner discuss their future holdings. Bernard Schwartz and Bernard Hodes (head of Loral) talk guided missiles.

Writer-director Nora Ephron (here with von Bidder) was one of the first to bring literary personalities to dine at The Four Seasons.

As blasé and unfazed by the sight of celebrities as the Grill Room regulars pretended to be, there was a dead silence in the room the first time Jacqueline Onassis walked in. She requested a table with her back to the window and sat down, and only then did conversation resume among the rich and powerful.

The powerful women of The Four Seasons have a long tradition here. When the Grill was first conceived, Margittai and Kovi pledged their allegiance to three goals: one, clubbishness; two, simple cuisine with unobtrusive service; and three, a haven for successful women. Lillian Hellman often lunched with Nora Ephron or her agent, Don Congdon, or her lawyer, Ephraim London, back in the days when smoking wasn't segregated or even mentioned. Just a few days ago, Jackie Onassis sat with Joan Ganz Cooney, the founder of Children's Television Workshop. Linda Wachner, C.E.O. of Warnaco and the only woman to head a Fortune 500 company, lunched with white-collar-crime litigator Stanley Arkin, and Mrs. Vincent Astor flirted with talk-show host Charlie Rose.

The genealogy of The Four Seasons is labyrinthine. Si Newhouse came because Condé Nast's creative director, Alex Liberman, came because Leo Lerman, *Vogue's* editor at large, not only came but raved about the food in the magazine. Walter Anderson, editor in chief of *Parade,* came because his friend and Santa Fe neighbor John Ehrlichman came; John Ehrlichman came because of his literary agent, Mort Janklow; Harry Evans came because his one-time boss (Atlantic Monthly Press owner and real estate baron) Mort Zuckerman came. Betty Prashker came because her author Lois Wyse came. Lois Wyse came because a fellow advertising guru, George Lois, came (and came so much that he created a number of memorable campaigns for the restaurant). Dr. Kissinger came because his literary agent, Marvin Josephson, came. Marvin Josephson came because his former colleague Lynn Nesbit came. Lynn Nesbit came because her client Michael Korda came. And so it goes.

The genealogy of defections is also legend. The nearby "21" Club had only to close its doors for a few months to lose Felix Rohatyn and Herb Seigal forever. The genealogy of lunching spouses is another infinite roster: Mrs. Leon Hess, Mrs. Bob Tisch, Mrs. John Veronis, Mrs. Carl Spielvogel (a.k.a. author Barbaralee Diamondstein), Mrs. Felix Rohatyn—the list is as long as the wives are powerful.

On this Tuesday, it is suddenly 2:00 P.M. and, just as suddenly, the Grill Room crowd is on its feet. This afternoon's conference call, boardroom meeting, interview, or press conference are all safely scheduled for 2:15, for the service in the Grill Room knows never to dawdle. House charge accounts are so commonplace that most of the guests have never bothered to signal for—much less sign for—their bills. At 2:10 P.M. all that is left of January 4th's lunch crowd is the faint whiff of power, still steaming long after the abandoned cups of double espresso have cooled.

Introduction

One of the first things that strikes people when they go to The Four Seasons for the first time is how quiet the dining rooms are. Even with its high ceilings and hard wood surfaces, the Grill Room seems particularly tranquil as guests are greeted and seated at the black leather banquettes and chairs, then served by a staff that seem to glide, rather than stride, through their ministrations. In the Pool Room, the water in the pool babbles soothingly like a mountain brook. Here men and women are regaling themselves, clinking glasses, laughing and carrying on quite the same as in any other restaurant in New York. Yet there is a composure about The Four Seasons found nowhere in the city.

Not far away at La Grenouille, the fashion crowd from *Women's Wear Daily* sits elbow to elbow and causes the air to ring with gossip. At Le Cirque an international assemblage of society figures and visiting dignitaries throws off enough exuberant energy and light to power the streetlamps along Park Avenue. And at the "21" Club the Bar Room is cheek by jowl with red-faced men and taut-faced women trying to be heard above the din.

Yet despite its seating more people than those three restaurants combined, The Four Seasons is an oasis of calm and discretion. It's part of the magic of the place, an acoustical trick built into the restaurant by master designers and craftsmen back when it opened in 1959. Actually, The Four Seasons is neither hushed nor stifled when customers dine there: there is in fact a hum of activity and the sound of people having a very good time. The marble pool actually throws off pacifying white noise that over-

The flick of a switch at the maître d's desk signifies when and where a guest will sit.

lays the other sounds in the room, and in the Grill the rippling metal curtains, thick carpets, and soft leather absorb whatever harsh sounds are emitted from tables set deliberately wide apart from one another—a profligate waste of expensive New York real estate space.

Go beyond the wide, swinging doors to the kitchen and you'll hear the same intense decibel level you'll find anywhere else—the crash of dishes, the mind-bending whir of exhaust fans, the shouts of waiters barking orders, and the bang-bang-bang of cooks slamming saucepans onto the stove and platters onto the heated metal counter for pickup. As in every kitchen, there are fires flaring up from the grill, captains stealing a cigarette in the corner, chefs expediting orders at the top of their lungs, and the heat, the heat, the heat.

Yet outside the controlled chaos of the kitchen, all is calm and still. The cacophony of life is muted, allowing people to converse and to bask in the warm light that filters through the twenty-foot windows and metal link curtains. Even at night the light at The Four Seasons is almost palpable. The pale blue-green of the pool reflects upward and softens shadows throughout the room, while from above recessed ceiling lights cast a mellow gray-gold glow on the tables, which are further illuminated by small, flickering votive candles. In such a light every complexion looks flawless, every woman attractive.

It is certainly true that many people find such an unusual atmosphere somewhat cold, almost forbidding. And it is also true that it took many years to find the exact balance of professionalism and intimacy to make the service here unique in New York and to attract people who give the room its character. Indeed, the story of The Four Seasons is as much a history of New York in the second half of the twentieth century as it is of a very special restaurant.

As New York emerged as the most powerful and important city in the world in the postwar era, New Yorkers began to forge a new urban sensibility that combined a real appetite for sophistication with a kind of brash giddiness at finding themselves the center of the world's attention. Like Molière's bourgeois gentleman, New Yorkers woke up one morning and discovered they were speaking prose!

For every refinement of taste and manners—however prosaic it might have been—New Yorkers of that period maintained a corresponding recklessness and love of the outlandish that manifested itself most obviously in the city's restaurants. No organization understood this better than Restaurant Associates, a gaggle of young, enthusiastic men who produced some of the grandest and some of the most contrived restaurants of the era, including the Hawaiian Room, the Forum of the Twelve Caesars, and La Fonda del Sol. Restaurant Associates executives like Jerry Brody and Joe Baum were businessmen first and iconoclasts second, determined to break free from the stodgy strictures of traditional restaurant design, menus, and service, and to have a great deal of exhausting fun doing it. The Four Seasons was to prove their most revolutionary idea.

Just as Mies van der Rohe's remarkable Seagram Building changed forever the face of New York architecture, so, too, did Restaurant Associates' opening of The Four Seasons within its elegant bronze framework change forever the way Americans looked at restaurants. The Four Seasons was not just a restaurant fit for the Seagram Building; it was a restaurant that signaled the increasing appreciation on the part of New Yorkers—and Americans in general—of the pleasures and importance of dining out.

One might almost date the American restaurant industry "B.F.S." (Before The Four Seasons) and "A.F.S." (After The Four Seasons). For even though The Four Seasons itself for many years was a failure at the bottom line, it was from the day it opened in July 1959 recognized as a radical, significant, and very beautiful departure from everything that had come before it.

It was, in a word, daunting. Everything had been envisioned, designed, cast, and calibrated to be the ultimate in modern design, cuisine, and service, from the ashtrays right up to the air-conditioning. There would be no compromises on silverware, ingredients, greenery, staffing, or the accommodation of customers' wishes. Here was a restaurant whose interior was actually *landscaped,* not just set with flowers and potted plants. Here was a restaurant where the sacrosanct industry standard for the height of a table from the floor was revised, a restaurant in which the designers installed a pool where any sensible restaurateur would have put six more tables, a restaurant whose showcasing of certain artwork granted the artists a wider public acceptance than at any museum in New York.

The Pool Room at lunch.

Saying that something is "ahead of its time" is often just another way of saying something was a flop. Nor does the mere endurance of The Four Seasons over more than three decades mean much in the face of New York institutions as disparate and venerable as Gallagher's Steak House, which started as a speakeasy back in 1927, the cavernous Grand Central Oyster Bar, opened in 1912, or The Old Homestead, which has been serving New Yorkers since 1868. That The Four Seasons's interior has remained almost unchanged for more than thirty years and has acquired rare landmark status is more a testament to the original conceptualizers than to those who tried merely to keep it afloat.

Though clearly a succès d'estime from the day it opened, The Four Seasons floundered for nearly two decades before its real value to New Yorkers became clear. For if any restaurant can be called a conceptual work of art, it is certainly The Four Seasons, not only because its vision was unlike anything known at the time of its opening, but also because it has continued to evolve and to mirror the changes in New York society by playing host to the most productive members of that society, from politicians and power brokers to the men and women who run the media and the arts. Much more so than the ill-named Forum of the Twelve Caesars, The Four Seasons came to function as a place where brilliant men and women exchanged ideas that would maintain New York's eminence as a crucible of modernism, a luminous city bursting with novel concepts and high standards.

At the tables of The Four Seasons plots were hatched, titanic projects were started or killed, and New York itself was either brought back from the brink of bankruptcy or plunged into it. By the 1980s, more than any other restaurant, it became the city's symbol of power and hubris, a place where men and women measured their mettle, where careers were made or lost over lunch. Even on that day in October 1987 when the stock market crashed, The Four Seasons was where many of the major players came to assure themselves that there was still one oasis of calm composure and civilized behavior amid the terrible hysteria outside. A banquette in the Grill Room seemed a cushion against pandemonium.

Even on that day it was quiet at The Four Seasons. Some might say it was somber or stunned silence. But there, at the top of the stairway, beneath the Picasso curtain and the trembling metal curtains, everyone carried on with a genteel grace that helped restore some needed perspective on the world. The pool continued to babble, wine was quietly poured into thin glassware, the dessert cart was wheeled smoothly across the carpet, and all was as one wished it to be.

Yet the strength of The Four Seasons is not about unchanging, immutable stasis. It is quite the opposite. Its strength has always been its ability to adapt and lead, to change and modify in tune with the fickle way New York vibrates. This is a story of visionaries and scalawags, promoters and self-servers, profligates and penny-pinchers, egos and ids. The best of them contributed mightily to make The Four Seasons a microcosm of New York's grandeur. Then again, as with everything else in New York, the worst of them did, too.

John Mariani

THE FOUR SEASONS

In one way or another, all great ideas start with a hole in the ground.

In the case of The Four Seasons restaurant, that hole was on the first floor of a controversial monolithic brown-black box called the Seagram Building on New York's Park Avenue and Fifty-second Street.

The Seagram Building had itself quite spectacularly filled a hole left by the Montana, a posh 1910 apartment building of a kind that once lined the avenue north of Grand Central Terminal. But the idea that this odd glass-faced "cereal box" would someday be hailed as a masterpiece of postwar International Style was hardly evident to those who watched it going up just blocks from the terminal's great beaux arts majesty, the Waldorf-Astoria's art deco glamour, and the neo-Byzantine beauty of St. Bartholomew's Episcopal Church.

Many people still had not gotten over the imposition of the Lever House, eighteen floors of blue-gray glass walls and metal columns erected in 1952 at Park and Fifty-third Street. Thus, the mere idea of another slablike tower across the street—this one to be thirty-eight stories and done in dark brown bronze and amber-tinted glass—seemed still another effrontery to the conservative elegance of Park Avenue. Besides, the owner of the land and building was not even American. He was Samuel Bronfman, a Canadian Jew who had made much of his fortune selling booze to Americans during Prohibition.

Chapter One

Splendor in the Glass, Glory in the Tower

How the Seagram Building Came to Be

PAGE *xviii: The Seagram
Building, designed by
Mies van der Rohe, opened
in 1958 on New York's
Park Avenue.*

Not that Bronfman had ever been accused of direct involvement with smuggling whiskey across the Canadian–U.S. border, but it got there one way or another and reaped enormous profits for Bronfman, a phenomenon he explained by saying, "We loaded carloads of goods, got out cash, and shipped it. We shipped a lot of goods. Of course, we knew where it went, but we had no legal proof. And I never went to the other side of the border to count the empty Seagram's bottles."

Bronfman was the son of a Russian immigrant who had fled the anti-Jewish pogroms of the late nineteenth century and settled in western Canada as a firewood salesman. By the time he was twenty-one, Sam Bronfman was owner of a hotel and began selling mail-order liquor. By 1924 he was making his own whiskey in Montreal, and four years later he bought out his main competitor, Joseph E. Seagram.

When Prohibition was finally repealed in 1933, Seagram stood to gain tremendously and within two months became the largest-selling brand of whiskey in the United States. Just to smooth over any hard feelings, Bronfman agreed to pay the U.S. Treasury $1.5 million in disputed taxes from profits accrued during the decade of the "Noble Experiment."

Bronfman, whom everyone called "Mr. Sam," was also successful amassing fortunes in other ventures like oil and real estate, and during and after World War II he devoted himself increasingly to philanthropy, particularly as a leading benefactor for Jewish and Zionist causes. His two sons, Edgar and Charles, came into the business, while his two daughters were educated and groomed for a life of privilege. One daughter, Minda, married Baron Alain de Gunsburg; the other, Phyllis, became the wife of French banker Jean Lambert.

In 1954 Bronfman decided to open an American subsidiary of Seagram and began considering plans for a corporate headquarters to be built in Manhattan. There was no question that Bronfman wanted his new headquarters to make an impressive architectural statement on Park Avenue, but he sought not to ruffle further the feathers of Park Avenue residents and corporate neighbors. Thus, the first design for the Seagram headquarters was fairly conservative and would have done nothing to raise the eyebrows of the New York zoning board, which regulated the height and placement of buildings that traditionally rose straight up, only a few feet from the curb. Thanks to a need for new office space, the zoning laws had been recently altered to allow buildings to be set back from the street, as was the eccentric Lever House, whose main tower sat atop a slab supported by stilts. Most new buildings, however, still started more or less at the curb, then zigzagged upward, with the tower allowed to be 25 percent the size of the property itself. The original plans for the Seagram headquarters were to be pretty much in this mold—until, that is, twenty-seven-year-old Phyllis Bronfman Lambert got a look at the drawings.

A Vassar graduate (class of 1948) who had studied architecture with Richard Krautheimer of New York University, Lambert had an interest in her father's new building that was more than routine. Short and stocky like her father, she was an intense, very serious, and temperamental young woman whom no one ever accused of having a sense of humor. She had grown up outside of Montreal, amid boundless wealth that both shielded and suffocated her, in a twenty-room mansion called Belvedere, whose heavy dark red decor gave her nightmares as a child.

Lambert, by then already divorced, was still abroad, living a safely bohemian life of painting and sculpture on the Left Bank. She had never been comfortable with such overweening wealth as her father had lavished upon her (he'd flown in fifteen thousand lilac blooms by private plane for her wedding in 1949), characterizing herself as a cat for whom money was "my tin can" tied to her tail.

Her decision to return to America was prompted by her seeing the first drawings for the Seagram Building plans. "I was living in Europe when Seagram's intent to build reached me in Paris in July through a rendering of a very mediocre building," she wrote in the Vassar alumni magazine in 1959. "I flew to New York and started to learn all I could about the good buildings built since the war, and I consulted with architectural critics. I felt that my task was to explain to my father, the president of the company, what the business's responsibility could mean in terms of architecture and to convince him of the validity of the new architectural thinking that started to mature in the twenties."

In considering her impassioned plea, which first came in the form of a transatlantic letter running to several thousand words, Bronfman saw a way to lure his daughter back to America. But while Mr. Sam may have been a man of simple tastes and a doting father to boot, he had small familiarity with the rarefied disciplines of modern architecture and so consulted the head of a large construction firm, Lou Crandall, to see if Phyllis's pleas for a radical architectural statement made any sense at all. Whether it was Crandall's respect for Lambert's passion and expertise, a way of keeping this formidable young woman busy, or just a means of pleasing Mr. Sam, the builder backed her up by suggesting she begin traveling around the country to interview several contemporary architects and see if any of them could come up with something acceptable to everyone.

Lambert was well aware that she operated under a certain paternal

After Philip Johnson finished work on The Four Seasons, he asked Mies van der Rohe what he thought of it. Mies said four words: "Ja, very good job."

license no one else at Seagram's could possibly have enjoyed ("A daughter who is interested in seeing that her father puts up a fine building has everyone's sympathy," she wrote), and when Bronfman gave her the go-ahead and title of "director of planning," she confided to a friend, "And now I must say my prayers every day to be able to do the job as it should be done. What a unique chance I have!"

One of Lambert's first stops was at New York's Museum of Modern Art, whose chairman of the architecture department, Philip Johnson, had, with Henry-Russell Hitchcock Jr., in 1932 published *The International Style—Architecture Since 1922,* a defining statement on the bold, clean, unadorned modern style exemplified by the work of German-born architect Ludwig Mies van der Rohe. Johnson joined Lambert on a carte blanche expedition to look at the work of those architects practicing the International Style—which included Skidmore, Owings & Merrill's Lever House; Eero Saarinen's auditorium and chapel at MIT and the General Motors Technical Center in Warren, Michigan; Walter Gropius's Harvard Graduate Center; Louis Kahn's Jewish Hospital in Philadelphia; I. M. Pei's Mile High Center in Denver; and Mies van der Rohe's Lake Shore Drive apartment buildings in Chicago—as well as Frank Lloyd Wright's Johnson Wax headquarters in Racine, Wisconsin, which Phyllis found "crazy as hell" and "magnificent" but also "not the statement that is needed now."

After two and a half months of research, looking and relating back to the Park Avenue property, Lambert chose Mies van der Rohe, arguing that he had "made poetry of technology" and "through superb detailing and clarifying and articulating the structural system . . . has given it artistic expression and created a language and vocabulary of architecture."

Mr. Sam was still not sure.

Ludwig Mies van der Rohe—whom everyone referred to simply as Mies—had already established himself as one of the most important and innovative architects in the world. Born in Aachen, Germany, in 1886, he was apprenticed to local architects there and in Berlin but had never actually studied for a degree in the field. After service in the German army in World War I, Mies became part of the avant-garde art and architecture movement in Germany and by the mid-1920s began designing residences and workers' apartments. His 1921 design for an all-glass skyscraper and his work on the German Pavilion at the 1929 International Exposition in Barcelona gave him an international reputation, so that in 1930 he succeeded Gropius as director of the Bauhaus school of design in Dessau.

Soon afterward the Nazis closed down the school as dangerously "radical," forcing Mies to emigrate to the United States, where he became professor and director of architectural studies at Chicago's Armour Institute, later renamed the Illinois Institute of Technology.

Mies insisted on exquisite spatial relationships, fine materials, and uncluttered lines that refined the concepts and designs of the more industrial Bauhaus school, and corporate clients allowed him to expand his own vision and adapt his ideas to the midwestern cityscape, as had Louis Sullivan and Frank Lloyd Wright before him. There had, however, been a considerable brouhaha over Mies's 1951 design for the Farnsworth House in Plano, Illinois; the glass house was so aesthetically severe and impersonal that the owner warned readers of *House Beautiful* not to be taken under Mies's spell—a sentiment even Frank Lloyd Wright supported in this eccentric instance.

So when Phyllis Lambert asked Mies if he would come to New York to design the Seagram headquarters, he did not exactly leap at the chance. Chicago was a crucible of modern architecture in the 1940s and early 1950s—far more so than New York—and Mies was both an acknowledged master of what became known as the "Second Chicago School" and entirely in his element. Furthermore, Mies was not licensed to practice architecture in New York (nor did he ever get a high school diploma), and he scoffed at the idea of having to pass a licensing exam. Yet the Bronfmans were clearly the answer to the universal architect's prayer: "Lord, send us clients with open pockets and open minds." Philip Johnson, who had helped bring Mies to the United States in the first place, somehow got him exempted from New York's licensing requirements, and with Johnson as co-architect, Mies signed the contract with Bronfman, whom Johnson called "the client of the century."

Architects Philip Johnson (left) and Mies van der Rohe worked closely with Sam Bronfman's daughter, Phyllis Lambert, to create the perfect modern design for her father's U.S. headquarters.

Once he had approved his daughter's choice, Bronfman specified his requirements of size and space—half a million square feet of usable office space—and then turned the project over to the architect, Crandall (who was there to mind the costs), and Lambert, who took on a Joan of Arc role by staying with the job "to fight for the concept" and ended up devoting herself to four years of hard work and the constant assuaging of Mr. Sam's fears. Indeed, on first meeting with Mies, Bronfman told the architect the one thing he didn't want was a "building on stilts," and upon seeing Mies's first renderings for precisely that, Mr. Sam was, according to Johnson, "appalled, because it didn't look like a baronial castle."

Mies's final design was for a rectangular building set one hundred feet back from Park Avenue on a grand open plaza—the first of its kind in the city—which allowed the viewer to see the entire building from the sidewalk, much as one would a Renaissance cathedral. Pools and ginkgo trees were set into the plaza to create a restful environment where workers could sit and contemplate the beauty of the building they worked in. The amber glass was specially created to allow for a lighting system dependent on an astronomical clock that regulated the interior light of the building as adjusted to the exterior light of day.

The lobby of the Seagram Building.

Although the Seagram Building looks austere on first glance, Mies enriched every surface and detail with wonderful materials few other architects were then using in skyscrapers, such as the bronze latticework "stretched" across the sides of the building, the Italian green marble used in the plaza's rails, and the textured granite of walkways. As had been the case in classic New York skyscrapers like the Empire State Building and the Chrysler, individual door handles, mail chutes, lighting fixtures, and fire alarms were designed from scratch and made from a wide variety of materials. Even stairwells were finished in brick rather than cheap cinder blocks.

If Crandall protested the cost of certain designs, Mies and Lambert devised ways around it. "For example," she wrote, "we wanted nine-foot ceilings instead of the present standard eight feet or less and fought bitterly for ten feet until we graciously accepted nine feet."

The work took four years and cost about a million dollars per floor, and when it was completed in 1958, Mies himself felt the Seagram Building was his "crowning glory" and the apotheosis of all that he had worked to achieve in the International Style. From the moment it opened, the skyscraper was called a "masterwork" and a testament to Mies's maxim (actually first pronounced by poet Robert Browning in 1855) that, indeed, "Less is more," especially if what seems to be "less" is the result of thousands of details and decisions that make up the "more."

There were, however, a few problems with the new building. Most crucial was the fact that Seagram was having trouble renting the office space in such an unorthodox structure. People were actually scared of working in a glass box whose windows, it was assumed, might just pop out if you leaned against them. Legend has it that the realtor would have a husky maintenance man run full tilt at the glass and smash into it, just to prove that it was safe.

The other problem was what to do with the building's lower floors, which sat under the front pillars and graduated down toward Lexington Avenue to the rear. This was a very expansive space—24,000 square feet, with twenty-foot ceilings and windows—unsuitable for offices yet dramatic in both size and shape. Mies had envisioned the area to be some sort of display space, but what went in there was up to the Bronfmans. By the time of groundbreaking, however, no decision had been made as to the lower floors. Some thought was given to making it into an art gallery or antique store, a bank showroom, or perhaps the home of the American Craft Museum. Others suggested that, since Frank Lloyd Wright had done a Mercedes-Benz showroom at Fifty-sixth Street and Park, a similar auto showroom would be good for the Seagram Building.

At one point Mr. Sam called Johnson and asked him to come to his office, telling him, "Don't tell Phyllis you're coming." When Johnson arrived, Bronfman showed him drawings for two prospective banks to be put in the first-floor space. "Would these hurt the look of the building?" Bronfman asked.

"I told him they would *ruin* the building," replied Johnson. "And neither I nor Phyllis ever heard another word about them."

No one knew quite what to do about the space. At the time the building opened, the notion of putting a restaurant in the Seagram Building never occurred to anyone at all.

The Famous *Hawaiian Room* · Hotel Lexington · New York

Dining out in New York in the early 1950s may well have been better than dining out in Boston, Chicago, or Washington, but not really by much. New Yorkers might well have considered their town the arts and financial center of the United States, but few would have thought to call it a citadel of fine restaurants, exquisite cuisine, and trend-setting taste. For despite the fact that in the 1950s New York had about twenty thousand restaurants—approximately the same number it had in the 1930s and that it has today—no more than a handful served anything approaching fine food, despite the extravagant praise heaped on them by the press agents and nightclub columnists who ate for free and covered the restaurant scene of the day, usually with reference to what celebrities ate where.

New York certainly had an enormous range of restaurants, from masculine steakhouses like Palm, Gallagher's, and Peter Luger's to ladies' lunchrooms like Zoe Chase, Passy, and the Salon de Thé of Rosemarie de Paris. You could get good seafood at the Gloucester House and Billy the Oysterman; wonderful sweets at Schrafft's, Hicks, and Rumpelmayer's; hearty Hungarian fare at Zimmerman's and Cafe Tokay; Viennese specialties at Blaue Donau and Cafe Weinecke; heart-stopping deli at Ratner's, Lindy's, and Howie's; shashlik and vodka at the Russian Bear and the Russian Tea Room; Spanish and Cuban

Chapter Two

Coffee Shops, Airports, and Roman Bacchanals

Restaurant Associates Defines Dining Out in the Fifties

PAGE 8, *Top: The Hawaiian Room in the Hotel Lexington. Bottom : Forum of the Twelve Caesars in the U. S. Rubber Building.*

food in between dances at El Flamenco, La Zambra, and El Chico; and curries at Ceylon-India Inn and the Rajah. Beyond all this, you could eat your way through Little Italy and the mazy streets of Chinatown and find any number of places around town to satisfy a craving for Mexican grub, German food, or Scandinavian smorgasbord.

You could dine at rooftop restaurants like the Waldorf-Astoria's Starlight Roof, where you'd go to hear Frank Sinatra croon; proletarian coffee shops like the Commodore; and expansive family restaurants like Toffenetti's, Patricia Murphy's, and the White Turkey. In Brooklyn there were colossal feedshops on the water, like Joe's, Lundy's, and Feltman's, where thousands of people each day could order just about anything they desired to eat.

Ever since the Swiss family Delmonico opened the first true restaurant in the United States on William Street in 1831, New York had pioneered most of the innovations and set most of the styles for restaurants in America. Delmonico's menus, based on Parisian models, were the prototypes other deluxe restaurants would follow for more than a hundred years, and one chronicler of New York life in 1898 wrote, "There is hardly one hotel in New York today whose chef did not learn his cooking at Delmonico's, every one of them."

Every celebrated personage who came through New York had to eat at "Del's," including Napoleon III, who was presented with a seven-page menu featuring nine soups, eight side dishes, fifteen seafood preparations, eleven beef items, twenty kinds of veal, eighteen vegetables, sixteen pastries, thirteen fruit dishes, and sixty-two imported wines. It was at Delmonico's that trenchermen like "Diamond Jim" Brady proved their mettle as men of substance, putting away gargantuan meals and holding parties of Lucullan excess. And it was Delmonico's that led the way in allowing unescorted women to dine, first at lunch, then at dinner.

After the Civil War fine dining became increasingly an elitist diversion. When Prohibition was imposed in 1919, fine dining was nearly destroyed, with deluxe restaurants like Delmonico's, Rector's, and Louis Sherry all gone by 1923, because their clientele deserted baroque dining rooms for grim speakeasies with sawdust on the floor and bathtub gin at the bar. As enforcement of the Volstead Act weakened in the 1920s, some "speaks" like the Colony and the "21" Club actually became rather swank, and they not only survived the rough-and-tumble era of Prohibition intact, but went on to become high society restaurants, where the outrageous expense of food and drink was an object not of scorn, but of amusement. Damon

Runyon used to crack that the owners of "21," Jack Kriendler and Charlie Berns, had a secret room where they met to laugh hysterically after presenting checks to their customers. The "21" Club drew the postwar captains of American industry, the newspaper columnists, the Broadway crowd, and other celebrities who gave as much excitement as they took from the restaurant, where favored customers had their own table and the less than famous were summarily sent upstairs to "Siberia"—a term actually coined to describe undesirable tables at El Morocco.

Fine food was definitely not the draw at such places, although "21" prided itself on the quality of ingredients it purchased and the extraordinary depth of its wine cellar, hidden behind a two-ton brick door never discovered by federal agents back in the speakeasy days. "Gourmets" and "connoisseurs" were considered rather effete epithets in the days following World War II. "Fancy" food, however, was quite all right, as long as it came in large portions, and if the dishes were dramatically flamed tableside or stuck full of sparklers and carried out in darkness, so much the better. Such menus were dubbed "continental," because there was a little of this from Italy, a bit of that from France, and some regional American favorites to round things out; thus the spectacularly glamorous Rainbow Room atop Rockefeller Center offered items like "Sliced Eggs Czarina," "Spaghetti Italienne," and "Supreme of Guinea Hen and Virginia Ham Eugenie" right along with "Gumbo Creole" and strawberry shortcake.

There were a number of high-toned French restaurants in Manhattan like Voisin, Marguery, Belle Meunière, Robert, Le Cafe Chambord, and Larue, but none of them had the cachet of Le Pavillon, a superlative French restaurant opened by Henri Soulé during the height of World War II. Soulé had come to the United States as manager of Le Restaurant du Pavillon of the French Pavilion at the 1939 World's Fair in New York. The fair hosted more than fifty restaurants, ranging from a Czech beer garden to a Formosan tea room, but Le Pavillon was clearly the most impressive, introducing Americans to a high degree of cuisine, decor, and service as had never been seen before on this side of the Atlantic.

When war broke out, many of the restaurant's staff stayed on in the United States. Soulé, then forty, was too old for military service on either side of the Atlantic, so with $14,000 he opened Le Pavillon restaurant in October 1941 at 5 East 55th Street. To everyone's surprise, Le Pavillon did remarkably well throughout the war, and by the time it was over, Soulé had singlehandedly set the standards for haute cuisine and fine dining in this country—so much so that his menu and decor were copied by every other French restaurant and his staff went off to open their own places in Le Pavillon's image. A severe perfectionist, Soulé expected herculean effort by his staff and tried in every way to give his clientele the best food and wine available. Yet, admitting that perfection was not possible in New York with what he had to work with, Soulé once confided, "Some of the richest men in the world are dining here tonight. And for all the money on earth I couldn't give them the simple, good things that every middle-class Frenchman can afford from time to time. Six *Marennes*. A partridge— very, very young. Some real *primeurs*—the first spring vegetables. A piece of Brie that is just right. . . . And some *fraises des bois*."

The fact was, despite its preeminence as America's great seaport and marketplace, New York simply did not receive the kinds of glorious foods one might have found in Europe even right after the war. Wild mushrooms were unavailable, all cheese and dairy products had to be pasteurized, and game, when available at all, was farm raised. In fact, food technology—much of it developed during the war—had ironically provided a wider range of foods in the market than ever before but at the same

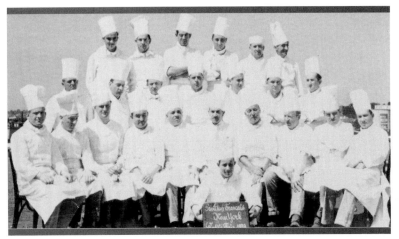

The brigade of chefs and cooks who opened the restaurant at the French Pavilion at the 1939 New York World's Fair—many of whom went on to work at the deluxe Le Pavillon on East Fifty-fifth Street under owner Henri Soulé.

time delivered it frozen, canned, homogenized, chemically treated, and otherwise adulterated so as to remove freshness and flavor. Tomatoes came to market green, tasteless chickens were raised by the millions, beef was shot full of hormones to build bulk, and fish came in already cooked, breaded, and frozen solid for easy use.

The years following World War II had also given Americans a giddy feeling that progress in and of itself was a wondrous thing and that such foods were miracles of the age and therefore desirable. Rationing was over, the economy was growing rapidly, and Americans were ready to indulge themselves with travel, food, and entertainment. Restaurants were places people went for fun, to see one's friends, to spy celebrities, to gorge a little, and to taste exotic foods, no matter how poorly they were made. Entrepreneurs catered to this new affluence by opening an array of gim-micky restaurants and franchises that ranged from McDonald's hamburger stands with golden arches to wacky pseudo-Polynesian restaurants like Trader Vic's, where customers sat under thatched roofs and sipped rum cocktails studded with paper umbrellas and maraschino cherries.

Often there would be entertainment—an oom-pah band at Lüchow's, a barbershop quartet at Bill's Gay Nineties, hula girls at the Hawaiian Room, and dagger dancers at Russian Yar. On any given night in New York Eddie Duchin played the Wedgewood Room at the Waldorf, Guy Lombardo was at the Roosevelt, and Tommy Dorsey was at the Cafe Rouge.

People came to depend on chains for the consistent quality of their food, service, and decor, so that customers got used to the look, feel, and fare of family places and coffee shops like Nedick's, Chock Full O' Nuts, Schrafft's, Horn & Hardart, and Howard Johnson's.

One not-so-successful coffee shop chain was called Riker's. It was taken over in 1942 by the Wechsler Coffee Company, the world's leading coffee importer at the time, headed by Abraham Wechsler. Three years later, two of Wechsler's partners died of heart attacks, followed a year later by his brother Edward, who had taken care of the Riker's chain. By 1946 Abe Wechsler was left with no one to run the branch of his company he knew nothing about but which increasingly was losing sales to competitors.

Wechsler turned to his brand-new, twenty-five-year-old son-in-law, Jerome Brody, who had just married his daughter Grace. Brody had graduated from Dartmouth College and Amos Tuck Business School, had served as a B-24 bomber pilot in the war, and was intending to go to Columbia Law School that fall when his father-in-law insisted Brody take over the failing Riker's chain, which then had two cafeterias and twenty-four lunch counters. It was a business about which Brody knew nothing.

Reluctantly, Brody threw himself into the job and found that despite gross sales of $4,500,000, the branch—now called Riker's Restaurant Associates—was making a profit of only $67,000 and had severe cash flow problems. Seeking to bring cash into the company, Brody went after management contracts like the Corner House restaurant chain (where he introduced hamburgers in burgundy wine sauce) and obtained a long-term lease to operate the lunch counter and employee cafeteria at Ohrbach's department store.

He also went after a lunch counter concession at Mitchell Air Force Base on Long Island and, as a result, received a call from Bob Curtiss of New York's Port Authority, asking if Restaurant Associates (by then known as "RA") might be interested in taking over Newark Airport's six-foot-wide hot dog stand since the owners had recently had a falling-out. This small concession sounded right up Brody's alley, so RA took over the lease, introduced a fifteen-cent foot-long hot dog, and doubled the business immediately—piling up $300,000 in annual sales.

When plans came to expand Newark Airport in 1952, Curtiss asked Brody if RA were interested in developing and building a full-service restaurant to be called The Newarker—an idea Abe Wechsler thought foolhardy. No one in his right mind, Wechsler believed, would drive all the way out to an airport to eat fine food. Nor did anyone at RA, including Brody, know anything about running a white-tablecloth restaurant. Brody accepted the challenge, however, and began looking for the kind of experienced restaurant talent that could accomplish such a task.

One of the first people he contacted was Joseph H. Baum, a dynamic, thirty-two-year-old professional out of Florida's Schine Hotels who wanted to return to New York anyway. Baum, the son of a Saratoga Springs hotelier, enjoyed the business, even though he found much of the work and personnel pretty seamy in many ways and lacking in any real imagination. After attending the Cornell Hotel Management School and then serving on a destroyer in World War II, Baum had taken a job as an accountant for a restaurant company, then become manager of New York's flamboyant Monte Carlo Hotel. Under the tutelage of Monte Carlo's William Zeckendorf, Baum learned a great deal about the show-biz aspect of running restaurants, which he put to use when he was hired to work for the Schine Hotels.

Tapping Baum for The Newarker set a pattern for RA that was to revolutionize the restaurant business in America. Like Brody himself, Baum was well educated, literate, and fiercely intelligent, and he had a vision of what the business *could* be at a time when the industry was expanding rapidly but without much focus or imagination at the high end. Up until then there was little sophistication among restaurateurs; most had little formal education and more often than not copied what had been done before rather than create new concepts of restaurant design and menus. In the postwar period there was a vital and provocative change going on in fast food, where fantasy themes and futuristic designs were part of the allure. But in the deluxe restaurant category, except for the influence of the New York World's Fair and the inspiration of Henri Soulé at Le Pavillon, little had really changed since the nineteenth century. Creativity was frowned upon, blind allegiance to tradition was enforced, and French was the lingua franca of restaurant kitchens.

Baum wanted to change all this, and The Newarker seemed like a good place to start. One of the first people he hired was a Swiss-born chef named Albert Stöckli, who had been trained in classical European techniques and had cooked on both the Holland-America and Grace steamship lines before settling in as chef at Atlantic City's Claridge Hotel. Baum found him working at a country club in New Jersey and hired him on the spot after tasting Stöckli's mushroom and barley soup. Good as the soup was, it was not the real reason Baum hired Stöckli (neither was it the fact that Stöckli could yodel). Baum sensed that the young Swiss had a good creative sense and was delighted by the prospect of breaking away from the tired Escoffier tradition of béarnaise and beef bourguignon, for decades the rule in deluxe restaurants. For although Stöckli was not himself a disciplined chef ("I don't think he was able to make a good hollandaise, and he put sugar in everything," said Brody), Baum also realized that he had enormous expertise in organizing a modern professional kitchen; so in addition to appointing him chef at The Newarker, he gave Stöckli the position of executive chef of RA.

This formidable young RA team tore into the project with verve and a belief that they were going to do something revolutionary, a stance that of course made Abe Wechsler uneasy. Baum stocked The Newarker with the finest silverware and china and had waiters brandish gigantic peppermills at the table, stick sparklers into the desserts, and flame everything in sight ("It didn't hurt the food much," said Baum). Stöckli came up with quirky ideas that Baum gave whimsical names, like a "three-clawed lobster" and a "knife-and-fork oyster" so large you had to use a knife and fork to eat it. But at the opening in 1953, it looked as if Wechsler's fears had been well founded: few people wanted to drive out to Newark Airport to eat high-priced food.

Business was terrible for the first few months—not helped by the negative publicity about several nearby plane crashes—yet Brody and company continued to pour their time, energy, and dreams into The Newarker. "People thought we were nuts to start a restaurant of this caliber in the swamps of Secaucus," Baum said, "[because] the public's image of airport restaurants was every bit as bad as its image of railroad-terminal restaurants. But Jerry Brody recognized the restaurant's value and supported it. We never cut corners. The more money we lost in those early days, the more trouble Albert Stöckli and I took to make the food good and cooking outstanding."

To stimulate traffic, Baum began inviting local business leaders and society people from New York to try the restaurant and, by bringing out the food press, began to generate favorable publicity about a kind of culinary "gem in the wilderness." Soon curiosity seekers, nearby suburbanites, and New Yorkers in search of an unusual setting started jamming the restaurant, and within a year The Newarker was being hailed as one of the finest modern restaurants in America. Within two years it was serving a thousand meals a day and had annual sales of $2 million.

RA had obviously hit on something new and different that tickled the public's fancy, and The Newarker gave a sudden boost to Brody's reputation as an innovative restaurant man. Although Wechsler still doubted the wisdom of further expansion into the white-tablecloth market, Brody saw a completely untapped public appetite for dazzling, uniquely designed full-service restaurants. Realizing that he and Baum shared the same vision of the future, Brody appointed Baum vice president in charge of the specialty restaurant division of RA, and the hunt was on for bigger projects and fatter contracts.

Encouraged by RA's general counsel, Lester Klepper (recruited from Ohrbach's), Brody also learned that the only way a cash-poor company like RA could develop large projects was to use other people's money—at the time a novel idea for restaurateurs—as they'd done with the Port Authority. It was also clear that other companies' outdated restaurant properties could, with a minimum investment on RA's part, be revived by modernization and promotion; this was how RA came to take over the failing Hawaiian Room in the Hotel Lexington, which had been losing more than $100,000 a year.

Klepper negotiated a deal extremely favorable to RA: by putting down only $25,000, RA got a twenty-year lease with rent based on a percentage of their gross sales—a percentage that would decrease as their volume increased. The deal set the pattern for future development, whereby RA's initial financial risk was minimal and its potential profits were cushioned against outrageous rent increases as their restaurants became more successful.

The Hawaiian Room was also the spur that sent RA executives traveling the world in search of ideas, recipes, decor, and inspiration—an unheard-of notion at a time when most restaurants followed proven formulas in menu and design, and travel budgets were out of the question for independent operators. Soon Brody and Baum were hopping on planes to Hawaii, where they researched local cooking and attended luaus, returning via Los Angeles and San Francisco to check out wacky Polynesian decor and crazy cocktails at the very successful Don the Beachcomber and Trader Vic's restaurants. Brody and Baum, both in their thirties, went full tilt and expected the same from the young executives they began to hire: Alan Lewis, who became the Hawaiian Room's first director; purchasing director Lee Jaffe; Tony Cabot, a Broadway director who became musical director for RA; Austin Cox, in charge of industrial relations and staff; and George Stich, who taught waiters about wine service.

Based on Brody's and Baum's Hawaiian research, Stöckli created new menus for the Hawaiian Room—again with lots of flaming dishes. RA hired a young Broadway public relations agent named Phil Miles, whose job it was to generate publicity for the restaurant by packing it with show business celebrities. Miles even got *Life* magazine to cover a party at the Hawaiian Room, at which he'd decked out the room with stars like Richard Burton, Liz Taylor, and Laurence Olivier. And when TV personalities Arthur Godfrey and Steve Allen broadcast their variety shows from the restaurant, business boomed and sales doubled within a year of RA's taking it over.

The house band and dancing girls at the Hawaiian Room.

By the mid-1950s Restaurant Associates was the hottest restaurant company in New York. Their reputation as innovators, experts in interior design, and savvy marketers attracted investors and developers, who came begging them to consider putting restaurants in their buildings. One night in March 1956, after a particularly festive evening at the Hawaiian Room, the president of Rockefeller Center, Inc., Gustav S. Eyssell, pulled Brody aside and said they should talk the next day.

Eyssell told him he was looking for a restaurant tenant for the new U.S. Rubber Building (which replaced the Center Theatre on West Forty-eighth Street). This was not the best site in the complex, but just being in Rockefeller Center itself would give RA enormous prestige. RA's challenge was to come up with something just as spectacular at ground level—using, of course, Rockefeller money to build it.

At the time RA had about $200,000 in cash at hand, so they borrowed $300,000 from Chase Manhattan, a Rockefeller-owned bank, and Lester

Klepper got to work on one of his extraordinary lease deals while Brody and Baum tried to think of what to do with the space.

Because the Center and neighboring buildings housed many of New York's top television, radio, and publishing companies, the idea of a "forum" where media people would exchange ideas over a good meal seemed to make good marketing sense. While Brody and Baum were turning this over in their corporate minds, RA's favorite interior decorator, William Pahlmann, informed them that he had recently purchased seventeenth-century portraits of the twelve Roman Caesars by Camillo Procaccini. By combining the idea of a forum with those portraits, they could create some stylized form of bacchanalia that would attract New York's most powerful corporate titans and the world's most beautiful women. "What an imposing setting it would make for a gutsy, masculine restaurant!" exulted Baum. Thus was born the idea of the Forum of the Twelve Caesars.

Off went Brody, Baum, and other RA associates to Italy (Alan Lewis alone made four trips), scouring Rome, Naples, and other cities for artifacts, ancient recipes, statuary, and anything else they thought would thrill a public whose impressions of ancient Rome were formed by 1950s CinemaScope "spectacle" movies like *Quo Vadis, The Robe,* and *Demetrius and the Gladiators.*

RA pulled out all the stops on the Forum of the Twelve Caesars, replicating the Appian Way in mural in the foyer, setting champagne into ice buckets made to look like centurions' helmets, and dressing waiters in pseudo-togas. Service plates were made of Milanese brass or copper imprinted with the head of Bacchus, god of wine. The ceiling was sixteen feet high, and the doors were made of carved wood and glass panels, with brass handles.

Baum, always trying to raise the sophistication level of his staff, had his busboys read the works of Suetonius and Apicius, chroniclers of the imperial gluttony in ancient Rome, and even enlisted the aid of poet Robert Graves, author of *I, Claudius,* to lecture the staff on Greek and Roman culture. The Forum's menu was translated into Latin under the eye of a Hunter College classics professor.

The ingredients used at the Forum's kitchen were the finest available at the time, but they were put to use in hilariously named dishes like "The Noblest Caesar Salad Of Them All," "Chicken Varius in a Shell of Centurion Almonds," "Sirloin in Red Wine, Marrow and Onions— a Gallic recipe Julius collected while there on business," "Tart Messalina,"

"Nubian Chocolate Roll," and "Piscatorian Roman Minutal," which turned out to be mousse of trout with lobster sauce. Nero himself would have wept with envy at the sight of so many dishes being flamed.

When the Forum of the Twelve Caesars opened in 1958, it had a strange effect on customers and critics. Its extravagance and unabashed ostentation clearly expressed what Baum called "a time of lusty elegance in which the good things of life are presented to the leaders of the world." But Baum also wondered out loud, "Could anyone possibly think I was serious?" Apparently many of the Forum's customers did and were willing to pay a high tab—$6 at lunch and $10 at dinner—for the privilege of dining at what became a destination restaurant. Yet despite its apparent success with the public and its initial low investment cost to RA, the Forum was not providing much cash for RA's coffers.

But at the moment no one seemed to be worrying much about the bottom line. To the public and the media, the privately owned company had made all the right moves, ran the most exciting restaurants in New York, and seemed like a sure bet for future investments. (They had also taken on the contract for the Corner House coffee shops along the entire New York State Thruway.) To work for RA in those days was a heady and exhausting experience, and to secure a job at RA was to plug into an industry Brody and Baum had made as respectable as Wall Street or automaking and as glamorous to a new generation of college-educated executives as anything in fashion or publishing. It might have been easier, therefore, for RA simply to duplicate Hawaiian Rooms and Forums of the Twelve Caesars all around the United States. But that was neither the company's style nor, to hear Baum speak, its mission. "We were vibrating, like a great athletic team," recalls Baum of those days. "We all wondered what can happen when you have all the talent in the world to work with and all the drive. And I just wanted to drive where I hadn't been."

RA also sensed that while New York was fast becoming a world capital of unparalleled grandeur, its restaurants were for the most part copies of European models and never as good as the originals. And, having entertained the public with luaus and Roman bacchanals, Brody and Baum thought Americans were ready for something unique—a restaurant that would express everything New York had come to represent: power, money, modernism, sophistication, eccentricity, and iconoclasm. RA just needed the perfect venue to develop such a vision. Perhaps the answer lay in that strange, dark building slowly growing out of a hole in the ground on Park Avenue.

As of the winter of 1956, Seagram was still pondering what to do with the lobby space of its headquarters, when the firm's rental agents, Cushman-Wakefield, received a call from Jerry Brody about the possibility of doing for Seagram what RA had done for the Rockefellers.

If the idea of putting a restaurant into the Seagram Building lobby had been considered at all, it was certainly not on the Bronfmans' "A" list, and Cushman-Wakefield's chairman, L'Huiller Shaef, had no idea if the Bronfmans would be responsive to such a concept. Brody argued that since Seagram was a spirits company and played such a big part in the American hospitality industry, a restaurant would be a natural extension of the Seagram image. Brody followed up with a formal proposal to Shaef, playing up the uniqueness of the building's design and asserting that any restaurants RA developed would be "just as unusual . . . [and would] even enhance the merchandising value of the building."

Shaef liked the idea but knew that before he even approached Sam Bronfman, any such notions about a restaurant would have to be presented to and passed on by the building's project director—Phyllis Bronfman Lambert, whose reluctance to compromise Mies's design in any way had already put the kibosh on many another plan. Aware of Lambert's reputation as a tough, inflexi-

Kids in the Candy Store

The Four Seasons Is Born

ble guardian of the Miesian vision, Brody knew that he would have to use all his powers of rational persuasion to win her over to the idea. "Good things don't get pulled out of a hat," she'd once said. "Only bad things get pulled out of a hat."

Brody had, of course, made a career of pulling things out of a hat and making them work, but he was well aware that the designs for the Hawaiian Room and the Forum of the Twelve Caesars were about as far from Miesian aesthetics as Lexington and Sixth avenues were from Park (Lambert thought the Forum was a "well-researched restaurant, but not a great one").

Assuming Lambert would at least expect, if not be impressed by, a show of luxury, Brody picked up Lambert in a limousine at Seagram's temporary offices in the Chrysler Building and headed out to lunch at The Newarker, then the least flamboyant of the RA properties. The Newarker's staff was alerted to be at their most genteel and to meet any request Lambert might have. But there was none.

"We sat down and ordered lunch, and I began to talk endlessly about what a terrific idea it would be to have restaurants in the Seagram Building," recalls Brody. "Lambert sat there, ate, but said nothing. She listened and listened, but just wasn't responding. At one point Alan Lewis came over to the table to see how it was going, and I whispered to him, 'Alan, I don't think she's heard a word I said.' Well, the lunch was a disaster. We rode back to New York in silence, and I phoned Shaef and told him I thought the whole idea was down the drain."

And so it seemed for six months. Then, in the middle of the summer, Shaef called Brody. "I don't know what will come of it," said Shaef, "but Sam Bronfman's son Edgar wants to talk with you about the restaurants." Edgar was, however, powerless to make any decision without the approval of either his father or his sister; he listened carefully to Brody's sales pitch and made another appointment for the two of them to meet with Mr. Sam. "But," he cautioned, "he wants you to come alone—no lawyers."

"I went over to the Chrysler Building to meet with them, and I was ushered into an empty office," Brody recalls of the meeting. "I was sitting there alone for a few moments, then in come Sam Bronfman and Edgar. Sam looks me straight in the eye, flops down in his chair, and says, 'So I understand you want to run a restaurant in my building.' That was all he said, and I knew I was expected to go into my spiel and not waste time. I was very nervous but well prepared, so I started to talk about how RA would build such unique restaurants that they'd do wonders for Seagram's corporate image, and how they would express everything that's wonderful about New York, and so on. And as I'm talking, I notice that Sam is nodding off to sleep! His head is drooping, and next thing I know, he's snoring. I look at Edgar. He says nothing. I start to speak louder, clear my throat, but it doesn't wake him up. Sam is out like a light, and I'm thinking, My God, I've just given the most important sales pitch of my life and I put the guy to sleep! Well, at that point Edgar asks a question and starts rapping his pencil on the desk till his father wakes up. Sam opens his eyes and, without missing a beat, waves his hand and says to me, 'All right, all right, I'll have my man contact you about working out a lease.' I was flabbergasted. Then, as I was leaving, I tried to break the tension by asking Sam, 'Well, Mr. Bronfman, since it's your building, what kind of food do you think we should serve?' "

Mr. Sam waved his hand again and replied, "All I want is to be able to get a good piece of flanken, okay?"

"That was it," says Brody. "I left the room not knowing if it had been Sam or I who was dreaming."

Brody went back to RA exultant and told everyone the news. No one was happier than Baum, who now saw the possibility of building the kind of restaurant he had long envisioned, a place where every single detail was to be researched, thought through, and designed with intelligence and a dedication to new standards of refinement never before imagined—or even possible—in a restaurant.

There would also be a smaller restaurant on the other side of the building that would have counter service, but the main restaurant, spread over three floors of the south side of the building, was to be a showcase for RA, Seagram, and everyone involved.

Lester Klepper went to work with Shaef, winning from the Bronfmans the right of final say on the design. There would, however, be several restrictions on Restaurant Associates' plans, not least of which was the necessity to work harmoniously with Phyllis Lambert on every aspect of the design. First and foremost was the need to find an architect whose design would be stringently complementary to Mies's. RA made some suggestions for architects, but Lambert insisted Brody get the input of Philip Johnson, Mies's associate on the Seagram project.

Born in Cleveland in 1906, Philip Cortelyou Johnson came into considerable wealth from shares of Alcoa Aluminum his lawyer father had given him at the age of eighteen. When the stocks quadrupled, the younger Johnson found himself a millionaire by his twentieth birthday. Having come close to a nervous breakdown while at Harvard, Johnson left school and toured Germany, where he became a convert to the new architecture of the Bauhaus then being promulgated by Walter Gropius and Mies van der Rohe. When the Bauhaus was closed down by the Nazis, the young acolyte helped his mentor emigrate from Germany and, on his return to America, began publishing some of the seminal essays on the new European architecture. At the age of twenty-four—despite never having earned a degree in architecture—Johnson became the first head of the architecture department for New York's new Museum of Modern Art, where in February 1932 he and architectural historian Henry-Russell Hitchcock mounted an exhibition entitled "Modern Architecture—International Exhibition," hailed at the time as a revolutionary challenge to existing concepts of American architecture.

Despite his new celebrity as a rising star in the arts, Johnson abandoned architecture in the 1930s for a brief flirtation with Ohio politics. After winning a seat and serving in the state legislature, he left office to write for a right-wing, anti-Semitic magazine called *Social Justice,* for which he filed front-line dispatches from Germany that were embarrassingly generous to the Nazis. It was a period in his life he later called "my terrible guilt," characterizing his sympathies of the time as "utter, unbelievable stupidity."

By 1940 he had returned to America and to architecture, earning a degree from Harvard's Graduate School of Design but flunking the design section of the New York State architect's license exam several times before finally passing it. When the United States entered the war, Johnson served stateside in the army, then returned to his unpaid job at the Museum of Modern Art as head of the architecture department while developing his own projects. One of the first structures to create a sensation for the now middle-aged architect was his own glass-walled house in New Canaan, Connecticut; this was followed by a New York City town house for the Rockefellers and a new wing and sculpture garden of the Museum of Modern Art.

Johnson worked within the International Style, which he had helped define back in 1932 as "characterized by flexibility, lightness, and simplicity. Ornament has no place, since hand-cut ornament is impracticable in the machine age. The beauty of the style rests in the free composition of volumes and surfaces, the adjustment of such elements as doors and windows, and the perfection of machined surfaces."

This was as good a description of Mies's work on the Seagram Building as any published since it went up, and Johnson, along with his ally

Lambert, wanted to make sure that the spirit of Mies's design was in no way violated by a routine restaurant decorator.

"We of course asked Mies if he had any interest in doing the restaurant for Seagram," said Johnson, "and he actually did some preliminary work on it, but soon got bored. So he turned to me and said, 'Philip, why don't you do it?' Well, I was startled. I was just a kid [Johnson was fifty years old at the time] trying to get ahead and had no idea what was required to design a restaurant."

So when Jerry Brody and Baum came to confer with Johnson on whom to use, he repeated what Mies had said and asked sheepishly, "Well, how about *my* firm?" With Mies's benediction and Lambert's imprimatur, RA had little choice but to accept. They were, however, legitimately concerned over Johnson's total lack of experience in restaurant design—an ignorance Johnson readily admitted—and therefore brought to bear all the talent RA possessed in areas that ranged from kitchen design to bathroom requirements.

Meanwhile RA's general counsel, Lester Klepper, was busy closing the deal with Cushman-Wakefield, which gave RA a twenty-year lease with an astoundingly low rent of only $25,000 for the first year, $50,000 the second, and $90,000 by the fifth. But the real sweetheart aspect of the deal involved Seagram's commitment to pour millions into the design and construction of the formal restaurant and provide the drapes, carpeting, kitchen costs (ultimately to be repaid by RA), and works of modern art from the Seagram collection. All RA had to pay for were tables, chairs, silverware, china, glassware, linen, and uniforms. With uncharacteristic nonchalance, Lambert called the deal basically "a turnkey operation."

While no one at Seagram was authorizing fiscal profligacy, RA got the clear message that this was to be a one-of-a-kind restaurant for New York and the world. Sam Bronfman might have known nothing about architecture or restaurant design, but he always knew the price of true excellence. Indeed, RA executive Stuart Levin recalled that Mr. Sam dismissed all talk of what anything was to cost. "Don't ask, Stuart," said Mr. Sam. "I never do. I can afford anything I want." In fact, it was rumored that the Seagram Building itself had been paid for in cold, hard cash.

The open-mindedness of the Bronfmans together with an open wallet and the lease of the century dazzled even RA's Joe Baum, for whom making money had never been a goal nor personal profit a motive. But the largesse of the Bronfmans enabled Baum and RA to fulfill all their dreams in one spectacular restaurant. "I felt like a kid in the candy store," he said.

"Here was the opportunity to build the greatest restaurant ever seen. And it was to be done at a time in New York when the city was coming into its own as a great world capital. It had become a seat of international government, a center of communications, transportation, art, theater, and fashion, and a mélange of many peoples. It was a place of youth, and optimism, and was constantly evolving, never staying the same, and our restaurant was going to reflect that. We would not draw on anything in the past, not even our own successes. We wanted to look at every detail, every piece of silverware, every matchbook, in a fresh way. It was not going to be French, we wouldn't use descriptive language on the menu, we wouldn't flame dishes, and we were all in on it together.

"You see, it was a magical time. We were all young and had this incredible pool of talent—the best designers, architects, artists, kitchen staff, landscapers, florists—everybody was working toward one common goal to do the best in its class. And here, finally, we had the money with which to do it."

Perhaps the most remarkable thing about the conceptualizing and construction of the restaurant was, in fact, the extraordinary working relationship among all who worked on it, which included everyone from Philip Johnson and Phyllis Lambert to Brody, Baum, and Stöckli; lighting expert Richard Kelly; industrial designers Garth and Ada Louise Huxtable; landscape architect Karl Linn; and horticulturist Everett Conklin. Ironically, while Lambert was kept informed of every detail of the project (her office was right next door to Johnson's), she exerted little of the force of her own character on the day-to-day details, allowing the organism to evolve according to a common goal.

To be sure, there were clashes of titanic egos. Baum could be a martinet on the one hand, yet he showed a flexible open-mindedness when presented with a good alternative idea. Johnson told the *Wall Street Journal,* "[Baum] can be quite unpleasant; he's very sure of himself, but so good," and noted that "without him, we couldn't have designed in this crazy space." Just to hedge their bets and protect their investment, RA insisted on bringing in their own favorite interior decorator, Bill Pahlmann, to work along with Johnson and, though Brody did not convey the sentiment to Johnson, to "warm things up a bit."

Lambert and Johnson went off to look at Pahlmann's work and were convinced the collaboration arrangement was not going to go smoothly. Lambert said the two men were "diametrically opposed in their attitudes" and took an immediate dislike to one another. At one pole was the minimalist Philip Johnson, who regarded the restaurant as a "space to be filled" in an elegant way that kept Mies's vision intact. At the other was Pahlmann, who believed that "good decoration is a design for living, not for looking" and should be "in the service of human needs." (Some years later, when asked what he thought of architects doing interiors, he sniffed, "I think it's for the birds. I think they just do it for the ten percent.")

In retrospect Johnson has said that Pahlmann was "very, very helpful with the interior," especially with concepts of table placement and chairs and kitchen layout, about which Johnson knew nothing. In any case, since RA had the final say on the project design, Pahlmann stayed.

As the initial stages of the design were thrashed out, everybody was invited to submit names for what the blueprints identified merely as the "Seagram Restaurant." Some of the names considered at the time—which included several allusions to the success of the Forum of the Twelve Caesars—were

> *The Imperator*
> *Restaurant of the Seven Wonders*
> *The Bronze Goddess*
> *The Roman Banquet*
> *Cleopatra's*
> *Plaza of the Twelve Fountains*
> *Avant Garde*
> *The Calendar Room*
> *The Time Table*
> *The Indoor-Outdoor Room*
> *Janus*
> *Le Passage du Temps*
> *The François Villon Room*

Clearly many of the names hinted at a theme of change and mutability. Baum had traveled through Germany and much admired the Vierjahrzeiten (Four Seasons) hotels in Munich and Hamburg. And at the time Baum had come under the spell of Japanese design, as articulated by his friend Elizabeth Gordon, then editor of *House Beautiful*.

"She was a lovely woman who brought *shibui* Japanese style to America," he recalled. "Her ideas and standards were very appealing to me, and Japanese design was so pure and simple, with a natural decorative line. Elizabeth gave me some haiku poetry to read on the passing of time and the four seasons. And that's where I came by the idea to use the theme of the four seasons for our restaurant, because everything we wanted to do with it represented change."

Suddenly all the pieces fell into place. "What could be more refreshing to a restaurant than change?" Baum exulted. "What is more foodlike and sophisticated than the seasons and what they bring to New York? Remember that song 'How About You': 'I Like New York in June . . .'? The theatrical season; the social season; the fall, spring, summer—all these have great emotional impact on a restaurant. The changing theme makes the cuisine imaginative and capitalizes on produce at its seasonal best, taking advantage of New York being the center of transportation and having all the markets. This happy idea of the seasons let us create an enduring style instead of a contemporary fashion."

The idea of change and evolution fit smoothly into the modernism of the Seagram Building, Mies van der Rohe's designs, and Philip Johnson's developing plans for a restaurant. A new set of possible names based on the four seasons theme was culled from RA personnel, some of whom obviously still had the Forum of the Twelve Caesars on their minds:

The Colonnade of the Four Seasons
The Gallery of the Four Seasons
The Coliseum of the Four Seasons
The Plaza of the Four Seasons
The Amphitheatre of the Four Seasons
The Harvest of the Four Seasons
The Enclave of the Four Seasons
The Table of the Four Seasons
The Orbit of the Four Seasons
The Four Seasons of the Zodiac
Rendezvous of the Four Seasons
The Symphony of the Four Seasons
C'est la Saisons
Season-o-Rama
Season-Go-Round

But RA ultimately decided that the simplest and most direct name was the best name, so the final decision was that the restaurant would be called The Four Seasons.

There was, however, a small problem with the name: two other restaurants listed in the Manhattan telephone directory already had it. One was an eatery in Harlem. This, Klepper offered to buy outright, but the deal never went through, and the place closed soon afterward. The other Four Seasons was a small midtown restaurant whose owners wanted money to change the name, but which not long afterward collapsed into an excavation pit. Thus the name became free and clear for RA's usage.

Deciding on a single theme helped focus everyone's energies on how best to manifest it, so that everything from plants to ashtrays would now be chosen and designed to fit the idea of passing seasons as well as adapted to the style and feeling Johnson and Pahlmann had thus far developed.

As the project moved along, Baum would take plans and blueprints home with him to South Orange, where he'd have Sunday morning meetings with RA colleagues. Fred Rufe, then director of The Newarker, recalls that Baum would get down on the floor and spread out the blueprints. "Albert Stöckli had given Baum a poodle puppy called Frivoli," says Rufe, "and it grew to be a very large dog. And every Sunday while we were having brunch at Joe's house, the dog would piss on the plans and we'd have

An early architectural floor plan of the restaurant gave ample room for the efficient flow of traffic between the kitchen and the dining rooms.

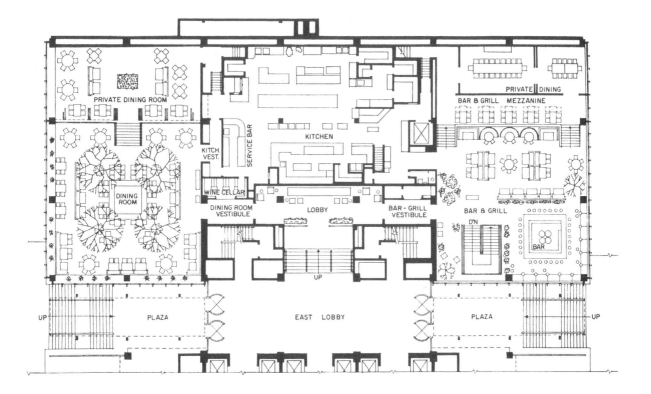

to get copies for the following week. Stöckli found this all hilarious, but it made Joe mad as hell."

The layout of the Seagram Building's first floor presented enormous problems in terms of both pure design and basic engineering. Johnson had to contend with three different levels, the first being the entrance on Fifty-second Street, the next the two dwarfing spaces for dining rooms connected by a hallway, and a third set back into the second. Since Mies had insisted that a crucial bearing column be removed from the space where the barroom area would eventually go, engineers had to create a specially reinforced beam hidden in the ceiling to bear the weight. There were also

The designers gave the restrooms as much attention as every other facet of the restaurant.

monumental problems with telephone lines that needed to be threaded over 43,000 square feet of space. Finally, there were to be two concealed projection rooms in the private dining rooms with 35-mm and 16-mm projectors.

"I was faced with all these fixed taboos about restaurant design," recalled Johnson. "They said that toilets must all be on the same floor as the dining area. They said the entrance to the dining room must be as far as possible from the service station and kitchen door. They told me putting a stairway leading to the dining room was a no-no. I certainly had no idea how to design a table. And, right from the start, I knew that the space was much too big for a restaurant. So really, I was just trying to fill the space somehow, stay true to Mies's designs for the building, and keep the commission. There's a *lot* of wasted space there, you know. But there is in a great cathedral, too, isn't there?"

The twenty-foot ceilings of the second floor had an inhuman scale that worked against any thought of intimacy in a restaurant, and lighting such spaces seemed impossible with existing technologies. At the time, there simply were no lighting fixtures to achieve the kinds of effects Johnson and RA desired, so consultant Richard Kelly, together with his assistant, Edison Price, had to devise all sorts of novel fixtures—some used only in this project and never again, such as a socket with fourteen facets milled with small bumps that would diffuse the light in what was to be an upstairs banquet room. In the downstairs lobby, fixtures were created to throw "dark" light downward without glaring in the eyes of those who walked under them—an idea that has since become standard. The ceiling was made of movable aluminum panels, which also functioned as air-conditioning ducts, that were actually held up by the lighting fixtures. The total cost of the ceilings and lighting came to more than $220,000.

Realizing the objections people had to entering a side entrance and ascending a staircase to a dining room, Johnson chose to make it a *spectacular* staircase. The guest is ushered through two sets of heavy glass doors into a large vestibule with floors and walls of travertine marble. Kelly's "dark lights" illuminate the area, which includes a coatroom, two restrooms, and two hidden telephone booths. The brass-railed staircase leads to a landing that prepares one for the final ascent into the magnificent Grill Room and bar area. The twenty-foot walls are covered with rectangular panels of stained French walnut echoed throughout in the ceiling's rectangular sheets of aluminum, the square bar, the tables, the windows, and the basic square of the room itself. Lights are subtly thrown against the walls to keep glare off the tables.

Artist Richard Lippold himself installed scores of bronze tubes above the bar to create his sculpture.

The Grill Room itself—a name never formally adopted and often interchangeably used for the "Bar Room"—has two levels, the lower one with coatroom and lounges and the upper one reached by another bronze-railed stairway that leads to a balcony with several tables. To the rear of the upper room is a small private dining room whose hundreds of diffused lights are randomly—and uniquely—set into the ceiling.

One of the most difficult challenges of the Grill Room was to somehow tame the effect of the twenty-foot ceiling without sacrificing the grandeur of the room. To drop the ceiling at any point would have been to introduce a solid mass that would overpower the bar and cut off the sightlines to the windows. There was momentary thought that Pablo Picasso might

When Marie Nichols's beaded aluminum drapes were hung, no one expected them to move gently in the air currents.

One night in Paris many years ago, John Galliher and I went to pick up Gloria Guiness at her beautiful flat on our way to a rather elegant, small dinner given by friends. Galliher, an American sophisticate known for his taste, was a great admirer of Gloria's and Gloria very much liked being admired. That evening she was wearing a slender column of black silk, its only ornament a bib of tiny gold chains from neck to waist, one of Yves St. Laurent's newest creations. She looked divine, and expectant.

When we arrived at our destination, her expression was still expectant

be commissioned to do a neon sculpture over the bar, but RA and Johnson instead turned to artist Richard Lippold, who was delighted to be asked because he believed strongly that "works of art rise to their noblest expression in collaboration with great architecture." Lippold proposed two sets of bronze tubes to hang above the bar itself and, as a balance, above the balcony area. Once the sketches were shown to his patrons, Kelly was brought in to light them and the surrounding area to take full advantage of their shimmer as they swayed softly in the air, thereby giving volume to the space without adding bulk.

Jerry Brody recalls watching Lippold setting the dozens of metal tubes to the ceiling. "Lippold would go up the ladder, put one up, adjust it, come back down the ladder, stare at it, then comb his hair. Then he'd go back up the ladder and put in another one."

Lippold felt that this particular work of art could exist nowhere else but at The Four Seasons. "It is not for me to say that the building would suffer through lack of the sculpture," he said, "but I would like to state that I feel the sculpture would surely lose most of its meaning without the building."

The enormous windows that looked out on three sides of the restaurant presented another challenge—how to keep them from appearing to be black "walls" at night. Johnson at first considered using draperies of silk but was told that the wear-and-tear of a restaurant and the bright New York sunlight would destroy them within six months. (The delicate and very expensive fabric first used as upholstery in the dining room did not, in fact, last out the year.) Lippold suggested instead that draperies of metal chains would not only block out the light and the night, but also echo the shimmering light from his own sculptures. There was some concern that such an eccentric curtain treatment might be too heavy, somber, or cold, but the designers took a chance. The drapes were fabricated by Marie Nichols from anodized aluminum fitted into vertical channels in the mullions.

On the day the draperies were put up, Johnson got a call from the installers, who told him he'd better come down quickly from his office in the Seagram Building and see something very odd and potentially disastrous. Johnson rushed down to find that the links in the drapery's chain mail rippled gently from top to bottom, a motion caused either by the heating and air-conditioning currents or by the rumble of railroad trains exiting Grand Central underneath Park Avenue—what Johnson preferred to call the "shock of New York." Though beautiful in an eerie and sensuous way, it was worrisome and, Johnson thought, might even make some diners sick. He anxiously called Baum to come over to look at this unexpected development. Baum arrived, looked at the draperies for a few moments, and turned to Johnson. "It's beautiful, Philip," he said. "I love it!"

"You know," Johnson said later, "I got the feeling that when Baum saw those lighted chain curtains, he was going to let me do whatever I wanted in the restaurant."

The other dining room was to have a different atmosphere from the Grill, something a bit lighter, less masculine, yet wholly in keeping with Mies's design for the building. This was a very large space whose integrity would have been violated by the installation of row after row of tables and chairs (the chairs themselves were based on Mies's own famous Brno design of chrome and leather). Here Pahlmann came up with a brilliant concept. Why not put a twenty-foot-square white Carrara marble pool in the middle of the dining room? Lighted softly from below and set at table level, a pool would have a softening effect on the geometry of the room, and the pleasant bubbling of the water would have a soothing effect on the diners. RA liked the idea and Johnson approved, so the plans were drawn up for what was to be called the Pool Room.

Here landscape architect Karl Linn was called in to create a harmony of interior design with interior plantings keyed to the four seasons theme. Having rejected the idea of placing Picasso sculptures around the pool, RA decided that trees could be used instead to serve as a kind of sheltering canopy. The species of trees would be changed four times a year to reflect the changing seasons—azaleas and birch in the spring, philodendrons and cocos palmosa in the summer, burnt orange and yellow mums, chrysanthemums, and oak leaf branches in autumn, and white chrysanthe-

but faintly annoyed. "John" she said, "you haven't mentioned my dress." Galliher, undaunted, looked at her from head to toe, appraising. "It's charming, darling," he said, "charming." That was not enough for the flawlessly dressed Madame Guiness. "You don't like it?" she persisted. "I do like it," he replied. "It's just that it reminds me a little bit of the window treatment at The Four Seasons."
Gloria Guiness never wore that dress again.

—Nancy Holmes, editor at large, *Worth* magazine

Richard Lippold's bronze sculpture hanging above the bar in the Grill Room.

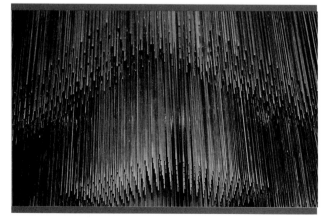

mums and white birch in winter—which required monumental research into how best to maintain living trees within a restaurant environment. Linn visited hundreds of nurseries to find matched trees—seventeen feet high—which then had to be carefully root-pruned in advance for shipment when needed. Together with plant physiologist Dr. O. Wesley Davidson and lighting consultant Kelly, Linn developed a system of providing consistent humidity, light, and temperature that would allow for proper maintenance. Using both natural and artificial light, they directed that all lighting be turned on high at sunrise and left that way until the restaurant opened for the day. To counteract spindly growth under muted light conditions, the temperature of the room was lowered each night by eight degrees after the restaurant closed.

Like every other detail at The Four Seasons, foliage and flowers are changed every three months to reflect the passing of the seasons.

The corridor leading from the Grill Room to the Pool Room also presented a problem, not only because it was just wasted space (although it did allow for access to the restaurant from Park Avenue). Once through the two glass doors, one was faced with a twenty-foot-high marble wall. Here, too, the resolution of the problem was the fortuitous result of a disagreement on the project.

As part of the deal on the restaurant, the Bronfmans intended to display the work of some of the finest modern artists, particularly the work of Pablo Picasso, who had been asked to do a large painting for the Pool Room. Picasso said he had no time for such a project but said the Bronfmans could have—at a price of about $50,000—a curtain designed for the Diaghilev ballet's 1920 Paris production of Manuel de Falla's *Le Tricorne* (*The Three-Cornered Hat*). The curtain, which had been intended for the Museum of Modern Art, was much too large for installation there, so the Bronfmans bought it with the intent of hanging it in the Pool Room of The Four Seasons. In fact, there had been some talk of decorating the room with Picasso artworks and perhaps calling it the Picasso Room. RA had already rejected six pieces of Picasso sculpture for the Pool Room (Brody flew to Paris to see them and pronounced them "ugly"), and now Baum objected to this extraordinary Picasso theater curtain as just not right for a dining room. "The Picasso depicted a bullfight," explained Baum, "and I just didn't think that would go down well with customers dining on tournedos of beef."

Johnson was furious, but RA still had the final say and compromised by hanging the Picasso in the corridor, which made for a magnificent surprise for those entering from Park Avenue or coming through from the Grill.

There was other fine art for the new restaurant, including a Jan Arp and three Mirós in the downstairs lobby. With Johnson's help, RA set up an exchange program with the Museum of Modern Art and Leo Castelli's art gallery, by which paintings and sculpture would be lent to RA and, as part of the theme of change and renewal, be exchanged for others throughout the year.

Meanwhile other artists and designers were turning their attention to everything from silverware to stationery. Mies's Brno chair had been adapted for restaurant seating, Johnson designed the banquettes, the private party chairs were by Charles Eames, and Eero Saarinen created the hassocks and taboret tables. Garth and Ada Louise Huxtable were hired to create more than a hundred pieces of serviceware (eighteen of

The downstairs lobby of The Four Seasons where four tapestries designed by Monica Correa hang.

which are in the Museum of Modern Art) in a nine-month period. Working closely with Brody, Baum, and Stöckli, the Huxtables designed everything that went from the kitchen to the table, including two kinds of champagne glasses, bread trays, and separate service for caviar, hot and cold appetizers, fruits, and vegetables. Ashtrays were colored and keyed to the seasons. The traditional lip on restaurant glassware was done away with in favor of a clean edge, and plates were designed to be as beautiful in profile as they were set on the table.

Carpets were hand-loomed by V'soske. Service wagons, based on a Baum idea, were made with hammered-silver tops and walnut cabinets, with a special drawer for cheeses and hooks from which to hang sausages. The graphics used on everything from the menus to matchbooks were created by Emilio Antonucci and, of course (like the waiters' uniforms and

When Philip Johnson first submitted his designs for the dining rooms' carpets, they were rejected because the carpets would become soiled too easily, especially if butter was dropped on them. Johnson merely sniffed, "Butter never crossed my mind." The carpets went in as he designed them.

even the typewriter ribbons), changed their colors every three months. Upholstery was changed, too: black for autumn and winter, beige for spring and summer. It was only because there wasn't enough time to design and make new molds for silverware that RA ordered standard pieces from I. Freeman. Uniforms for waiters, busboys, and doormen were designed by Eleanor Charles and Monte Streitfield.

For their part, RA spent a million dollars on The Four Seasons, made possible by the success of their recent takeover of the gargantuan Mamma Leone's Italian restaurant, which was grossing $4 million by 1959. Seagram's expenditure for the restaurant was to total $4.5 million—by far the largest amount of money ever lavished on a restaurant. Indeed, the entire Guggenheim Museum, which opened the same year, cost only $3 million.

Meanwhile Lambert and Johnson were in discussion with Mark Rothko to do a series of paintings intended solely for the large enclosed dining room above the Pool Room. This was a tremendous commitment on Lambert's part, not because of the fee, which was only $40,000, but because, of all the New York School abstractionists of the period, Rothko—given his temperament and ideas—seemed inimical to the serene aesthetics of The Four Seasons. After all, it was Rothko who listed "tragedy, doom, and ecstasy" as the three major preoccupations of his art, and corporate wealth and social elitism ran counter to everything he stood for. Still, he admired Mies van der Rohe's work immensely, and the thought of having a large space entirely to himself, free from the commercial atmosphere of the galleries, led him to accept the commission, which was to cover one long interrupted wall and about half of a smaller wall that included an entrance to the kitchen. By autumn he had fitted out a studio on the Bowery to the exact dimensions of the Four Seasons room—fifty-six by twenty-seven feet—set up his scaffolding, and begun to paint.

Rothko did something like thirty paintings in three different series, many of which were rejected by the restaurant and sold separately. Most of them were quite somber and contemplative, fuzzy rectangles within rectangles, with no more than two colors or tones of a single color.

By the spring of 1959 Rothko apparently had developed a sinister intent for the use of his paintings. In June—one month before the restaurant was to open—he confided to a friend that he'd been "commissioned to paint a series of canvases for the walls of the most exclusive restaurant in the Seagram Building . . . a place where the richest bastards in New York

come to feed and show off. . . . I accepted this assignment as a challenge, with strictly malicious intentions. I hope to paint something that will ruin the appetite of every son of a bitch who ever eats in that room."

Referring to Michelangelo's designs for the walls in the Laurentian Library in Florence, Rothko described what he intended at The Four Seasons: "[Michelangelo] makes the viewers feel that they are trapped in a room where all the doors and windows are bricked up." Not exactly what Lambert, Johnson, Brody, or Baum had in mind for their airy dining room with a twenty-foot-high window overlooking Park Avenue.

At the time, Rothko insisted he never had realized the dining room was to be used to feed the "richest bastards in New York," believing instead that it was to be a "workers' cafeteria." Of course, there had never been any such plan in Johnson's designs.

Garth and Ada Louise Huxtable designed more than a hundred pieces of serviceware for The Four Seasons—eighteen of which are in the permanent collection of New York's Museum of Modern Art.

When asked why he dined at The Four Seasons so often, Philip Johnson replied, "To patronize my own work."

Suddenly, with the work uncompleted, Rothko and his family took off for Italy, not to return for months. By that time The Four Seasons was finished and the staff was in rehearsals, but the upper dining room was still bare. Desperate, Jerry Brody asked art collector Ben Heller if he had something appropriate to fill up the gigantic fifty-six-foot-long wall. Heller said he did own a rather large abstract work his kids were going to destroy if he didn't do something with, and perhaps the restaurant would like to borrow it until the Rothkos were delivered. Brody accepted, donated $3,500 to Heller's favorite charity, and hung the large painting, called *Blue Poles,* in the upper room. The artist was Jackson Pollock.

After returning to New York, Rothko continued to work on the paintings, even though he had already decided not to sell them to Seagram. When the artist came to dinner at The Four Seasons and saw Pollock's work hanging in the room, he snorted, "I don't like it." The next day Rothko pounded the table and screamed, "Anybody who will eat that kind of food for those kinds of prices will never look at a painting of mine!" Soon afterward he told Seagram he could not complete the commission and sent back his $40,000 fee.

The murals were then sold or given to others, including the Tate Gallery and Houston's Menil Collection, where they reside today.

With the exception of the Rothko murals, everything was in readiness for the opening of The Four Seasons on July 29, 1959. The anticipation in the New York media was tremendous over this, the most expensive restaurant ever built, especially since it was in a building already praised as a masterpiece of twentieth-century architecture. No one knew what kind of reception the new restaurant would get, and the publication in the powerful *New York Times* of an article entitled "$4.5 Million Restaurant to Open Here," by food editor Craig Claiborne, just a few days before the opening, worried RA executives, who were concerned that people might be put off by the expense of it all.

The opening, therefore, was kept deliberately anticlimactic. Contrary to the usual policy of having PR agent Phil Miles mount a glamorous party filled with Broadway and Hollywood stars and plenty of press, RA planned a very soft debut. For three weeks prior to the opening, RA held small lunches and dinners for friends and had waiters and captains serve each other, in order to develop a certain Four Seasons style.

By late afternoon of July 29, everything was set and in place. Twenty captains oversaw fifty waiters and fifteen busboys in green summer tunics as they polished and shined the glassware and silver. The 1,300 cases of

wine in the air-conditioned rooms off the Pool Room were at perfect temperature for service. Lighting was adjusted for the last time while a maintenance crew clipped and trimmed the ficus trees of all imperfect leaves.

A typical restrained but elegant table setting in a private dining room, circa 1960.

At one point Mrs. Samuel Bronfman came to tour the premises and seemed in awe of what she beheld. "May I bring down Mr. Sam now?" she asked Brody. Her husband—the man who two years earlier had told Brody all he wanted was to be able to get a nice piece of flanken—came down from his office, entered the restaurant, turned to Brody and the assembled RA personnel, nodded, said, "Thank you very much," and went back upstairs to work.

As the time approached for the doors to open to the public, Philip Johnson came through the glass doors on Fifty-second Street, climbed the broad stairway, entered the majestic Grill Room, watched as the beaded metal curtains swayed in the windows, walked across the marble floor past the Picasso curtain, and entered the Pool Room, where the quiet was broken only by the gentle babbling of the blue-green water. The architect looked up and around him, shook his head a little, and sighed, "Isn't it beautiful? It's a shame to spoil it with people."

The Four Seasons opened in pieces: first the Grill Room, then a week later the Pool Room. (The separate, casual, twenty-four-hour-a-day eatery called the Brasserie opened at the same time on the other side of the building.)

No one knew what kind of reception the new restaurant would get, and Brody feared that the city's food writers—especially Craig Claiborne of the *New York Times*—might not understand everything RA was trying to do at The Four Seasons. Claiborne, who had been trained at a Swiss hotel school in the intractable traditions of French haute cuisine and service, had joined the *Times* in 1957 and developed his craft on the job, becoming in the process the most formidable food critic in America, although he did not become a weekly restaurant reviewer until 1963. Claiborne was also known as a Francophile whose favorite restaurant was Le Pavillon, and early in 1959 he had written a devastating article on the dining scene in New York, which he found generally to have more style than substance. And that included some of RA's properties.

Thus, on hearing a rumor that Claiborne was going to savage The Four Seasons, Brody took the bold step of asking the food editor to lunch at the restaurant to explain how The Four Seasons had been developed, how it was a new kind of restaurant for a new age in New York, and how all the effort, the architectural detail, the artwork, and the idea of evolution was very different from anything that had ever been done.

PAGE 40, Top left: Albert Kumin, The Four Seasons' original pastry chef. Top right: Tasting at La Fonda del Sol are Fred Rufe (left), chef Albert Stöckli, and Joe Baum. Bottom left: Tableside food preparation in the Pool Room. Bottom right: The original pastry cart from 1959 with the restaurant's signature Fancy Cake on top and Chocolate Velvet cake on the second tier.

RA had made every effort to gather the best ingredients, the best talent, the best designers, and the best service staff to be found in America. And Baum was insistent that The Four Seasons was *not* to be a French restaurant; it was to be a *New York* restaurant—whatever that meant in 1959. Baum therefore went against the entrenched policy of hiring French personnel (although he did steal a few from Le Pavillon), preferring instead Americans and a good number of British plucked from the service staff of the *Queen Mary.*

In fact, Baum sought to challenge every accepted notion about fine dining as developed since the nineteenth century according to Parisian models adapted by Delmonico's. Baum's sense of sophistication did not necessarily mean numbing formality, and he questioned everything about every ingredient, every piece of silverware, even the height of tables when people sat down behind them (tables at The Four Seasons are deliberately adjusted three-quarters of an inch lower than the industry standard). When associates defended sacrosanct traditions of table placement, settings, napkin folding, or anything else that had to do with service, Baum would ask them *why* it had always been done that way. Was there any good reason not to try *another* way that seemed to make more sense in the modern world?

Nevertheless, the emphasis Baum and his associates put on the food and wine at The Four Seasons was extraordinary, even beyond what Henri Soulé had done at Le Pavillon. In fact, when the news of the menu innovations at The Four Seasons reached Soulé's ears, he forbade his kitchen staff to eat there on pain of being fired from their jobs.

The development of recipes was an arduous process in which all RA personnel participated, with Albert Stöckli absorbing ideas from Baum, Brody, Alan Lewis, Stuart Levin, and others, then translating them into modern concepts of cooking. Much of the early experimentation was done in the kitchens of the Hawaiian Room, and Stöckli would bring Baum and his colleagues dozens of variations of a dish before everyone agreed on its excellence and appropriateness for The Four Seasons. Levin recalled once testing thirty-seven different soufflés developed by pastry chef Albert Kumin before finding an acceptable one—all in one day! During the process, the kitchen ran out of soufflé dishes and resorted to pouring the batter into bottle caps.

RA had earlier hired James Beard, then considered the "dean" of American cookbook writers, to consult on their restaurants' menus and to train the waiters about the history, varieties, and service of wine. A man of daunting size and girth, Beard had long played the part of the merry gastronome with unbridled gusto, and his spirit was infectious among RA personnel.

Beard added enormous prestige to the project. Even Baum was in awe of the man's breadth of knowledge on subjects ranging from the culinary arts to theater, literature, and ballet. Still, RA executives (few had real titles, and most were called "directors") who were present when Beard tasted recipes along with Baum and Stöckli recalled with some bemusement how the gargantuan eminence would simply nod in agreement with whatever anyone else approved or discarded. But Baum protested that assumption, telling Beard's biographer, Evan Jones, "People say he always agreed with you. Well, he didn't—he sounded as if he did, but people jump to first impressions. It's a matter of taking the trouble to hear what he was saying. You know, sometimes you have to peel something off to know what it is. I'd know that he'd maintained his position completely, and it was not a question of making trouble—it was just that he knew a lot of confrontation was not necessary, if there was another way to make the point."

More than anything else and in contrast with all he had done before at The Newarker and the Forum, Baum had come to believe that a man and a menu should tell the truth and do it without any flowery language. He therefore banned descriptive phrases on the menus—no more "lusciously prepared young duckling with garden-fresh peaches" and no more outrageous culinary puns like "The Noblest Caesar Salad Of Them All." No more gimmicks, period: if The Four Seasons listed an ingredient on its menu, the guest need not ask if it was fresh or sweet or ripe.

Stöckli was extremely open to new ideas, ingredients, and spices (he loved curried dishes in particular), but he was also adamant that classic European dishes be made according to strict rules—something not always done in other American restaurant kitchens: "I believe in making [beef] Stroganoff the way they make it in Russia," he insisted, "and coq au vin as they prepare it in Paris." This often meant the importation of the finest foreign ingredients, like foie gras from Strasbourg, caviar from the Caspian Sea, smoked salmon and fresh grouse from Scotland, Dutch herrings, Milanese truffles, and an array of wild mushrooms almost unknown in the United States until The Four Seasons imported them. He also had an RA man in the Midwest specially select his beef, which was then aged and slaughtered to Stöckli's specifications. Baby vegetables were raised to order on Long Island truck farms, and an array of flowers like nasturtiums were used as salad ingredients.

In the autumn of 1961, I was invited to dinner at The Four Seasons by a very special gentleman, who was later to become my husband. Even then I was an avid follower of fine dining, and The Four Seasons' reputation had already been established: sophisticated elegance. At the mature age of nineteen, this was indeed a major step.

The evening arrived, and we were ushered into the magnificent Pool Room. It was everything the critics said and more. We busied ourselves with the impressive menu and began ordering. Everything was fine until we ordered asparagus and the captain asked, "White or green?" Immediate and mutual panic: neither of us had ever heard of white asparagus, and our silence became obvious. Our captain, sensitive to our plight, saved the day by saying, "But of course, you want to select them yourself," and promptly brought forth a basket of fresh green and white asparagus. We contentedly chose each piece—white, of course.
—Barbara Barton,
    New York City

RA developed resources around the United States for the best freshwater and seawater fish, as many as possible kept alive in custom-built water tanks in the kitchen. Trout was brought in from Colorado, geese from Wisconsin, blue crabs from Virginia. Herbs were grown on the premises. Tomatoes were vine ripened, and menus emphasized the seasonal availability of fruits and vegetables.

Nothing was too good for the Four Seasons kitchen, and no expense was spared, not even the purchase of a cotton candy machine used to create fanciful presentations for customers celebrating a birthday or other event. Stöckli designed the kitchen to be the most technologically modern workplace of any restaurant in the world, with state-of-the-art rotisseries, grills, exhaust systems, and refrigeration.

The first menus at The Four Seasons were amazing documents, beautifully designed and fronted with rice paper. The dinner menu listed at least twenty-six cold appetizers, twenty-two hot appetizers, and twenty-five entrées, in addition to any special request a customer might make of the kitchen. Baskets of seasonal vegetables were brought to each table, and guests picked which they wanted to have that evening.

In 1959 such dishes as coriander prosciutto, French-fried baby shrimp in Japanese shoyu sauce, mustard fruits, minted lobster parfait, smoked salmon soufflé with onion sauce, julep of crabmeat in sweet pepperoni, larded pigeon with candied figs, salads made with nasturtium leaves, artichoke soufflé, Amish ham steak with hot rhubarb, and pomegranate sherbet were unknown in American restaurants, and desserts such as chocolate velvet cake were much copied around the country.

Despite Baum's earlier claim that there would be no flaming dishes, a few were eventually added to the menu, but the grill items formed a large part of the menu. Many dishes were still accompanied with sweet sauces or garnishes, according to the taste of the era, and richness was considered

An early menu indicated the style and direction The Four Seasons intended to take with modern American and Continental cuisine. The prices were among the highest of any restaurant in the world.

a virtue in dishes like beef marrow in "bouillon or cream," pheasant en salmis, and quail en brochette with chestnut gnocchi.

Yet Stöckli never strayed into culinary exoticism for its own sake, nor did he mask the essential flavors of crab, veal, trout, or venison with cloyingly heavy sauces. Most of the menu, in fact, was composed of simply grilled or roasted steaks, chops, and game.

Four times a year the menus were completely redone, according to the availability of fresh ingredients. In winter there would be Iceland herring, smoked goose with pickled walnuts, stone crabs flown in from Miami, a New England lobster tartlet, and roast boar with apple dressing. In the spring would arrive a tureen of April fruits, new potatoes with dill, and shad roe. In the heat of summer the kitchen offered lobster with sorrel, cream of chicken soup with new oats, bouillabaisse salad, and a soufflé of spinach. For dessert there were primrose beignets and kumquat ice cream. And come harvesttime, the menu listed mussels glazed with Vermont cheddar cheese, curried crabmeat crepes, Swiss chard soufflé, skillet steak with smothered onions, gosling with rosemary leaves, and grouse with bread sauce.

In many ways the early menus of The Four Seasons were the inspiration for what much later came to be called "New American Cuisine" (a term nonchalantly used by Silas Spitzer in a December 1959 article about Stöckli in *Holiday* magazine), whose hallmarks were a reliance on the freshest produce, poultry, seafood, and game, prepared with a respect for their tastes, textures, and seasonal range. The Four Seasons' commitment to carrying California wines was also unusual for a deluxe restaurant at a time when most others stocked only French bottlings. RA did, however, have wine expert Frank Schoonmaker choose a V.S.O.P. Cognac as a special reserve bottling with a Four Seasons label.

So much of what The Four Seasons was doing with their cuisine was so revolutionary in 1959 that RA had good reason to wonder if a sufficient number of people—and critics—were capable of appreciating it. Baum insisted that it was RA's mission to "educate the public," but Brody preferred arm twisting to missionary zeal and, using every bit of his professional and personal charm, went off to lunch with Craig Claiborne.

Whatever he said that afternoon must have had some effect, because, to RA's delight, the *Times* food editor wrote a very respectable review of the restaurant on October 2. It began with the amazing statement:

When gastronome Gregory Thomas hosted a dinner at The Four Seasons, his guests were left to wonder at the unusual taste and texture of the garniture in a sauce that accompanied the turkey. With the tone of someone surprised at others' ignorance, Thomas replied, "Those are cockscombs and diced rooster testicles."

The uniqueness of The Four Seasons was immediately recognized, as shown by this ad for a restaurant guide, which appeared the year after The Four Seasons opened.

Read about
The Four Seasons
in the new book...
GREAT RESTAURANTS OF AMERICA
100 superb places to dine personally selected by
TED PATRICK
Editor of Holiday
and
SILAS SPITZER

There has never been a restaurant better keyed to the tempo of Manhattan than The Four Seasons, which opened recently at 99 East 52nd Street.

Both in decor and in menu, it is spectacular, modern, and audacious. It is expensive and opulent, and it is perhaps the most exciting restaurant to open in New York within the last two decades. On the whole, the cuisine is not exquisite in the sense that la grande cuisine française at its superlative best is exquisite.

One of the most creditable features of this new restaurant is the table service. In a city where waiters are noted for their Olympic detachment, it is a revelation to find a corps with the pride and enthusiasm that their occupation demands. Judged on the basis of recent visits, there is probably no dining establishment in New York where training for table service is more thorough.

Like most facets of The Four Seasons, the decor is a conversation piece sufficient in itself to sustain lively causerie throughout a leisurely lunch. There are massive plants that reflect seasonal changes; from the ceiling in the bar area are hung thousands of brass rods to produce what is called a "sculptured chandelier" effect. . . . Both the luncheon and dinner menus at The Four Seasons are extensive and, to a degree, bewildering. For example, the evening card lists more than a score of cold appetizers and nearly as many hot hors d'oeuvres. Typical in the cold selection is an "herbed lobster parfait." If memory serves, this contains large chunks of lobster enrobed in a devastatingly rich blend of whipped cream and hollandaise sauce.

It is not too derisive to say that the vast majority of the dishes can be categorized as "à la minute," or made on the spot. That is to say that there are many grillades, sautéed dishes, spit-roasted meats, and chafing dish specialties.

Flaming dishes are among the most popular items. One of the best of these is the traditional beef Stroganoff, which is prepared tableside in a somewhat unconventional but thoroughly tempting fashion. It is made of quarter-inch slices of prime tenderloin seasoned with sweet paprika. The meat is then sautéed in butter, flamed with Cognac, and bathed in a sauce containing meat glaze and sour cream.

An admirable feature of the restaurant is its extensive use of fresh herbs. Although herbs are used increasingly throughout America, they are not employed frequently in a fresh state.

At The Four Seasons freshly picked rosemary, chervil, and sage, among many other herbs, are available to give character to dishes on customer demand. In a similar vein, guests may dine on several varieties of fresh mushrooms generally unknown in this country. There are

Tableside omelet-making in the Pool Room.

cèpes, morels, and chanterelles, all beloved in Europe, these appearing almost daily on toast, on filets mignons, in sauces or in salads.

Then Claiborne threw out a few pointed caveats:

There are several valid criticisms that may be leveled at the preparation and presentation of the food at The Four Seasons.

In the opinion of this reviewer, it is vulgar to surcharge plates with food. The service of gross portions of edibles is a barbaric custom that is all too common in American dining places. Judged on the basis of recent visits, The Four Seasons is no exception.

There is also a tendency to serve overly sweet sauces with game. A roast grouse that represented perfection in itself was presented with a sauce totally lacking in finesse. This is because the sauce was heavily loaded with a conserve, bar-le-duc perhaps. It was accompanied, too, with a heavy dumpling that was less than tempting.

Some of the dishes are garnished with less than expertly "sculptured" vegetables. Ideally such items as potatoes and carrots are trimmed to a most attractive uniform shape and enhance a dish. It is hoped that the kitchen staff at The Four Seasons will become more skillful in this art in the future.

And a minor point, but annoying. Why does such a restaurant, so dedicated to seasonal themes, permit iceberg lettuce on the premises? Oak leaf lettuce, cos salad, and Bibb are now available in this era.

There is certainly no question that Albert Stöckli, the executive chef at The Four Seasons, has a talent to equal his imagination. At a dinner this week for an organization known as the Parlement de Bordeaux, he created a quenelle de brochet deserving of the highest praise.

This is a sublime creation made with a poached forcemeat of pike and smothered in a rich sauce made with a fish bouillon and heavy cream reduced almost to an essence. As prepared by Mr. Stöckli, the pike was as gossamer as a cloud; the sauce was capable of ravishing the palate.

The wine list at The Four Seasons ranks among the best in the city. It is also one of the most handsome in design. It's almost pointless to cite a few wines of the many, but those that were enjoyed recently were a Nuit-St.-Georges, Clos des Corvées, 1953, a Fixin, Clos du Chapitre, 1955, and a Chassagne-Montrachet, les Ruchottes, 1955. The average cost for an excellent Burgundy or Bordeaux of recent vintage is about $7. Excellent domestic wines are available at $3.50 a bottle.

It is estimated that the average luncheon check for food with wines and without cocktails totals about $25. Dinner on the same basis is about $40.

A petulant restaurant reviewer named Seymour Britchky once criticized just about everything he saw, met, and ate at The Four Seasons, noting, "The attendant in the ladies' room should not inform healthy customers that they appear ill, it should never require fifteen minutes to obtain a bottle of soda water, the pages should be trained not to trip over the wire of the Princess phones they are delivering to the tables, and, most important, get rid of those rubber trees."

Given the prejudices of food writers of the day, RA could hardly have hoped for better. Claiborne's praise gave The Four Seasons a legitimacy it needed to make it in the New York marketplace, and the write-up drew enormous attention to the restaurant, which immediately filled up with curiosity seekers, gourmets, and some of the most important people in New York. On one overbooked night, the reservationist had to refuse a table to Arthur Ochs Sulzberger, publisher of the *New York Times.*

Within months other critics chimed in. The *Herald Tribune's* Clementine Paddleford called the restaurant "fabulous, spectacular, amazing," and Ted Patrick and Silas Spitzer of *Holiday* magazine extolled it as "a restaurant of undoubted gastronomical importance, the only one of the top dozen restaurants in American which is not French or Italian, either in management or in the food it serves," also noting that it was very probably the most expensive restaurant in the world. Patrick and Spitzer caught the spirit of the menu, too, saying that many of the novel dishes and presentations were "bound to disappoint the man who is strictly and solely impressed by the traditional cuisine of France, and who regards all departures as an outrage against good taste. But gourmets who have an adventurous viewpoint approve this striking out in new directions."

Not all food critics understood what the new restaurant was supposed to be, however. One Francophile carped, "There is no excuse for such an odd combination of foods, and besides, the rooms don't even have any decorations—it looks as if they ran out of money." But for most of the writers and columnists of the day, The Four Seasons was nothing if not spectacular. It was also considered outrageously expensive. Wine merchant Bill Sokolin was at the restaurant's opening and recalls that all he could afford to drink was an $8 bottle of New York State Taylor champagne.

So, too, the architecture critics were duly impressed with what they beheld. *Architectural Record* did an extensive photo layout of the restaurant in their November issue, complete with Johnson's floor plans, and the novel usage of plants and trees throughout the restaurant won a special award in the annual Industrial and Institutional Landscaping and Beautification Committee competition that fall. The December number of *Interiors* carried a breathless review by Olga Gueft of the restaurant's decor. "The Guggenheim [Museum] is Beethoven's Ninth and The Four Seasons is Mozart's *Magic Flute,"* Gueft wrote. "Both are works of joy." She went on to expound on the restaurant's "understated strength and masculine nobility" and called the space "dignified as a bank . . . [but]

the dignity of The Four Seasons is combined with romanticism, its discipline with serenity, its sober magnificence with lightness of heart."

Highfalutin as such praise was, it expressed pretty much what Philip Johnson and RA had intended. New York was impressed, and a certain reverence accrued for what was achieved. So when Jerry Brody casually mentioned to James Rockefeller that the lights from his bank across Park Avenue glared through the restaurant's metal curtains, Rockefeller had them turned off at night, so as not to disturb that "sober magnificence" of the Pool Room.

Romantic as The Four Seasons was, there was never any question that the restaurant had been planned, in fact, as a masculine haunt. In the late 1950s it could hardly have been otherwise, since the overwhelming majority of paying customers at deluxe restaurants were business*men.* Those women who could afford to eat at such establishments favored Le Pavillon, the Colony, Voisin, and other salons that catered to them at lunch. But at night it was still a rare thing to see women dining alone and paying for their own meals.

The Four Seasons' Grill Room in particular had almost a corporate boardroom look, with its French walnut wall paneling, metal curtains, manifest bar area, and leather-and-chrome chairs. There was nothing soft about the room really, nothing feminine, and RA's executives, every one of them male, expected to attract the same, like-minded expense-account rich corporate crowd, not the "ladies who lunch."

Brody also wanted The Four Seasons to attract first and foremost a local market, believing that out-of-towners might not appreciate the sophistication of the restaurant and would prefer instead the more operatic atmosphere of the Forum of the Twelve Caesars and Mamma Leone's. RA was already at work on another extravagant project in the Time & Life Building on Sixth Avenue: called La Fonda del Sol, it would have a bright, colorful, highly developed Central and South American theme that would be more accessible for everyone.

RA cared little about attracting either the fickle show business crowd—although it developed a formidable clientele among Hollywood and Broadway stars of the day—or New York's ultraconservative high society, much preferring to lure in the city's power brokers and a new class of young executives in industries like publishing, advertising, and fashion. RA thereupon attempted to give their new restaurant the appeal of a private club opened to a discriminating segment of the public. To heighten this aura of exclusivity, The Four Seasons would not accept credit cards

A bad thunderstorm hit New York during lunchtime at The Four Seasons. As George Lois entered the restaurant soaking wet, he overheard one of the "Silver Bear" Hunt brothers tell someone on the phone, "Well, the weather's foul, but the wheeling-dealing's fine."

The Pool Room (above) and Grill Room (opposite), largely unchanged since opening in 1959.

(then still a relatively new concept anyway) and welcomed house accounts in an effort to develop a regular clientele base. House accounts encouraged frequent dining at a restaurant, since clients left all the inconveniences of checks, gratuities, and billing to RA's accountants, who would send a statement once a month. By the turn of the year RA boasted to *Fortune* magazine that The Four Seasons had more than seven thousand such accounts, with only 20 percent out-of-towners.

The value of publicity and promotion was not lost on RA, however, and their PR agents, Philip Miles and Roger Martin, had great fun coming up with snappy ideas to bring The Four Seasons to the public's attention. A few weeks after opening, they arranged for a fashion show *in* the pool, with the models stepping from box to box. Miles actually wanted a model to slip deliberately into the water, but Baum nixed the idea in order to attract more fashion shows in the future. On another occasion the pool was covered with a sheet of ice for the introduction of a new soft drink named Fresca.

RA also hired a young, irreverent art director named George Lois, of Papert Koenig Lois, to promote all their restaurants in the media.

Lois, who had already done ads for Seagram products and had his office in the building, was immediately taken with the idea and saw a certain poetic justice in accepting the account, even though it was not for big bucks: when The Four Seasons opened, Lois had taken his wife there for dinner, and he remembered how they had sat counting their money to see if they had enough to pay the bill.

At the time restaurant advertising was undertaken conservatively, usually consisting of a small box in a magazine with nothing more than the establishment's name, address, and phone number. But Lois, who would go on to do more than 1,200 ads for RA over the years, wanted the arrival of The Four Seasons to seem more like an event. His advertisement read, "THE FOUR SEASONS. THE NEW RESTAURANT ON 52ND STREET," with Emilio Antonucci's graphic of four stylized trees beneath it. The ad was forthright and to the point, but to cognoscenti, it signaled

When George Lois first dined at The Four Seasons, he balked at paying $1.50 for mashed potatoes. Today The Four Seasons serves a baked potato with olive oil for $9.75.

Susan Rudin, the imagina-
tive and gracious wife
of real estate tycoon Jack
Rudin, wanted to encour-
age her husband's tradi-
tion of donating exotic
animals to the zoo. To help
his cause, at his seventi-
eth birthday dinner she
presented him with a gift
of three llamas and
announced that each was
to be named for three
places he can be found at
mealtime: Brasserie,
Parma, and Four Seasons.

As everyone laughed,
Susan noticed that one of
their guests, restaurateur
Pete Kriendler, wasn't as
amused as the others.
Quickly realizing the problem, she diplomatically
assured him that the very
first llama offspring would
be named "21."

—Regina Macmenamin,
Assistant to the
Vice President and
General Manager of
The Four Seasons

that The Four Seasons was going head to head with that *other* restaurant on Fifty-second Street—the "21" Club.

To most observers in 1960, RA's fortunes seemed to be soaring and its success rate astounding in the rough-and-tumble restaurant world. Indeed, RA told *Fortune* that The Four Seasons had gone into the black within six months of its opening and was grossing $250,000 a month. If that was true, it certainly was not translating into net profits, for the cost of running The Four Seasons was extraordinary, and Baum, though careful to price out every item in detail, never worried about the cost of anything if it met his high standards. And despite his often fearsome demeanor, Baum paid his employees high salaries and found it almost impossible to fire anyone.

Whenever Baum thought something was going stale, he reacted, often vehemently, without necessarily knowing how he wanted it changed. He visited all the RA properties almost daily and on occasion would call up George Lois and say, "Let's go bust balls."

Many RA employees recall the time Baum walked into the restaurant and demanded to know, "What's wrong with the consommé?" The staff, bewildered because he had not even yet tasted the soup, asked him how he could tell there was something wrong with it. Baum furrowed his brow, leaned forward, and said, "There's *always* something wrong with the consommé."

"Baum didn't always know when something was right," said Stuart Levin, then The Four Seasons' manager, "but he always knew when it was wrong." Alan Reyburn, who came to RA in 1962, recalls how Baum would come into the restaurant, see something that displeased him, curl his lip, and snarl, "That's not what I had in mind," then storm out. Reyburn and his associates would then wonder, "What the hell *did* he have in mind?"

On the occasion of a $10,000 grand dinner held for an exclusive gastro-nomic society known as the Confrérie des Chevaliers du Tastevin (of which Baum was a member), The Four Seasons pulled out all the stops in an attempt to achieve absolute perfection. The six-course dinner included three kinds of oysters and other shellfish, oxtail soup, grilled wolffish with fennel, Bresse chicken with truffles under the skin and sauce suprême, French cheeses, and pineapple sorbet. The wines were just as impressive: Krug Brut Reserve Champagne, Muscadet Clos des Orfeuilles '61, Chablis Grand Cru Les Clos '59, Chassagne-Montrachet Clos Saint-Jean '57, Latricières-Chambertin '49, and various *digestifs.*

The next day Baum asked Roger Martin how it went.

"Well, at our press conference after the meal, they resolved unanimously that it was the finest meal ever served in the history of the world," answered Martin.

Baum paused for a moment, then snapped, "Goddammit, that's not good enough!"

It probably never would be with Baum, who in any case was already on to other projects. As significant a statement as The Four Seasons had been, it was only one of many projects RA had under development by the time it opened in 1959, and Baum was getting starry-eyed again. The plans for La Fonda del Sol were well under way, Baum and other executives had already been on extended research trips to South America, and, though completely different in style and atmosphere from The Four Seasons, La Fonda was planned to be equally spectacular, with rows of open ovens and rotisseries, folk art figures made from bread, and hundreds of folk art dolls. La Fonda was designed by Alexander Girard (who had been recommended to RA by Philip Johnson), and Baum even told a *New Yorker* interviewer, "I think that of all our places La Fonda is the one I love the most."

Joe Baum (center) tasting dishes with Restaurant Associates personnel Lee Jaffe (far left), Jerry Brody (left), Alexander Girard (right), and Fred Rufe (far right) for the menu at La Fonda del Sol, their South American theme restaurant in the Time and Life Building.

Baum was never one to look back, and La Fonda occupied much of his and RA's time and money. The company's reputation for creating unique, high-profile restaurants was unquestioned, but in fact only Mamma Leone's was a cash cow, and in 1961 RA was forced to raise money for La Fonda and other projects by going public.

Meanwhile The Four Seasons was eating up its own profits and adding little or nothing to RA's coffers. Business in the glamorous Pool Room was consistently good, but they were not exactly packing them in at the Grill Room. In fact, regular customer George Lois recalled that often at lunch he would wave at Philip Johnson—who would never again design a restaurant—across an empty dining room.

Farmhouse Duckling au Poivre

1 medium duckling, about 6 pounds, trimmed for roasting
6 tablespoons coarsely crushed black peppercorns
¼ cup Cognac
2 cups veal or chicken stock
1 cup heavy cream
1 teaspoon *glace de viande* (optional; see Note)
Salt

1. Preheat the oven to 350° F. Place the duckling breast-side up in a large roasting pan. Roast for 1¼ hours, pricking the skin frequently with a fork to allow the fat to escape. Remove the pan from the oven and use the back of a spoon to press the crushed pepper into the skin of the duckling. Return to the oven and cook 15 minutes longer or until the juices run clear when the thigh is pierced with the tip of a sharp knife.

2. Pour off all the fat from the pan. Pour the Cognac over the duckling and, standing back, carefully ignite with a long kitchen match. Allow the flames to subside.

3. Remove the duckling to a carving board and cover with foil to keep warm. Place the roasting pan on top of the stove over medium-high heat. Pour in the veal or chicken stock and bring to a boil, scraping up the bits clinging to the bottom of the pan. Add the cream and bring back to a boil. Stir in the *glace de viande,* if using. Season to taste with salt. Strain the sauce and keep warm until ready to serve.

4. Carve the duckling into 4 to 6 serving pieces and pass the sauce separately.

Serves 4

NOTE: *Glace de viande* is a strong reduction of hearty veal or beef stock used in some professional kitchens. It can be purchased by mail order from Maison Glass, 1111 East 58th Street, New York, NY 10022 (telephone 212–755–3316).

Crisp Shrimp with Mustard Fruits

For the sauce

2 cups milk
3 tablespoons unsalted butter
3 tablespoons all-purpose flour
2 tablespoons dry mustard
6 tablespoons imported Italian mustard fruit, coarsely chopped (see Note)
Salt and pepper

For the shrimp

24 large shrimp, about 2½ pounds
1 cup mustard fruits, coarsely chopped
Oil for deep-frying
4 cups all-purpose flour plus about 1 cup additional for rolling
1 teaspoon baking powder
2 tablespoons vegetable oil
3 cups water
2 egg yolks
Salt
Deep-fried parsley for garnish, optional

1. To prepare the sauce, place the milk in a medium saucepan and bring to a boil over medium-high heat. In a separate medium saucepan, melt the butter over medium-high heat. Whisk in the flour and cook, stirring often, for 1 to 2 minutes or until foaming and lemon-colored. Do not brown. Pour in the hot milk, whisk well, and bring to a boil. Reduce heat to medium and simmer, stirring often, for 3 to 5 minutes. Stir in the mustard and chopped mustard fruits. Season to taste with salt and pepper. Remove from the heat and cover. Reheat gently over low heat just before serving.

2. To prepare the shrimp, bring a large pot of salted water to a boil over high heat. Add the shrimp and bring back to a boil. Cook until the shrimp are bright pink and firm, 2 to 3 minutes. Drain, cool, then peel and devein the shrimp.

3. Slit the shrimp about halfway through to butterfly. Fill each slit with a small amount of the chopped mustard fruits. Pat firmly to stuff the shrimp. Set aside.

4. Prepare a deep-fat fryer or electric skillet with oil for frying. Heat to

NOTE: Mustard fruits can be found in many specialty food stores. It can be obtained through mail order from Dean & DeLuca, 560 Broadway, New York, NY 10012 (telephone 212–431–1691, extension 270).

(Continued on next page)

400° F. In a large bowl, combine the 4 cups of flour with the baking powder, oil, water, egg yolks, and salt to taste. Stir briefly to form a thick batter.

5. Roll the stuffed shrimp in the additional flour and then dip them into the batter. Transfer to the hot oil and cook, a few at a time, for 4 to 6 minutes or until well browned. Drain on paper towels. Serve hot with the sauce on the side. Garnish with fried parsley if desired.

Serves 6 as an appetizer or 4 as a main course

Tiny Shrimp in Potato Baskets with Sauce Shoyu

Oil for deep-frying
4 large potatoes, about ½ pound each, peeled
Salt and pepper
1 pound tiny shrimp
2 tablespoons shoyu powder (available in Asian markets)
2 tablespoons cold water
2 tablespoons mayonnaise

1. Fill a deep-fat fryer or electric skillet with a deep layer of oil. Heat to 350° F.

2. Slice the potatoes paper-thin, preferably using a mandoline slicer. Dry the slices thoroughly on paper towels. Using a metal potato basket with clamps, line the larger basket with potato rounds, overlapping them thickly at the bottom. Clamp the smaller basket on top. Immerse the basket in the hot oil and fry for 3 to 4 minutes or until the potatoes start to brown. Lift out the basket, open it, and gently pry out the formed potatoes. Drop them back into the fat and continue to fry until golden brown, 1 to 2 minutes longer. Drain on paper towels and season to taste with salt and pepper. Repeat with the remaining potato slices.

3. Season the shrimp with salt and pepper. Fry in the same oil at 350° F. until golden, about 3 minutes. Drain on paper towels.

4. In a small bowl, mix the shoyu powder with the water to form a paste. Stir in the mayonnaise.

5. Fill the potato baskets with the shrimp. Serve the baskets with the sauce on the side.

Serves 4

Beef Stroganoff

2 tablespoons vegetable oil
2½ to 3 pounds fillet of beef, cut into 12 slices
3 teaspoons imported sweet paprika
Salt
1 cup beef stock
2 teaspoons lemon juice
¼ cup dry sherry
¼ cup Cognac
½ cup sour cream

1. Place the oil in a skillet large enough to hold the slices of beef in one flat layer. Add the beef and set the heat at high. Cook, turning constantly, until lightly browned, about 3 minutes. Add the paprika and salt to taste. Immediately remove the pan from the heat to prevent the paprika from burning. Turn the meat until well coated, then remove to a plate. Cover to keep warm.

2. Pour the beef stock, lemon juice, sherry, and Cognac into the pan. Bring to a boil over high heat. Boil rapidly, stirring often, until reduced by half. Remove the pan from the heat and cool slightly. Stir in the sour cream.

3. Just before serving, gently heat the sauce over low heat. Do not boil. Return the meat to the sauce and turn to coat and warm through. Serve at once over rice or noodles.

Serves 6

🌳 🌳 🌳 🌳

The Four Seasons Fancy Cake

This cake is a "signature" of The Four Seasons. The Fancy Cake is actually a layer of orange chiffon cake topped by a dome of Bavarian cream with the whole affair then encased in chocolate. It has been an offering on the dessert cart ever since the restaurant opened. You cannot exactly duplicate it in your home kitchen, but you can come very close. In the restaurant kitchen, for example, special machines are used to roll out the chocolate coating. For the home cook, who has no such facilities, we have devised a different chocolate coating which closely resembles the original.

Allow two days to make the Fancy Cake. Make the Bavarian cream the day before you intend to serve the cake. The next day make the cake layer and the chocolate coating and assemble the whole.

For the Bavarian cream
3¾ cups milk
3 scant tablespoons (3 envelopes) unflavored gelatin
6 large eggs, separated
¼ teaspoon salt
1¼ cups sugar
¼ cup dark rum
1 cup heavy cream, whipped stiff
¾ cup crushed almond macaroons or vanilla wafers (about 10–12 small cookies)
⅓ cup finely chopped walnuts or pecans

For the orange chiffon cake
1 cup plus 2 tablespoons sifted cake flour
¾ cup sugar
1½ teaspoons baking powder
½ teaspoon salt
¼ cup vegetable oil
2 egg yolks
6 tablespoons fresh orange juice
1½ tablespoons finely chopped orange peel
½ cup egg whites (from 3 to 4 large eggs), at room temperature
¼ teaspoon cream of tartar
½ cup heavy cream, whipped stiff

For the chocolate almond cream coating
2 pounds almond paste
1 cup cocoa
Confectioners' sugar for sprinkling

1. To prepare the Bavarian cream, place 1 cup of the milk in a medium bowl and sprinkle the gelatin over the milk. Let stand for 5 minutes to soften. In a medium saucepan over medium-high heat, warm the remaining milk until tiny bubbles appear around the edge.

2. Meanwhile, beat the egg yolks with the salt and ½ cup of the sugar until blended. Stir in the milk and gelatin mixture. Gradually stir in the warm milk. Place the mixture in the top part of a double boiler. Cook over hot but not boiling water, stirring often, until the mixture coats the back of a spoon, about 15 minutes. Remove from the heat, cool slightly, and stir in the rum. Refrigerate, covered, until the mixture mounds slightly when

lifted with a spoon, about 3 hours. (Alternatively, place the pan over ice water to hasten the chilling. Stir occasionally until the mixture mounds slightly when lifted with a spoon, about 30 minutes.)

3. Line a 2½-quart bowl, no wider than 9 inches in diameter, with plastic wrap or foil. Set aside.

4. In the bowl of a large electric mixer, beat the egg whites on high speed until soft peaks are formed. Gradually add the remaining ¾ cup of sugar and beat until stiff but not dry. Add the whipped cream and the gelatin mixture. Beat at low speed until just combined, about 1 minute. Turn into the prepared bowl.

5. In a small bowl, combine the crushed macaroons or wafers with the nuts. Mix well. Sprinkle over the top of the mixture in the bowl and gently press down. Cover and refrigerate for at least eight hours or overnight.

6. To prepare the orange chiffon cake, preheat the oven to 350° F. Sift the flour with the sugar, baking powder, and salt into a large bowl. Make a well in the center. Add the oil, egg yolks, orange juice, and orange peel. Beat with a spoon until smooth.

7. Beat the egg whites with the cream of tartar on high speed until stiff but not dry. With an under and over motion, use a wire whisk or rubber spatula to gradually fold the orange batter into the egg whites. Mix just until blended. Do not stir. Pour into an ungreased 9 by 1½-inch round cake pan. Bake for 30 to 35 minutes or until a cake tester inserted in the center comes out clean. Place the cake upside down on a dry, clean kitchen towel. Cool completely, about 1 hour. With a spatula, carefully loosen the cake from the pan. Hit the pan sharply on a table. Remove the cake and place it on a serving platter.

8. Spread the whipped cream over the top of the orange chiffon cake. Invert the bowl of Bavarian cream over the whipped cream-topped cake. Remove the bowl and peel off the plastic wrap. The Bavarian cream will form a dome over the cake. Refrigerate until ready to coat.

9. To prepare the chocolate almond cream coating, in a large bowl knead the almond paste with the cocoa until thoroughly mixed and softened. Divide into 5 portions, 4 of equal size and 1 smaller portion for the topknot. On a large board sprinkled with confectioners' sugar, roll the 4 uniform pieces out, one at a time, into 8 by 7-inch sheets that measure about ⅛ inch thick. As each sheet is rolled out, place it on the domed Bavarian-orange cake, working from the bottom up and pinching the top to make gathers in it. Break off any excess that sticks out at the top. The whole cake should be covered by the 4 rolled-out sheets.

(Continued on next page)

10. Roll out the remaining portion of chocolate almond cream coating into an oblong that measures about ¼ inch thick. Gather into a topknot and place on top of the Fancy Cake. Refrigerate until ready to serve. Let the cake stand at room temperature for 20 minutes before slicing.

Makes about 16 portions

Chocolate Velvet

This adaptation of The Four Seasons' popular dessert comes from Maida Heatter's *Book of Great Desserts*. As she says at the beginning of the recipe, it takes a lot of time but the result is worth the effort.

For the sponge cake
    10 eggs, separated
    ½ cup sugar
    2 teaspoons vanilla extract
    6 tablespoons all-purpose flour
    ¼ teaspoon salt

For the filling
    1½ pounds semisweet chocolate, coarsely chopped
    1 tablespoon instant coffee
    ½ cup boiling water
    ½ cup orange-flavored liqueur
    3 large eggs, separated
    ⅛ teaspoon salt
    ¼ cup sugar
    1 cup heavy cream, whipped stiff

For the icing
    6 ounces semisweet chocolate
    ½ cup boiling water

1. To prepare the cake, preheat the oven to 375° F. Butter two jelly roll pans that measure 10½ by 15½ by 1. Line the pans with wax paper and butter the paper. Dust the pans lightly with flour.

2. In the bowl of a large electric mixer, beat the egg yolks on high speed until lemon-colored, about 4 minutes. Add ¼ cup of the sugar and all of the vanilla. Beat 4 minutes longer or until the mixture forms a thick ribbon when the beaters are lifted. Gently fold in the flour with a rubber spatula.

3. Clean the beaters and, in a clean bowl, beat the egg whites on high

speed with the salt until soft peaks are formed. Add the remaining ¼ cup of sugar and beat until the mixture is firm and stiff but not dry.

4. Fold the whites into the yolk mixture. Divide the batter between the two pans, smoothing the batter flat. Bake for about 15 minutes or until golden brown. Turn the cakes out onto dry clean kitchen towels to cool.

5. Line the bottom of a 9 by 3-inch round springform pan with wax paper. Place the pan on one of the sponge cakes at one short side and, using the tip of a sharp knife, trace around the pan. Use scissors to cut out the circle of cake (using scissors will keep the cake from tearing). Repeat with the second sponge cake, making a second circle of cake. Place one of the circles in the bottom of the pan. Set the other circle aside. With a ruler and toothpicks, on the remaining pieces of cake mark off three even slices 2¾ inches wide by 9½ inches long (two from one piece of cake, one from the other). Cut 1 inch off from one of the strips to make it 8½ inches long. Place it and the other two longer strips standing up around the sides of the pan. Fit the strips together tightly to form a solid lining of cake.

6. To prepare the filling, in the top of a double boiler over hot but not boiling water stir the chocolate until evenly melted. Dissolve the coffee in the ½ cup boiling water and set aside. Transfer the melted chocolate to the bowl of an electric mixer and cool. On lowest speed, gradually beat in the prepared coffee and the orange liqueur. Add the egg yolks and beat just until smooth. Set aside.

7. Clean the beaters and, in a clean bowl, beat the egg whites with the salt until soft peaks are formed. Gradually beat in the sugar and continue beating until the whites are stiff but not dry. Gently fold the whites into the chocolate mixture. Fold in the whipped cream.

8. Pour the filling into the cake-lined pan. Top with the remaining circle of cake. Cover with plastic wrap and refrigerate for several hours or overnight.

9. To prepare the icing, chop the chocolate into small pieces. In a small, heavy saucepan over low heat, combine the chocolate and water. Stir until smooth. Remove from the heat and cool to room temperature, stirring occasionally.

10. To ice the cake, remove the sides of the springform pan and carefully invert the cake onto a large serving platter. Remove the wax paper. Pour the icing over the cake, completely covering the top and letting a little excess run down the sides. Refrigerate until ready to serve.

Makes about 16 portions

There's a new restaurant in Manhattan
With the Four Seasons as its theme.
They have trees and a pool there,
But you look quite the fool there,
Unless you blend in with the scheme.
Every season they change the decor there
From the trees to the finger bowls, too;
As Cue said in their issue
Even the tissue
Acquires a seasonal hue.

Suddenly, last summer
I fell beneath its charm
But in that leafy bower
I had a close alarm.
They have a Venus Fly Trap
That fed upon my arm,
   At the Four Seasons
      In the Seagram.

. . . My love fell in the pool there
Beneath a cypress tree.
The pool has frozen over,
I'm waiting patiently.
In Spring they'll drain it out
And she'll come through the Brasserie,
But Spring will be
      A little late this year
      At the Four Seasons,
      The Four Seasons
         in the Seagram.

Glory Days

The Four Seasons Makes Its Mark

*The Four Seasons courted
the media, including the
ladies who lunch here—
editors of some of the
nation's top women's
magazines. From left to
right: Miss Eleanor Crook
of* American Weekly,
Mrs. Sylvia Humphrey of
Women's Home Service,
*Mrs. Hyman Shanok,
Mrs. Lillian Poses, and
Mr. Hyman Shanok.*

True renown may best be gauged at that point when people begin to write doggerel about you. Thus, by the end of 1959 a downtown musical review already contained a skit (excerpted above) entitled "The Four Seasons at the Seagram" (with lyrics by Louis Botto), lampooning the restaurant's highly publicized theme.

Miles and Martin were certainly earning their pay, placing almost daily items in the tabloid columns and getting RA spokesmen on all the top radio talk shows of the day. They were also successful in courting New York's fashion industry, which was delighted to show off its seasonal collections at this spectacular, stylish new restaurant on Park Avenue.

Yet in all the media attention, scant mention was ever made of the Grill Room, which continued to do poorly. There were as many theories given as to why the Grill Room did not catch on as there had been directors of The Four Seasons. For despite several changes in personnel, each with his own distinctive style, RA could never get the Grill to work.

Some believed that New York's WASP corporate establishment would not favor a restaurant paid for by a Jewish-Canadian bootlegger and run by slick Jewish saloonkeepers like Wechsler, Brody, Baum, and others, although it had never made any difference that the owners of the former speakeasy across town—"21" Club—were named Kriendler and Berns.

Others whispered that the bar had become a hangout for homosexuals—a rumor mentioned in the gay guide *Screw*. In fact, The Four Seasons' bartender, Jim Kelly, was jolted on finding a discarded underground bulletin that recommended the bar as a discreet meeting place for gay men—a notion that infuriated Baum.

The problems were not quite so simple, however. From the start, the public had been led to believe that the Pool Room was the "A" room and a far more glamorous place to dine, especially after a lavish spread in *Look* magazine pictured the room as *the* place to sit. After that, most photo shoots were done in the Pool Room, and New York's society and gossip columnists reported that everyone from Chubby Checkers to Jacqueline Kennedy dined there, rarely mentioning the Grill at all. Thus it was perceived that only out-of-towners or newcomers were seated in the Grill, while regulars and celebrities were awarded the privilege of dining at the Pool.

To be sure, the atmosphere in the Grill was far more sedate, with nothing particularly soft or romantic about its decor. Years later, when asked about the Grill, Johnson admitted, "It was a miserable failure. I often sat in there alone at lunch." And when queried as to why he'd never designed another restaurant after The Four Seasons, he replied, "I was never again asked to do one," adding that restaurants require "too much hard work and not enough satisfaction."

A visitor to The Four Seasons in those days hoped his party would be seated in the Pool Room—what one columnist called "the world's largest finger bowl." After doffing your coat in the downstairs lobby hung with artwork by Miró, you would turn upward to the reception desk, where a very handsome and very smooth maître d' named Jacques Casanova stood to greet you. Casanova had been recruited from the Monte Carlo Club because he knew everyone in town and could quickly size up a guest's self-assurance. He would look for your name in his book, note if there were any special symbols next to your name, acknowledge you by name, smile, then turn your party over to an usher, who would walk you through the awesome "Picasso Alley" to the Pool Room.

There, Casanova's cousin, John Laumier, already alerted by means of a signal light set atop his station desk, greeted you by name and seated you. He would then flick a switch that lit up a bulb back at Casanova's desk, indicating which table was taken for the evening. After taking your order from the two-foot-high menu wrapped in rice paper, waiters would bring over vegetable baskets from which you could choose whatever you wanted cooked with your entrées. When your order was ready, a captain in the dining room would be alerted by a small transmitter attached discreetly to his pocket.

Soon after the restaurant was up and running, a new director was appointed who imparted a demeanor of worldliness to The Four Seasons and a sense that guests were part of a glamorous party that went on night after night. His name was Stuart Levin, and he was a suave, handsome New Yorker who had risen through the RA ranks as assistant manager of The Newarker, assistant director of the Forum, and director of the Lexington Hotel and Hawaiian Room before taking over as resident manager of The Four Seasons.

Levin was a man of boundless energies, and his instincts for building

After becoming a regular at The Four Seasons, Jackie Onassis still seemed oblivious of her celebrity. One day, when wine writer Charles Rubinstein found himself in back of a long line of people at the cloakroom and in front of Mrs. Onassis, he kindly offered to check her coat for her and to bring her ticket up to her. "That's very nice of you," said the most famous woman in the world, "but however will you find me?"

the banquet business at the restaurant not only were sound, but fit in with his own love of a good party. "The Four Seasons was my home for years," said Levin. "I worked hard and played hard, and it cost me my marriage in the end. But it was a glorious time. And The Four Seasons was simply the most glamorous place to be."

Levin was as much a perfectionist as Baum, but more gregarious and concerned about day-to-day details that affected the bottom line. Alan Reyburn, who came from London's Connaught and Montreal's Windsor Hotel to work for RA, had a two-week training session in RA management style under Levin.

"Stuart would walk me up and down through the restaurant," Reyburn recalls, "and question me on all sorts of arcane subjects. What percentage of our linen is rejected? How many covers did I estimate for tomorrow based on the last three days' observations? What was the average time customers spent in the dining room? He made me very conscious of things I already knew, and he taught me that you should have as few people between the management and the customers as possible if you want to personalize service."

From the beginning, Levin, together with his assistant, George Stich, was very much a hands-on director, and he spent an enormous amount of time writing service manuals and lengthy memos, even explaining the astronomical reasons a specific date and time signaled a change of season.

"Officially spring came to New York at 9:43 A.M. yesterday morning," he would begin. "This meant that at that time the position of the sun was directly over the equator and the day and the night were of equal length. This is known as the spring equinox." Then, more rhapsodically, he went on to say, "Spring is a season of gentle weather and more pleasant living. It injects into everything a sense of newness and optimism. Here at The Four Seasons, it also represents our fourth seasonal change and completes the cycle of the seasons for our first year." Next he would describe in detail how captains' winter gray coats would now be spring beige and the doorman's would be pink. Upholstery, china, matchbooks, coat checks, menus, and stationery would all be replaced.

Levin labored hard to make The Four Seasons a showplace, encouraging fashion shows, art exhibits, and banquets for the glamour industries. Too often, however, the parties were being given away almost free of charge, with high-profile companies paying only for the food costs; The Four Seasons swallowed all others. Certain regulars even had a special RA "999" credit card that allowed them to eat free and pay only for gratuities to the waiters in trade for ad space in magazines. Of course, the magazines traded their credits to others, so there was a constant parade of people eating free of charge in the restaurant. Even the Commanderie de Bordeaux paid next to nothing for their grand dinners, and The Four Seasons made nothing off wine sales on those nights because members brought their own bottles with them. Even RA employees got 25 percent discounts to eat in RA restaurants.

In retrospect such policies were abused, and later they came to haunt RA, but in those early years they seemed a reasonable, if eccentric, way to build rapport with the most powerful movers and shakers of New York.

While capable of exhaustive long-term planning for an upcoming event, Levin was also resilient and resourceful enough to mount a grandiose affair on a moment's notice, as when movie producer Joe Levine called him one afternoon to inquire if it was possible to have a black-tie dinner at midnight for two hundred people—none of whom had yet been invited—to celebrate the opening of his movie *Boccaccio 70* that evening. Levin told the tycoon simply to invite the guests and that everything else would be taken care of. Of course, it was.

> Movie mogul Joe Levine was so cheap, he would always sit at other people's tables just to get a cup of free coffee. He also told every waitress he met at The Four Seasons that he'd make her a star.

In the Pool Room Sophia Loren (left), columnist Dorothy Kilgallen, and producer Joe Levine celebrated the actress's Oscar-winning performance in the movie "Two Women."

"The staff loved doing Joe Levine's parties," recalls Levin. "He brought in all the movie stars. So everybody pitched in and agreed to stay on to work. I ordered up an enormous floral centerpiece for the Pool Room, covered the pool for dancing, and at midnight Levine, Marcello Mastroianni, Romy Schneider, and two hundred guests arrived. They dined on shrimp with mustard fruits, tournedos of beef with woodland mushrooms—all cooked tableside—and an ice-cream dessert set with sparklers and carried around the room by waiters."

On another occasion Reyburn and Alan Lewis arrived one Sunday morning to prepare for a fashion show, only to find that no one had notified the kitchen crew to come in. "So we started breaking cases of eggs to make enough omelets for a hundred and fifty people," remembers

Reyburn, "while we waited for emergency staff. Yet when the guests arrived, no one noticed anything amiss."

Four Seasons banquets were always something out of the ordinary. When England's Princess Margaret and Lord Snowdon opted to hold a private party, Levin made the unheard-of suggestion that they have a midnight supper in The Four Seasons' kitchen.

Elaborate preparations were made and plans worthy of a military tactician drawn up. Levin met with British officials to glean every nuance of royal protocol and found out Princess Margaret's favorite dishes and cocktail (gin and tonic). He replaced the gray carpet with a gold one, and a Lucite panel was placed over the pool for dancing to Peter Duchin's orchestra.

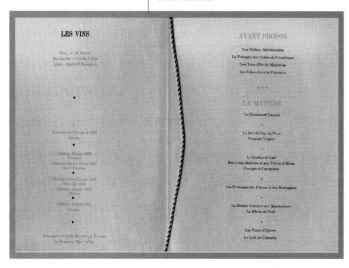

A special Christmas menu created for the Commanderie de Bordeaux in 1961.

Reservations from the public would be accepted only up until seven P.M., and customers would be graciously escorted out by nine in order to accommodate the arrival of the royal party at eleven-thirty. The kitchen, then headed by chef Louis Fessy, was set up with seven stations. The buffet table would offer creamed chicken hash, sourbread toast, lamb curry, and mango rice. At the next table would be three kinds of eggs and hashed browns, then on to a shellfish station heaped with oysters, clams, mussels, and lobsters. There was a single station just for two trout preparations; the pantry was set up for roast chicken, roast beef, salmon in aspic, and other delicacies; and the grill station was for sausages, bacon, and "small hamburgers" on sesame seed buns. Then there were cheeses and, of course, flaming crêpes Suzette—all part of what was billed as an "American kitchen party."

Miles and Martin revved up the publicity machine for this singular event, which promised to rouse enormous press interest. The international guest list included Alfred Bloomingdale, Leonard Bernstein, Harry Belafonte, Carter Burden, Sammy Davis Jr., John Lindsay, Ray Milland, Joshua Logan, Harold Prince, Robert Sarnoff, Truman Capote, Gene Kelly, Prince Amyn Aga Khan, Oakley Rhinelander, Stephen Sondheim, Dean Witter, Bette Davis, Henry and Anne Ford, Danny Kaye, Peggy Lee, Bea Lillie, Ethel Merman, and Robert Salant.

Then, to their horror, Miles and Martin got word from the royal family that there was to be *no* press coverage of the event whatsoever. At the risk of infuriating the rest of the media but determined to get some print from the inside, the resourceful PR men arranged to sneak gossip columnist Earl Wilson into the kitchen dressed as a cook; he ended up taking his notes while pretending to slave over a hot stove.

Everyone who worked for RA in those days remembers it as not just a special time, but as a time not likely to be repeated ever again. Jim Tsighis, who joined The Four Seasons fresh out of Cornell Hotel School, remembered his time there as "a dream," insisting, "I was absolutely thrilled to work from six A.M. to six P.M. seven days a week."

Left: Paul Kovi greets New York mayor John Lindsay. Right: Truman Capote.

"It was a golden era, another world," said Levin, who would go to Europe to buy silverware with a $10,000 letter of credit in his pocket. "We tried to do everything to perfection and make it all seem effortless. One night former president Truman just walked in off the street from his hotel. A terrific rainstorm began, and by the time he finished his dinner, every limo in New York was taken. I had to borrow a limousine from Eddie Fisher and Elizabeth Taylor without being able to tell them why. Afterward, when the limo returned, I told them, 'The President was very grateful.'"

On another occasion Phyllis Lambert held a party attended by actor Montgomery Clift, who quickly proceeded to get potted and disappear. He was not found until the next morning, asleep on a couch, undisturbed, in the ladies' room.

Possibly the most famous party of the early 1960s was that thrown for President John F. Kennedy's forty-fifth birthday on May 19, 1962. Four hundred people coughed up $1,000 each to attend the dinner, and the list included everyone from Averell Harriman to Jennie Grossinger. The party began at six-thirty, and guests were startled to peer through the glassed-in wine room and see an incandescent Marilyn Monroe strolling among the Bordeaux and Burgundies.

The newspapers reported that Kennedy worked the room tirelessly and never got to eat a morsel of the dinner (composed of crabmeat baked in a

The Four Seasons staff could not keep a straight face whenever Truman Capote ordered grapefruit juice, because he couldn't pronounce it.

When a reunion of cast members of the 1950s TV show *Leave It to Beaver* signed The Four Seasons' guest book, they all wrote in character. Ken Osmond, who played the duplicitous Eddie Haskell, wrote, "My, what a handsome restaurant you have." And Tony Dow, who played Beaver's brother, Wally, wrote, "Golly, Beaver! Let's call Lumpy and Eddie and head on down to the Four Seasons for a burger and malt."

Stairway from the Fifty-second Street lobby to the Grill Room.

shell, chicken broth with spring wheat, medallions of beef glazed in Madeira with herbed carrots and woodland mushrooms, and a presidential birthday cake). "That's not true," says Levin. "He did shake everybody's hand that night, and he seemed to have this amazing ability to connect with everyone on a personal basis, even those like Joe Baum, Jerry Brody, and me, whom he'd never met before, so that he would meet you, shake another hundred hands, see you again, and say something to you as if you were an old friend. I've never seen anyone like that. But then he asked if we could have dinner in a private room with Alan Jay Lerner, Bob Wagner, and myself. He immediately asked someone to get him a beer, then ordered cream of asparagus soup. Afterward he left by limo and we all got into buses and went off to Madison Square Garden, where I saw something I'll never forget—the sight of Marilyn Monroe singing 'Happy Birthday' to the president of the United States."

The next day Miles reported to Brody, Baum, and Levin that "the news clips came in boxes."

The whole theme of change used up incredible resources and meant exhaustive planning months in advance. So, too, the changing art in the restaurant took time-consuming negotiations on RA's part, even though many artists and gallery owners were dying to get their work into such a public space as The Four Seasons.

For a long while artwork hung in the downstairs lobby, until one Saturday morning a man came in, picked up a painting by surrealist Jean Arp, and walked out with it on his back. At one time the exhibited works—many owned by the Bronfmans—included the Picasso curtain, Pollock's *Blue Poles,* the two Lippold sculptures, Willem de Kooning's *Id,* Grace Hartigan's *Montauk Highway,* Franz Kline's *Mahonig,* Larry Rivers's *Me Too,* Joan Miró's *Femme Fleur Étoile, Hirondelle d'Amour,* and *Composition,* a bronze by Jean Arp, Jacques Lipchitz's *Guitar Player,* Frank Stella's *Railroad,* and Fernand Léger's *Watermelon.*

Levin worked with Johnson in selecting much of what was to be displayed,

and in 1961, with the help of Edith Scull (who showed up wearing a white cowboy outfit), The Four Seasons was the scene of one of the most important art exhibits of the decade, showcasing many of the brightest talents then emerging on the New York scene, including Andy Warhol, Robert Rauschenberg, James Rosenquist, and Helen Frankenthaler.

On one of his annual trips to Europe, Levin rented a villa on the Riviera, where he met Leonard Lyons on his way to visit Marc Chagall in Venice. Levin went along. "Leonard introduced me to Chagall," Levin recalls, "and told him, 'Stuart here runs The Four Seasons restaurant in New York. Why don't you lend him one of your paintings?' When Chagall demurred for a moment, Lyons told him, 'You know, they already have a Picasso at the restaurant.' Chagall stood up and said, 'If Picasso can be there, Chagall must be there. Call my agent, Lucia Chase, in New York and tell her to give you the stage curtain from the Aleko ballet. You can hang it in the private dining room.' And that's how we got the Chagall."

A formal dinner party held in the upstairs private dining room by the all-male Commanderie de Bordeaux. Note the Joseph Stella painting on the wall (left) and the Miró (right).

Corbusier once called New York "a beautiful disaster," and in the postwar building boom, it was not a place for anyone to feel complacent. The profile of the city was constantly being altered, sometimes radically, and as travel writer Horace Sutton quipped in 1961, "the pneumatic noisemaker is becoming the emblematic sound of New York, the way the bells of Big Ben are the sound of London."

Chapter Six

Cutting Corners in Paradise

The Sixties Turn Sour

New York had become an international capital with unlimited possibilities for the future. Its population totaled almost eight million people. Not only was New York America's financial and artistic center, but new industries like television, radio, publishing, advertising, and fashion had given it a global clout unlike anything ever seen before. There was plenty of money to go around, and plenty of ways to spend it, which included dining out for both business and pleasure at an array of modern restaurants that promised not just good food, but entertainment as well. Restaurants functioned as stages upon which people played out their fantasies of the high life or manifested their new affluence.

The theme restaurant pioneered by RA was becoming commonplace in New York. At an eatery called the Autopub in the General Motors Building, customers sat on the bucket seats of actual cars while served by pretty waitresses in racing uniforms. Camelot, on Third Avenue, was done up like a mythical Arthurian castle, while at the Cattleman, on Fifty-fourth Street, you were greeted by a cowboy and fed amid an atmosphere of a boisterous Wild West saloon. At the Library, on Broadway, guests sat in rooms whose walls were lined with books, and for those nostalgic for the swagger of World War I fighter pilots, the Red Baron was decked out with all the accoutrements of an aerodrome circa 1917. At a restaurant called the Salum Sanctorum, sacramental candles burned in a hushed medieval atmosphere and menus looked like illuminated manuscripts.

"Singles' bars" like T.G.I. Friday's and Maxwell's Plum, done up in outrageous Victoriana and Tiffany glass, were popping up all over town. Men bought "keys" to visit the Playboy Club, where voluptuous young women dressed in abbreviated bunny costumes served them big steaks and strong cocktails.

No company did theme restaurants better or with more polish than RA, a perception that brought the expanding corporation bigger and better contracts. In the early 1960s it seemed that the company was grabbing up every glamour project in New York. Soon after opening both La Fonda del Sol and a swank penthouse restaurant called the Tower Suite in the Time and Life Building, RA was asked to develop three separate restaurants in the new Pan Am Building (designed by Walter Gropius), which included a "jet age" Italian eatery called Trattoria, a German lunch counter named Zum Zum, and an Irish tavern named Charlie Brown's Ale & Chop House. Elsewhere RA opened a small chain of bars and grills under the names Charley O's and the Paul Revere Chop House, a restaurant at LaGuardia Airport, and a nostalgic tavern called the Lord Jeffrey Inn in Amherst, Massachusetts. Of course, exacting research went into each and every project, from the pewter accessories and recipes for cock-a-leekie soup at Charlie Brown's to the pasta cutters and massive brass espresso machine at Trattoria. Zum Zum had its own butchers and bakers, who made every item fresh, from several types of German sausage to flaky Austrian strudels.

The reports of RA's success were daunting. A long profile of the company in the *New Yorker* in 1964 made everything sound rosy: RA was said to be doing $30 million in annual sales. Still, since the public sale of 245,000 of its 750,408 shares in 1961, RA had yet to pay a dividend to anyone, and the author of the article, Geoffrey Hellman, noted that "in little more than a decade [RA] has come to project the most confused corporate image on the gastronomic scene, and possibly in the Western Hemisphere, that has been projected in *any* line of endeavor."

In the face of such opportunities for expansion, goodwill, and profit potential, the fact that RA's own monetary resources were stretched to the limit hardly seemed to matter. What money they did make—and it was certainly not coming from sales at the Forum, La Fonda or The Four Seasons—was plowed back into the new projects. Nevertheless the company's stock (which in 1961 was at $6 a share) began to rise, fueling the possibility of even bigger projects, both in and outside of New York. The biggest plum of all was the New York World's Fair of 1964, which awarded RA the contract to develop fifteen different restaurants at a sprawling Flushing Meadows site. There had even been overtures abroad to open restaurants at the Paris airport and in Monte Carlo.

But there was trouble in paradise, instigated, as in the Garden of Eden, by the temptation of forbidden fruit. While working in France to develop a hotel casino in Divonne-les-Bains, Jerry Brody met and fell in love with a secretary-translator named Marlene Gray. Brody's wife, Grace, sued for divorce, an act he knew would result in a confrontation with her father, Abe Wechsler. Wechsler was furious over the divorce and used the incident to rid himself of Brody one way or the other. Ironically, Wechsler at first offered to sell his shares of RA to Brody. After so many years, the old coffee magnate had still not developed any affinity for the deluxe restaurant business and would have been just as happy to have Brody take it off his hands. Brody could not raise enough money to purchase the shares, however, and under pressure from Wechsler's wife, the offer was withdrawn and Brody was fired.

To fill the void left by Brody, Wechsler asked another son-in-law, James Slater, to find a new president for RA, one who was less a conceptualizer than a brass tacks businessman. Slater turned to Martin Brody (no relation to Jerry Brody), formerly head of an industrial catering company called Rain or Shine Food Box. The shift was to alter completely the future direction of RA. For one thing, Jerry Brody's departure and Martin Brody's arrival immediately affected RA's stocks for the better. Indeed, by the mid-1960s RA's stocks rose to 43 and showed no signs of slowing down as Brody expanded the company into an astounding number of new ventures.

Then, in May 1965 Waldorf Systems, Inc., which ran an unprofitable chain of eighty-three cafeterias, drive-ins, and pancake houses in eight states, announced a plan to merge with RA. On the surface this marriage of high- and low-end restaurant companies seemed an odd one, until one realized that Abe Wechsler himself had major holdings in Waldorf and that a merger would give RA about two-thirds control of both companies.

As an article in *Time* magazine noted at the time, "Restaurant Associates feels it can do something to vitalize the Waldorf chain without compromising the attractive image of its expensive restaurants," but those, like Baum and Levin, who had created that attractive image had a certain sinking feeling about how the new company would evolve. By the time the merger was completed, Martin Brody and Slater were the largest stockholders.

Now six years old, The Four Seasons was no longer perceived as the most novel of Manhattan restaurants—Joe Baum once quipped that a "classic" restaurant is one that renews its first lease—but it was still testament to the kind of majesty RA could mount when its communal genius was applied. And there were still ongoing innovations, like instituting a pretheater menu—the first for a deluxe restaurant beyond the immediate theater district. Still, The Four Seasons was not making any money, and the cost of maintaining its eminence was becoming harder and harder to defend.

As a result, Martin Brody thought it no great loss when Stuart Levin and his co-director at The Four Seasons, Bob Gifford, left the company in 1966 to develop the restaurants at the new Lincoln Center. Two years later Levin went on to realize his dream of owning his own deluxe restaurant: he bought the most famous of them all, Le Pavillon, which had been limping along after the death of Henri Soulé in 1966.

Other defections radically changed the old RA team and spirit. Stöckli left to open an inn in Connecticut called Stonehenge. Alan Lewis and Philip Miles went to Longchamps. Jim Armstrong, who had headed up RA's airport restaurant division, left to work at Disneyland in Anaheim, California, eventually becoming director of food service at the gigantic new Walt Disney World in Orlando, Florida. Patrick Terrail, director of the Brasserie, left to run El Morocco. Brian Daley, The Four Seasons' kitchen manager, and Fred Platzer at The Newarker, signed on with Jerry Brody at the Rainbow Room.

In casting about for a replacement for director of The Four Seasons, Baum, who himself was fighting daily battles with his new bosses, turned to a dynamic young Hungarian named George Lang, who had come aboard at RA in 1960 and whom Baum regarded as a civilized buttress among RA's corporate vulgarians. Lang was a formidable presence whose steely eyes, stocky build, rock-solid jaw, and impressive forehead (which became more impressive the balder he got) gave him an intimidating demeanor, buoyed by an even more intimidating command of several languages and an erudition Baum himself found daunting. Lang also possessed credentials no other restaurateur in the world could claim.

He had grown up in Hungary in a middle-class family committed to their son's liberal arts education and supportive of his passion for the violin. Indeed, for a time it seemed the young man might consider a career in music. The war intervened, and at one point during the Russian occupation of Hungary, a group of soldiers forced the terrified boy to play for them at gunpoint for eight hours straight. As soon as possible after the war, Lang emigrated from his beloved Hungary, hitching a ride on a GI troopship bound for the United States.

Lang was astounded at the opportunities America presented to a young man of his talents and energies. On arrival in New York he became enthralled with the diversity and imagination that went into American food service, especially the Horn & Hardart Automats, and, after a brief stint playing violin with the Dallas Symphony Orchestra, he found himself working in restaurants in every capacity from busboy to short-order cook. Within a few years he knew everything about the restaurant industry, from making a textbook-perfect béarnaise to balancing a reservations book. At the Waldorf-Astoria he trained under the fearsome Claudius Charles Philippe, who, Lang recalled, showed him "how to sell what were cheese blintzes on Wednesday morning as crêpes Suzette on Saturday night."

With a wealth of experience under his belt and an ability to converse on almost any subject under the sun, Lang had, by the mid-1950s, become a well-known figure in the industry as vice president of the Brass Rail restaurant company, for whom he'd developed the imaginative restaurants at Kennedy Airport. It was there that he came to the attention of Baum, who in 1960 hired the young man as project director for the Tower Suite and the Hemisphere Club. When RA got the contract to design and run the restaurants at the New York World's Fair of 1964, Lang was tapped to coordinate everything, which included several pavilion restaurants, an employee cafeteria, a private dining room for Henry Ford, and a first-class restaurant called Festival 64/65.

Lang's imagination leapt: three sides of this innovative restaurant of the future were walls of glass overlooking a reflecting pool set with islands of floating flowers. Outdoor tables were made of unbreakable glass that picked up the shimmer of light and water. And the food was a celebration of American traditional cooking—somewhat less fancy than the novel American cuisine then being created at The Four Seasons. For dinner at the Festival one might begin with shrimp rémoulade, chilled cherry soup, or New England scallop chowder. For the main course there were deviled crabs à la Creole, California abalone steak, green corn pie with shrimp, stuffed Maryland baked ham, beef stew cooked in an iron kettle, and a double veal chop with mushrooms and freshly made ketchup. Cheeses were American farmhouse varieties. Breads, rolls, and biscuits were baked on the premises, and desserts included apricot ice cream, sugar pie, "plantation wedding cake," and banana fritters.

By the time the Fair ended in 1966, Levin had left RA, and Lang reluctantly took over The Four Seasons at a time when its future looked dim. Costs simply didn't balance with the amount of money coming into the restaurant. Expenditures had to be trimmed and concepts had to be

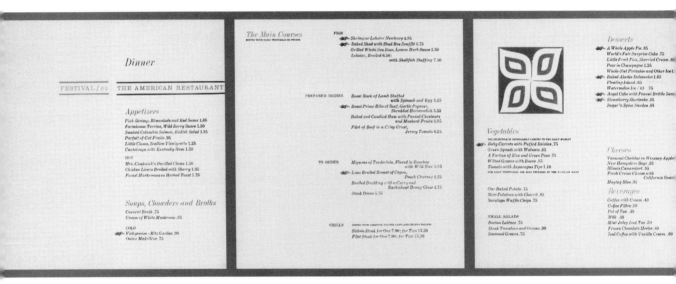

The Festival 64/65 restaurant managed by George Lang at the New York World's Fair in 1964 heralded what came to be called the "New American Cuisine," as shown by a menu of the day.

rethought. While few at RA would dare at that time to compromise Baum's original vision, everyone agreed that change was needed to keep The Four Seasons at the forefront of modern American restaurants.

The fact was, other, newer restaurants had begun to steal The Four Seasons' thunder, and its innovative menus had, quite simply, never really caught on with a general public far more used to classic French and continental cooking.

Lang set to work, cutting costs where possible and bringing in a new chef, Maurice Chantreau, who had been with him at Festival 64/65, to rework the menu. Because Chantreau was known for his extraordinary cooking technique, Lang would challenge him to reproduce famous complex dishes from history, and Chantreau would always come through. One day Lang asked the chef to reproduce a dish made by deboning an oxtail whole, then stuffing it with a marrow dumpling farce and serving it as part of a pot-au-feu, with the meat sliced in front of the guests. Chantreau tried to make the dish for weeks before he perfected the technique. "Not wanting to die by a stab with a twelve-inch French cook's knife," said Lang years later, "I never told Chantreau that I had never actually seen or eaten such a dish."

Lang tried hard to turn things around, introducing a trio to play at the Grill Room and bringing in many of his friends from the music world. Lang, always the raconteur, tried to build rapport with new customers, coming to their tables and talking about every subject under the sun, causing one Jacob Javits, then U.S. senator from New York, to complain, "George Lang knows how to speak twelve languages, but he doesn't know how to say good-bye in any of them."

The food press was still respectful toward the restaurant, which by the mid-1960s had become more an establishment than a revolutionary monument to change. *Gourmet* magazine's Alvin Kerr wrote of the design, "A scheme of decoration that was once considered very avant-garde has now been tempered by time. Even the strikingly lighted brass stalactites that form the two Lippold sculptures . . . now seem quite traditional." Kerr went on to describe, though mostly to list, the offerings on The Four Seasons' 1967 menu, which was still very much tied to the changing seasons. Prices remained among the highest in the United States, with appetizers averaging $2.50, soups $1.25, main courses from $6.00 to $9.00, and the famous chocolate velvet cake $1.50.

The Four Seasons had certainly been well established in the minds of corporate America (though not so much New York) as *the* place to celebrate in grand style (especially since many still dined there for next to nothing by special arrangement with RA), and if a company could not go to the The Four Seasons, on occasion The Four Seasons would go to them. When the Ford Motor Company wanted to introduce its new luxury Lincoln-Continental, five Ford execs traveled to New York to consult with Alan Reyburn as to the feasibility of reproducing the look, feel, and food of The Four Seasons on an assembly-line floor back in Detroit. Although the logistics were mind-boggling, Reyburn was able to pack up enough of The Four Seasons' tables, chairs, and serviceware and take waiters and cooks to Michigan to approximate the restaurant's atmosphere. "It was a big success," recalls Reyburn, "despite the fact that the chairman of Lincoln-Mercury complained that the gazpacho was 'cold' and everybody

The publication in 1971 of The Four Seasons Cookbook signaled a more international style to the menus at the restaurant.

complained the lamb was cooked too rare because everybody out there ate their meat well done."

As the restaurant's reputation crystallized in the late 1960s (even though it was still not making a profit), it seemed reasonable to publish a *Four Seasons Cookbook,* which appeared in 1971. The official author, whose name appeared on the cover, was Charlotte Adams, who functioned for the most part as a tester of recipes provided her by Lang (who by publication date had left RA to run his own restaurant company), Chantreau, and James Beard. Sadly, Albert Stöckli's name never appeared anywhere in the book.

The sumptuous volume, printed in Italy on various colors of heavy-stock paper, had a foreword by Beard, who credited Baum with the original "dream," and wrote, "Although [The Four Seasons] has been called an American restaurant, a French restaurant, and even a Hungarian restaurant, it is basically without national ties. It embraces every nationality. Its cuisine owes allegiance only to the seasons and to the serving of food at its peak."

Such sentiments were a departure, however subtle it might seem to those who frequented The Four Seasons, that signaled how the original concept of a quintessential New York restaurant had been altered for a new page in its history. The photographs in the book were evocative, sometimes surreal, but in no way tied to any New York theme.

The foreword certainly gave the impression that The Four Seasons was a lavish place dedicated to the highest standards of gastronomy, with ample recipes for signature dishes like the chocolate velvet cake, the duckling au poivre, and the crisp shrimp with mustard fruits. But there was also an array of international dishes—mostly French—ranging from Basque chicken and tripes à la mode de Caen to moussaka and mulligatawny soup. Oddly enough, there was not even a single picture of the restaurant in the book, and none of the china and silver used in the photo layouts were The Four Seasons designs.

In many ways, the book seemed to exemplify a kind of Old World gentility rather than evolution of The Four Seasons modernity. But since the mid-1960s, promoting The Four Seasons had not been among RA's main concerns. The company was gobbling up properties and contracts gluttonously and, for the most part, very successfully. By 1967 the company's stock was up to $43 a share and sales were $100 million. Martin Brody, a man who once described his palate in three words—"I eat plain"—was, as he put it, "extending our spokes outward." By this he meant the expansion not only of chain restaurants—including the Zum Zum concept that began in the Pan Am Building—but of all kinds of eateries on thruways and in airline terminals, ball parks, theme parks, private clubs, and employee cafeterias. RA picked up the Publick House restaurant in Old Sturbridge Village, Massachusetts, took over the operation of Tavern on the Green in New York, ran the cafe in the Museum of Modern Art, and grabbed up the food and souvenir concessions at the Orange Bowl in Miami.

RA was restructuring itself for a new age and a new generation of young Americans who at worst hated or at the very least ignored the genteel traditions of fine dining. Mobile, restless, and affluent, the youth of the 1960s were also rebellious and no longer content or desirous to take their place in a so-called establishment that feasted on two-inch steaks and three-martini lunches. For such people the whole idea of a restaurant called the Forum of the Twelve Caesars was anathema, and they would probably have been able to enlist the support of Mark Rothko in a protest march against the excesses of a restaurant like The Four Seasons, where the cost of a meal could feed a family in Biafra or Chile for a month.

The counterculture celebrated the virtues of "ethnic" cooking, and "junk food" became synonymous with "prole" (for "proletarian") food. The new generation of executives at RA recognized this sea change in American society and worked hard to cater to it. No longer were RA restaurants spoken of in lyrical flights of idealistic fantasy à la Joe Baum. No longer were employees required to read Suetonius and travel to Milan to choose silverware. Now, RA execs like Martin Brody and his marketing vice president, Sandy Bain, spoke of "fast food," "retreat to the suburbs," and "automated waiters." In order to improve employee training, industrial psychologists were hired to "develop programs and routines of management corrections."

In interviews Bain would castigate any restaurateur who affected "snob appeal" in an attempt to draw "duke and duchess, prince and princess, Jackie and Ari, Dick and Liz," asserting that "the kind of publicity appearing on the photo-pages of newspapers and every haute couture magazine in the country with attending, superfab, cutesy-poo prose can easily become the kiss of death for a restaurant."

Clearly Bain was not talking about RA hits like Zum Zum, Charley O's, and Mamma Leone's. For while RA paid a certain lip service to the great RA restaurants of the past, the company had no intention of ever building

The first time I went to The Four Seasons for lunch, I felt compelled to order the much vaunted $9.75 baked potato. It came unadorned on a white plate, without so much as a sprig of parsley to garnish it. It was by far the most self-confident potato I had ever encountered. That night, I wrote to a friend of mine who was living in Prague at the time. Pam and I always told one another about notable meals and thus I shared my potato story with her. Two weeks later I received her response: $9.75 would buy enough potatoes to feed a Czech family of four for a month.

—Erica Marcus,
   New York publishing
   executive

another remotely like them. To put it as bluntly as possible, Bain told *Hospitality* magazine, "Look, if you want to just sit someplace in pleasant surroundings, do nothing, don't eat, just contemplate your navel if you like, there couldn't be a nicer place to do it than The Four Seasons. That's what it is, in addition to being a place where there is heavy emphasis on quality food properly prepared and served."

The view from RA's bottom line seemed to prove Brody right. For while The Four Seasons was not making much money in the late 1960s, RA's fortunes were rising in the fast-food eateries and family restaurants they owned, ran, or managed around the United States. Nothing seemed beyond RA's grasp in 1967.

Then, in January of 1968, RA plunged in over its head with the purchase of the Barricini Candy Company, which had 128 retail stores in addition to candy factories, followed two months later by their takeover of the Treadway Inns Corporation (with 31 units) and in June the acquisition of Al Green Enterprises, Inc., in Detroit, which gave RA entry into in-flight food service. A family restaurant chain called Alice's Wonderful Kitchens, themed to Lewis Carroll's children's fantasy, was planned to replace the International House of Pancake units in New England, and RA contracted to build Big Alice Country Kitchens in three hundred Citgo Villages along the interstate highways. Branches of Mamma Leone's and Zum Zum were opened in Boston.

Things quickly started to go wrong, and RA had neither the resources nor the money to keep their titanic empire afloat. The hands-on management that once characterized the Jerry Brody–Joe Baum era was dissipated and replaced by a corporate mentality that regarded every unit with dispassion. The once visionary themes of the glory days were being replaced with concepts designed to "fill a niche." And, worst of all, the American economy went into the Dumpster.

In November of that year RA's image was still bustling and positive enough to rate a highly favorable story in *Newsweek* magazine, the cover of which was a photo of executives in gray flannel and matrons with bouffant hairdos dining elegantly in the Pool Room of The Four Seasons. Within months, however, everything began to deflate like a badly made soufflé. An unexpected hike in the price of cocoa hurt the candy industry badly. The Detroit operation was severely compromised by a strike at Ford Motor Company. An interstate highway was built in the wrong direction from the routes to the Atlanta Big Alice Country Kitchen, and the Treadway Inns were hit hard by a bad economy.

By the first quarter of 1970, the company lost $1.3 million and the stock had slipped to 4.

Barricini and Treadway were among the first to be cut loose, five Zum Zums were sold, and many RA personnel were eliminated, including long-time PR head Roger Martin.

Throughout this period Baum had battled tooth and nail with Martin Brody over every new acquisition and every old property. Baum would not stand by while Brody destroyed the very soul of what RA had built over a dynamic decade of growth. The way RA had let The Four Seasons drift was particularly odious to Baum, who by 1970 had been removed from the presidency of the company and replaced by Richard Blumenthal. For a while longer Baum was accommodated, but he was reduced to what Grace Wechsler Brody described as "nothing more than an interior decorator."

Baum's $75,000 salary, his $50,000 expense account, his stock options and research allocations, his access to a Park Avenue apartment—all were looking more and more like unearned expenditures that served just to keep him at bay. It was hardly unexpected, then, that Martin Brody began to regard Baum as extravagant and unrealistic. More important, Brody found him extraneous.

Working harder than ever, Baum found himself increasingly frustrated and under stress, smoking heavily and ignoring a chronic pain in his lower abdomen. Then, one morning on the way to a board meeting, the pain increased sharply and he skipped the meeting to go to a doctor. By the time he got to the physician's office, the pain was so excruciating that Baum collapsed on the floor and had to be taken in an unconscious state to the hospital. Doctors there found that his appendix had exploded and begun to infect his entire system. An emergency operation was undertaken immediately to save his life.

When Baum woke up, he learned that not only had the doctors removed his appendix, but Brody and Blumenthal had cut him out of RA.

While he was still recovering in the hospital, The Four Seasons, looking tatty for the first time in its eleven-year history, with dirty carpets and holes in the tablecloths, a reduced staff, and hiked-up menu prices, had its biggest June, July, and August in its history. RA's new president, Richard Blumenthal, a thirty-three-year-old executive whom one colleague described as "incredible cunning covered with a lot of fat tissue, a blend of Lucretia Borgia and Machiavelli," predicted brashly, "Barring an atomic bomb, [The Four Seasons] may make a profit for the first time ever."

Now all RA had to do was get rid of the old dinosaur once and for all.

Things were going from bad to worse at RA, as typified by the publication of a scathing article in *New York* magazine by restaurant critic Gael Greene entitled "Restaurant Associates: Twilight of the Gods," which portrayed Baum as martyr and RA board members as heathens out to dismantle the empire. "The philistines sit in the driver's seat," she cried. "Excellence is frowned, nay, spat upon."

Greene, whose first meal at The Four Seasons in the early 1960s was so expensive—$40—she went into sticker shock at the presentation of the bill, used all her considerable critical and journalistic powers to chart RA's decline and inveighed against fallen standards, calling the Forum of the Twelve Caesars "shabby," its brocade "faded," its rack of lamb "bone dry," and its boiled beef "a barbaric specimen." And, driving the sword deep into RA's gut, Greene quoted Grace Forrest—the former Mrs. Jerry Brody—as telling RA's board, "You're killing [Baum] and stamping on his grave."

Other reports on The Four Seasons were not as personal, but the important Forbes magazine, while generally praising the Pool Room, noted that "the trees, menu, uniforms, flowers, tableware, and other trappings no longer change with the four seasons," and even that self-described "capitalist tool" called the prices at the restaurant "one of the most stupendous things about the Four Seasons."

Chapter Seven

Raising the Titanic

The Four Seasons Changes Hands

RA took more hits: the Boston branches of Mamma Leone's and Zum Zum were failing. La Fonda del Sol was closed, only to reopen at half its size, sharing its space with a bank. RA sold its airport restaurants back to New York's Port Authority. A fearsome recession was cutting deeply into restaurant profits nationwide. An oil embargo raised gas and oil prices. New York was particularly hard hit because of a massive blizzard that winter, followed by a newspaper strike and a theater strike, all of which affected business negatively and drastically. Yet RA's New York restaurants like Mamma Leone's, Trattoria, and Charley O's continued to keep the company solvent; all of them were under the direction of forty-year-old Tom Margittai, who had joined RA in 1962 after a stint at the Mark Hopkins in San Francisco. Recruited by fellow Hungarian George Lang, Margittai spent a month at The Four Seasons to learn RA's management style and by 1972 had risen to become vice president in charge of "tablecloth" restaurant operations.

Though not a member of the RA team of the glory days, Margittai shared the belief of men like Jerry Brody, Joe Baum, and Stuart Levin that places like The Four Seasons were symbolic not only of what *could* be done in American restaurants, but of what *should* be done in a society whose sophistication and taste level were rising rapidly, right along with a growing affluence that promised even better days to come, recession or no recession.

Margittai had never liked corporate life, preferring instead the hands-on management of a property to the boardroom politics of RA, which had become increasingly divisive and accusatory. Margittai was more than once called "soft" on landlords by Brody and Blumenthal and knew they had no intention of throwing any more money into supporting his side of the business.

There were other complications: The Four Seasons' staff was becoming increasingly angry over the way things were being run. When the Grill Room was changed to a supper club with music, captains and waiters from the Pool Room were shifted into the Grill, thereby losing their lucrative tips from regular Pool Room customers. For a while there was no maître d' at all, and director Paul Kovi interviewed thirty-seven people for the job.

"No one wanted it," said Kovi, whom Margittai had appointed to hold things together after Lang's departure. "They knew it was much too difficult and had heard that The Four Seasons was not a peaceful place to work. We'd had a maître d'—a Frenchman—who terrorized the staff and

could no longer control the crew and had violent arguments constantly. At one point we had the union coming in every day to complain about one thing or another."

In every sense The Four Seasons was losing its soul, its personality and its allure. RA had not delegated enough authority to Kovi or his staff to allow them to respond to customers' complaints about shoddy premises, poor service, and mediocre food. "If a customer had a complaint, we had to tell them to call or write RA's corporate offices on Broadway," said Kovi.

Nevertheless, Blumenthal was asking his directors to make even deeper cuts. There were days when no butter was placed on tables because it had not been delivered or perhaps not even ordered. One day Blumenthal called Margittai into the office and told him RA had to get more money out of the New York units by raising prices and giving less for the money. "Take the garnishes off the plate," he told Margittai. "Make the portions smaller. Do whatever you have to do, but I want our costs cut and our profits up." A popular Saturday lunch was dropped. Flowers were kept for days or not replaced at all. Cleaning of carpets and the metal draperies was postponed indefinitely. Rather than buy new tablecloths, management patched the holes in the old ones.

Margittai argued that he'd already done all he could without completely compromising the New York restaurants' images. "I thought Blumenthal was dead wrong," Margittai says, "but I had to do it and hated every minute of it. Even so, profits did not materialize."

By this time Seagram was becoming increasingly dissatisfied with the way RA was managing what had once been intended to promote Seagram's image of sophistication, good taste, and commitment to the highest standards of art, architecture, food, and service. It seemed they were supporting a dying institution whose only real appeal was the enduring beauty of the original design. Seagram expressed its disenchantment to Brody and said they were willing to allow RA to sublet the space (there were still nine years left on the lease), provided a tenant suitable to Seagram's standards could be found. Preferably this would be another restaurant client, but nothing prevented The Four Seasons from being taken over by any other kind of enterprise and turned into an auto dealership, art gallery, or retail store. The problem was, no one in his right mind wanted to take over this failing giant of a restaurant, whose upkeep was still very costly and whose future was very dim.

It was no secret that RA would have loved to unload The Four

Working for The Four Seasons can be a highly stressful job. One evening it got to a waiter, who pushed open the kitchen doors, ripped off his waiter's jacket, shirt, and tie, and shouted, "You can take this job and shove it!" A year later he came back and applied for a manager's position. He didn't get it, so instead he became an architect in Houston.

Seasons—as well as the Forum—despite Sandy Bain's astounding public assertion in the May 1972 issue of *Restaurant Hospitality* magazine that "The Four Seasons just came off its most successful year. Closing it would be a lot like J. Paul Getty committing suicide after watching yet another oil well come in." Compared to a decade of losses, the little profits The Four Seasons was then making (sales were said to be only $1.5 million) might have been reason enough for Bain to crow, but the restaurant was no gusher, as Tom Margittai well knew.

Things had gotten so bad that Margittai had already accepted the inevitablity that his head would soon be on RA's chopping block, a move that would at the very least save the company $100,000 a year in salary payments, benefits, and expenses. "I hated what I was being asked to do to the tablecloth restaurants," recalls Margittai. "I started to think seriously about resigning and looking for other work."

There were several offers, including a job managing the then successful Playboy Clubs, but the idea of running his own restaurant began to take hold of him. Every restaurateur ultimately dreams of owning his own restaurant, and most try it—and fail at it—at one time or another in their careers. At forty-three Margittai was in the prime of his life and at a crisis in his career. Having survived adversity, he was not a man to back down from a fight, nor one to avoid a challenge. The son of a Jewish Hungarian industrialist, Margittai had been born in Transylvania and educated in Switzerland, and he had been imprisoned in a Nazi concentration camp before the war ended. After the war he came to the United States to work at the Waldorf-Astoria, rose through the hospitality ranks at the Park Lane and the Sherry-Netherland, and became director of sales and catering at the Mark Hopkins in San Francisco at a time when it was designated as a "State Department hotel" for visiting dignitaries like Charles de Gaulle, Konrad Adenauer, and Nikita Khrushchev. Broad-shouldered and possessed of thick, jet-black eyebrows he could use to wither an opponent or employee as he dressed them down in any of five languages, Margittai was considered a formidable taskmaster who did not shrink from the nuts and bolts of running a restaurant.

He had, however, long been cushioned by corporate life and was skittish and doubtful that he could run a restaurant all by himself. Unsure which way to turn, he asked advice of James Beard, who recognized that Margittai didn't just need another job, but a change of direction in his life. "I can't imagine you'd be very happy running the Playboy Clubs, Tom," said Beard, "but I could see you running The Four Seasons. At the very least you couldn't do any worse than RA is now."

The idea had enormous appeal to Margittai but seemed like pure fantasy. He had made a good living at RA, and back in the 1960s Jerry Brody had given him a gift of one thousand shares of RA stock, which he sold very profitably at 43 (two weeks before it dropped to 22). But he had nothing like the hundreds of thousands of dollars he thought it would take to swing the deal.

He knew he'd need help, both financial and professional, so he asked his fellow Transylvanian, Paul Kovi (whom he'd reappointed as director of The Four Seasons when Lang left), if he'd have any interest in becoming a partner in such a crazy venture.

Four years Margittai's senior, Kovi was a more gregarious fellow than his boss and fully enjoyed the hand-on-hand contact restaurateurs build with their customers. A native of Balassagyarmat, Hungary, he had graduated from the University of Transylvania with a degree in economy and architecture, moved to Italy after the war, and pursued a career in professional soccer. In 1951 he came to the United States, where he attended New York City Community College, graduating with a degree in hotel and restaurant management.

From there it was on to the Waldorf, where he first met Margittai, and then to the Sherry-Netherland, where he was head of food and beverage and banquets. He also taught courses on banquet management and wines at New York City College for four years before joining RA in 1964 as director of the Tower Suite. Two years later Margittai tapped him to be director of The Four Seasons when Levin left the company, then again after Lang's tenure.

Better than anyone else Paul Kovi, director of The Four Seasons, knew the gamble it would be to take over the running of a restaurant in sharp decline.

Kovi was a man of culture and refinement, with a demeanor that bespoke both breeding and connoisseurship. He too had a pair of remarkable eyebrows that could register both disdain and sympathy on the same face at the same time. He was well regarded and highly respected by the staff at The Four Seasons.

Kovi knew that his days at RA were dependent upon The Four Seasons' survival, and Margittai's offer struck him as a way to salvage a great institution and to leave RA behind. "No one really knew the operation of the restaurant the way I did," says Kovi, "and I had worked hard to build rapport with customers. Tom and I were still young men at the height of our strength, and we knew we could handle the kind of work and hours it would take to make a living. But I was well aware that it was a very risky undertaking for us both, especially since neither of us had much cash to throw around and nothing as collateral."

"So what do you think, Paul?" asked Margittai. "Can we possibly make this thing fly?"

Kovi considered the question for a moment, pressed his hands together as if praying, and replied, "If the two of us work like four men, maybe so."

The two men thereupon went to see Brody and asked him about the possibility of taking over The Four Seasons. Not entirely to their surprise, Brody thought highly of the idea—with one proviso: the two suitors had to

Left: Peter Gogolak, pictured here just after college (1970), became an eight-year place kicker for the New York Giants. He stands next to Paul Kovi. Right: Jesse Owens, circa 1968, winner of several Olympic gold medals.

marry not one, but two over-the-hill dowagers—The Four Seasons and the Forum of the Twelve Caesars—at book value (an unremarkable $230,000) and pay all RA's obligations under a lease that still had a few years to run.

Margittai didn't know whether to laugh or scoff at the idea. His dark eyebrows shot upward. "Look, Martin," he said, "you know Paul and I don't have that kind of money, and the Forum is in even worse shape than the Seasons. The Forum was a great gimmick, but it's outlived its time, and The Four Seasons needs all of our energies to bring it back to health, if that's possible at this point."

"Relax, Tom," replied Brody. "I just want the water to come up to here"—he raised his hand to his neck—"not up to here," he said, raising his hand to his nose. "You don't have to come up with the whole amount. I just want both places off RA's books and my own head above water."

Margittai and Kovi next talked with Jack Yogman, then president of

Seagram, who was delighted that the two seasoned Transylvanians would take on the challenge. This was key, because without Seagram's approval the deal would never have gone through. When the papers were finally signed on October 13, 1973, Margittai and Kovi agreed to take over the running of both The Four Seasons and the Forum and to continue paying off the original lease—which on the surface sounded like an intolerable burden for the two of them to bear alone. But that was just on paper. The fact was, Margittai and Kovi got two of the most famous institutions in American restaurant history by putting up only $15,000 in cash. "We got a bargain all right," Margittai said later, "but it was one that was very difficult to live with.

"The first thing we did," recalls Margittai, "was to have an all-day

 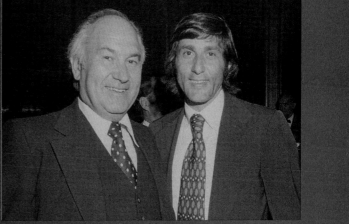

Sunday meeting with the restaurants' staffs. We told them that none of them would lose their jobs and that we were all in this together. It could only get better if we all worked hard. The second thing we did was call George Lois."

Lois, who had been doing RA ads since the opening of The Four Seasons, accepted the challenge "in a flash" and quit the RA account. (Ironically, Baum had begged Lois to stay with RA because the company was doing so badly and Baum still had so much stock in it.) Nevertheless, Lois played devil's advocate to the new owners' evangelical zeal.

"So what are you going to do with the old lady?" Lois asked with characteristic forthrightness. "What's going to be any different?"

Margittai and Kovi were full of cautious optimism built on a change of strategy. Margittai spoke first.

"We're going after New Yorkers first and foremost, George. One of the

Left: Olympic figure skater Peggy Fleming being interviewed in 1968 at The Four Seasons. Right: Paul Kovi and Ilie Nastase, circa 1970.

Paul Kovi (second from right) on the Joe Franklin television show in 1969.

problems with The Four Seasons is that New Yorkers have come to think of it as a tourist restaurant for out-of-towners. We want the kind of customer the '21' Club has, the old, established guys, but we also want young New Yorkers, the guys just coming up."

Kovi chimed in, "If we're going to survive, it has to be on the basis of a strong, faithful clientele who knows that Tom and I will do anything to please them. Before we took over there was never a real presence at the restaurant. It was a place owned by a corporation. So we want everybody to know that we're going to change the service, the food, the whole kitchen if necessary, and that Tom and I will be there at all times. Now, how do we get that message across?"

Lois shrugged and raised his palms. "We announce it to the world like it was some goddamn momentous event. We put a full-page ad in the fucking *New York Times.*"

Margittai and Kovi looked at each other and laughed out loud.

"George," explained Margittai, "we haven't got two cents left to spend on ads like that. I'm not even sure we can afford you."

Lois stuck out his chin. "So I'll eat off my fees at lunch."

Not only did Lois "eat off" his fees, but he charged Kovi and Margittai nothing for the artwork, asked for no cash commissions, and even pressured the publisher of *Book Digest,* John Veronis, to give The Four Seasons two free pages.

Within days Lois had drawn up an ad for the May 15 edition of the *Times* that was actually a two-page spread costing $10,000. It was a picture of Margittai and Kovi standing and shaking hands on the steps of the Park Avenue entrance. The ad read "We breathlessly announce that the two of us have taken over The Four Seasons." The two Hungarians-turned-New Yorkers looked urbane, smug, even victorious, and the faint smile on their lips suggested a kind of triumph. In reality, the two of them were nearly broke and terrified at what they'd taken on, and they sent out a press release that told friends and colleagues, "In our wildest dreams we never thought this could happen. But it happened."

The thrust of the ad, which Lois also ran in *New York* magazine, was to tell New Yorkers that The Four Seasons was no longer a unit restaurant of a faceless corporation, but that there were now two men who would greet, receive, and make a fuss over you and make you happy in any way they could.

Mailings went out to executives at every top company in New York, and Margittai and Kovi put the word out through their regulars that things had changed at The Four Seasons. Two weeks after the ads ran, the phone started ringing with reservations from people who had previously regarded the restaurant as an expensive tourist trap.

Margittai and Kovi started hiring new staff members better suited to their style for the "new" Four Seasons. They appointed Joe Scialom, who had made a name for himself at Shepherd's Hotel in Cairo as one of the great dining room greeters, to man the reservations desk at the top of the stairs. Scialom was known for his extraordinary ability to make both old-timers and newcomers feel comfortable and cosseted. The hauteur that characterized the "clubbish" atmosphere of earlier days was exchanged for a welcoming attitude that encouraged repeat visits.

Margittai and Kovi kept on Oreste Carnevali, who had been the valued maître d' of the Pool Room for the past five years and knew everyone in town worth knowing.

Meanwhile new expenditures, new menus, and new chefs would have to wait. The fact was, despite The Four Seasons' listing condition, it was the Forum of the Twelve Caesars that was fast slipping beneath waves of red ink. At least twice a day Margittai and Kovi rotated between the two restaurants, sometimes bicycling from Park Avenue to Rockefeller Center, trying to establish their presence and personality at both places and keep things from breaking up at either. Like characters in a French farce, the two owners darted back and forth, always seeming to be in two places at once, and guests would catch sight of both men during a meal, sometimes twice, but rarely ever together.

In order to bolster the kitchen at the Forum, Margittai and Kovi had lured away RA's executive chef, Joseph "Seppi" Renggli, a highly versatile Swiss who was always willing to innovate in order to turn things around. Renggli had broad training in Europe's finest hotels, including the Chalet Petite Suisse in Amsterdam as *poissonier,* the Grand Hotel in Stockholm as *rôtisseur,* the Hotel de la Paix in Lucerne as *saucier,* and the Carlton Elite in Zurich as *garde-manger,* before emigrating to the United States in 1966. Together with his assistant and fellow Swiss, Christian "Hitsch" Albin, he

Chefs Seppi Renglli (right) and Hitsch Albin were given the task of reviving the luster of the kitchen at The Four Seasons in the 1970s.

began doing an extensive buffet at lunch every day to bring in local business and people who had thought the Forum too posh and expensive for lunch. The Four Seasons staff was told to encourage customers to try out the Forum, too. "It backfired," says Carnevali. "Every time we'd send a customer to the Forum, we lost a table at the Seasons."

Nothing really worked, and the Forum continued to drain the few resources Margittai and Kovi had. "We were working twelve to fourteen hours seven days a week," recalls Margittai. "But we were so broke we couldn't even pay our legal bills. Fortunately we did have cash flow from the Seasons, so we were always able to meet our payroll, even when we couldn't afford to pay our own salaries, which we'd cut down to twenty-five thousand dollars each."

The two restaurants desperately needed an infusion of cash to get them through the year. "The natural thing to do was go to Citibank," says Margittai, "which we'd worked with for years at RA. So we went to see them and asked for a revolving, unsecured credit of a hundred thousand dollars. They refused because they said we were so expensive not even their own executives were allowed to eat at The Four Seasons, which was on the top of their list of prohibited restaurants."

They approached Yogman at Seagram, and he agreed to lend them $50,000 for maintenance of the restaurant, to be "eaten up" over the course of a year by Seagram executives.

By 1974 it was obvious that the Forum was dying and had to be closed. But Margittai and Kovi's deal with RA stipulated that they had to run both restaurants or lose both.

"Things dragged on for months," says Margittai. "Nobody wanted to take over the Forum, and finally Paul and I had no alternative but to close the place. We sent a letter to RA, telling them we'd lock it up on June 1, 1975, and give them the key." In the meantime Seagram agreed to pay cash to RA to give up The Four Seasons' lease; Seagram then renegotiated with Margittai and Kovi, tacking on an additional $150,000 loan for future maintenance of the $4.5 million interior.

Meeting with Jack Yogman and Seagram's real estate expert, Harold Fieldstiel, Margittai was both grateful for and exasperated by the deal. "It's an extraordinarily generous deal," he told the Seagram representative, "but Paul and I don't think we can afford the rate of interest you want on the loan. Sadly, I'm afraid we're going to have to refuse your offer."

Yogman could hardly believe what Margittai had told him, shook his head, sat there for a minute, then waved his hand and said, "Ah, the hell with the interest!"

Tom Margittai (left) and Paul Kovi intended to show that The Four Seasons now had hands-on ownership and management in place for a new era in the restaurant's history, beginning in October 1973.

Fieldstiel balked. "Jack, what's Edgar [Bronfman] going to say to a deal like that with no interest?"

Yogman folded his cards. "Gentlemen, the fact is, all Edgar wants out of this is a three-star restaurant in the Seagram Building. So, we got a deal, then?"

Margittai had played well. He knew that under New York State alcohol laws, Seagram, a spirits distributor, could not operate a restaurant. He also knew that since the death of Sam Bronfman in 1971 at the age of eighty, Seagram had recently expanded its investments in wine and Edgar Bronfman had plans to make the company as well known for its import of fine Bordeaux as it was for Seagram's 7 Crown. The younger Bronfman was also a man of more refined tastes than his father, so the change of taste from "a nice piece of flanken" to three-star cuisine was inevitable.

The terms of the new lease were the same as for the old one, but Seagram demanded it hold the rights to the trademark for The Four Seasons.

"Why would you want that?" asked Margittai.

"You never know," answered Yogman. "We may want to control what goes on in that restaurant."

However forbidding that sounded, Margittai and Kovi accepted the terms and shook hands. "Only at that moment," recalls Margittai, "did I truly believe that Paul and I owned The Four Seasons."

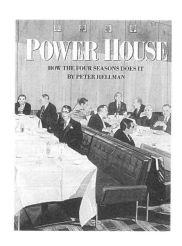

The decade of the 1970s was not one to give any New Yorker much to cheer about, with the resignation of a corrupt president, inflation running 13 percent a year, oil prices soaring, and a deficit that was beginning to restrain American productivity.

There were, however, a few reasons to hope for better times. After publicly browbeating New York, the federal government reluctantly agreed to save the city from bankruptcy to the tune of an annual bailout of $2.3 billion from 1975 to mid-1978. A year later the New York Stock Exchange set a trading record of 63.5 million shares. And the Yankees took the pennant two years in a row, beating the L.A. Dodgers four games to two in the 1977 World Series.

But it was an event of national exultation that boosted New York's image and self-pride more than anything else had in what Tom Wolfe called the "me decade": the bicentennial birthday of the United States, which was celebrated in New York with a kind of spectacle unimaginable anywhere else. On July 4, 1976, scores of tall-masted ships from around the world arrived in New York Harbor as part of Operation Sail, and the party that went on throughout that momentous day made the city seem like the most wonderful, most exuberant, most exciting, and most powerful place to be in the world.

Chapter Eight

Almost As Good As Money

The Four Seasons Survives and the Power Lunch Begins

PAGE 96: *Bringing in young professionals like Julian Niccolini (left) and Alex von Bidder (right) to help manage The Four Seasons brought new energy to the restaurant.*

More than a century ago Oliver Wendell Holmes mused, "How many people live on the reputation of the reputation they might have had!" He may well have been talking about New York and about The Four Seasons in the mid-1970s.

Freed of the Forum albatross and sensing that New York was destined to renew itself after a long recession, Kovi and Margittai set to work to change everything at The Four Seasons without people noticing any change at all. For although Margittai and Kovi sought desperately to attract new customers—especially the diehards at "21"—they did not want to alienate any of the old. Favorite dishes, like the shrimp with mustard fruits and the chocolate velvet cake, were retained, but the menu itself was shortened and geared more to a new breed of younger executives who

Left: Paul Kovi leaning over Diane von Furstenberg with an unidentified guest in the early 1970s. Right: The Duke and Duchess of Windsor, circa 1972.

did not take three-hour lunches or two-hour cocktail hours. The kitchen was told to gear up for lunches that would take one hour from appetizer to dessert. George Lois suggested getting rid of the expensive, pretentious, velvet-covered wine books in exchange for a single broadsheet, printed on imported German paper called "elephant hide," that had the menu on the front and the wine list on the back.

The theme of seasonal change was not only carried on, but amplified by the explosion of new products and ingredients in the American marketplace, of which New York was the central distributor. The kinds of foods Henri Soulé could only have dreamed of serving at Le Pavillon were now available in profusion for restaurants like The Four Seasons that were willing to pay for them—domestic baby lamb, field greens, goat's cheese, a wide variety of oysters and seafood, and an enormous cornucopia of fruits and vegetables. Margittai and Kovi even consulted with an amateur mushroom expert named John Cage, perhaps better known as a composer of aleatoric music.

For the first few months of their proprietorship, Kovi and Margittai had no formal chef creating new menus for the restaurant; they were forced to get along with overseers and cooks who were nothing if not robotic. When they could afford to do so, they persuaded Renggli, under great duress, and Albin to come over from the defunct Forum. The two Swiss first had to win over The Four Seasons' established kitchen staff and then make changes very slowly in the methods of cooking and service of food. They looked at every ingredient in the kitchen, threw out everything that was not fresh, and bought only the finest in the marketplace.

Renggli was not only exceptionally gifted as a working chef, but he had iron discipline and was a superb organizer. He had the priceless ability to buy the best and still save money. He knew how to improve efficiency, streamline operations in the kitchen, and move food out at the moment it was ready to be served.

Left: Ingrid Bergman with Paul Kovi, 1970.
Right: Nelson and Happy Rockefeller, 1968.

Kovi and Margittai consulted with everyone, listened to everyone, and tried anything. On a trip to Venice, Margittai fell in love with the raffish atmosphere at the renowned Harry's Bar, which attracted precisely the kind of affluent, well-traveled, and sophisticated clientele he craved for The Four Seasons. So he decided to add pastas and risottos to the menu— an idea unheard of in an American restaurant at the time.

Since both Kovi and Margittai were by then divorced, they were able to spend all their time and energies on the restaurant, splitting their responsi-

Every year our friends Fran and Jerry join my wife, Bobbie, and me to celebrate our anniversary with a dinner at a fine restaurant. For our twentieth anniversary in 1974, we ate at The Four Seasons. In the middle of the meal, I was quite surprised when the captain came over and said, "Sir, your shoes are sadly missing from your feet." I have a habit of taking my shoes off under the table at restaurants. I am, I believe, most unobtrusive about it. In this case, however, the gentleman spotted the offending feet—I'm sure nobody else noticed—and, in the most polite terms, asked me to desist, which I did with dispatch.

A few years later, the fine writer John McPhee wrote a restaurant review in the *New Yorker* in which he included a sentence about The Four Seasons. He praised the restaurant, saying it was the kind of place where you could be comfortable taking your shoes off under the table without worrying about censure.
—Stan Isaacs,
    Freelance sports writer,
    New York

bilities according to their own strengths. Margittai oversaw finance, bookkeeping, cashiering, maintenance, food and beverage controls, insurance, purchasing, advertising, and housekeeping. He plowed $30,000 into refurbishing the woodwork and $40,000 on upholstery, and he finally replaced the ten-year-old carpet at a cost of $30,000. He became manic about every detail of the furnishings. Recalling Gael Greene's remarks about the holes in the linen, he would inspect every inch of the tablecloths, carpets, and upholstery for tears, nicks, or wear. On one occasion he noticed a tiny tear in the fabric that covered a chair and told the staff he wanted it removed from the floor immediately. When Margittai noticed the next day that his orders had not been followed, he pushed the chair through the kitchen doors and, to the astonishment of the staff, threw it across the room. Always dressed impeccably in a dark business suit, he was just as meticulous about the way his staff looked and required managers to bring in their suits to make sure they matched the colors of the banquettes and carpet.

Margittai also dispensed with the old barter cards that allowed so many customers to eat free of charge, although he did offer certain influential members of the press a 25 percent discount card on food and beverage.

Kovi meanwhile took care of banquet sales, public relations, office administration, uniforms, linen, laundry, purchasing, reservations, promotions, and expansion of the wine list. These last two functions coalesced in Kovi's desire to make The Four Seasons a restaurant known for its cellar, its service, and its devotion to the marriage of food and wine. And wines were priced fairly—at 100 percent plus a dollar above retail.

Both men knew that parties and banquets were where the real profits lay, yet despite working fourteen hours a day, there was simply not enough time to go after that part of the business. For this reason, Kovi began casting about for a banquet manager. Rather than rely on any of the old RA personnel, he wanted someone young, dynamic, and conversant in several languages.

He got wind of a young food and beverage manager at the Park Lane named Alex von Bidder, who was learning quickly and ready for a move up. Tall, slender, and extremely boyish-looking, but a deadpan serious professional, the twenty-six-year-old Swiss had trained with the Mövenpick hotel and restaurant company, then emigrated to the United States "to learn English" (he already spoke German and French) and enrolled in the Hotel School of Cornell University. After a stint with the Loews Hotel Company, he went over to the Park Lane in New York, owned by Harry and Leona Helmsley. He was being primed to take over the food and beverage operations at the Helmsley's new Palace Hotel when he received an invitation to have lunch with Kovi at The Four Seasons.

"Everybody told me to stay away from The Four Seasons," said von Bidder, who enjoyed hotel work and had no particular interest in working for a restaurant anyway. "I was told that Tom and Paul had a partnership like a marriage rather than a corporation, and my colleagues said that Tom Margittai was a 'man-eater.' The smart money said that they were just not going to succeed. People pointed out that any East Side restaurant that instituted a pretheater dinner had to be doing poorly."

Von Bidder listened to Kovi's salary offer—which at $16,000 matched Helmsley's—but refused it. Margittai was, however, impressed with the young man, citing his meticulousness, honesty, and "good middle-class virtues," all of which were needed at The Four Seasons.

Margittai called von Bidder back. "What'll it take, Alex?"

Von Bidder, whose Italian wife had recently become pregnant and had stopped working as a flight attendant, wanted security more than anything else—something he was not likely to obtain from Leona Helmsley.

"It'll take a contract," he told Margittai. "I'm not interested in a tryout position, and if I come aboard, I have to have the authority to make changes and to believe I have a hand in the future of this place."

Young Swiss hotelier Alex von Bidder (right) was hired away from Leona Helmsley by Margittai to boost banquet business at The Four Seasons.

Margittai and Kovi accepted his terms, appointing von Bidder banquet manager of The Four Seasons. Within months of his arrival, the restaurant's party business, which had for years stagnated, started to grow. Von Bidder began by adding to his telephone book the names of every important person in New York whom The Four Seasons wished to attract. He had a reputation for providing pretty much anything a party giver might require at a moment's notice, whether it was a tap-dance floor to place over the pool for a fashion show or a wedding runner for an impromptu wedding.

Von Bidder became known for his grace under pressure, and his ability to remain in control under the most trying circumstances became legendary. He was adept at disarming a patron bent on making a scene by

When a New York gangster tried to pay for his daughter's $50,000 wedding with someone else's endorsed check, von Bidder refused to accept it and went to the man's apartment to collect, only to be given a suitcase full of cash and an offer to be driven back to the restaurant. Von Bidder refused both and the next morning extracted a cashier's check from the gangster.

making whatever mishap occurred seem perfectly normal. For example, one time a waiter accidentally dropped a platter of Dover sole in front of a couple and sent the fish sailing out over the pool. Von Bidder merely turned to the offended table and said, "Why, there must be some mistake, sir. You didn't order the flying fish, did you?"

His professional discretion was often tested in the most bizarre ways, such as the time he had to help extract two large women stuck in an intimate embrace in the downstairs telephone booth.

Von Bidder was especially good when it came to stiffs. One Saturday at lunch a gargantuan man suddenly collapsed and died while passing from the Bar Room to the Pool Room. His enormous three-hundred-pound frame was splayed beneath the Picasso curtain, which meant moving him would be extremely difficult, not to mention illegal, since a dead body must remain untouched until the police can investigate. The problem was, the lunch crowd was starting to appear, walking up the steps to the Bar Room. "We couldn't very well have them enter the Pool Room by stepping over this guy's body," recalls von Bidder, "so we told people there was a little problem with the Picasso and invited every guest to take a spontaneously arranged tour of our kitchen, whose back door enters onto the Pool Room."

On another occasion a customer slumped over and inconveniently died at the bar. This time, with as little fuss as possible, von Bidder arranged for the body to be removed to one of the banquettes and covered with a tablecloth. Some regulars may have wondered if there was a leak from the ceiling that required covering the banquette, but no one who came in from that point on had any notion of the corpse's presence, and cocktail hour went on as usual.

Sometimes it was the less-than-terminal cases that tried von Bidder's patience most of all. "One Saturday night an older lady was sitting on one of the inside chairs against the pool and suddenly fainted," recalls von Bidder. "She started to slide under the table, her wig came off, her friends jumped up, and her husband screamed, 'Julia, don't leave me!' So I rushed over to see if she was still breathing. Suddenly her husband shouted at me, 'Don't you touch my wife!' I tried to explain that I was trying to help her and that an ambulance was already on its way. The guy screamed, 'I didn't ask for an ambulance!' Then he took a glass of water off the table and poured it on top of his wife's head, and the woman woke up. Just then the ambulance paramedics arrived with the stretcher, and the husband said, 'Get them away from her!' The ambulance guys insisted that I had to sign a release that they were prevented from attending to her. Meanwhile she was slowly coming to, and her husband helped her up and out to a cab. I never heard a word from them again."

In addition to his dual duties as banquet manager and fire extinguisher, von Bidder also helped focus the staff's consciousness on every detail and every ingredient. Once, having tasted an array of the most expensive Asian teas in the market for possible purchase, von Bidder took more than two months testing his choices at home before putting any on The Four Seasons' menu.

Kovi and Margittai's gamble on von Bidder soon paid off in more measurable ways: a year after he'd taken over banqueting, sales, which had been a slow $200,000 a year, soared to $524,000 and by 1983 they reached $1,370,000.

Things were certainly looking a bit better by the mid-1970s, though the Grill Room was still a loser. In fact, Kovi and Margittai had closed the room for a while and used it only for the cocktail hour. Their failure to make a success of the Grill gnawed at Margittai and Kovi, who wondered why the room could not attract the same kind of people who dropped into Harry's Bar or the Savoy Grill in London, people who wanted to dine well without making an "event" out of a meal.

In fact, The Four Seasons' Grill Room had never really been developed according to the traditions of other grill rooms, where men would meet for simply cooked steaks, chops, and seafood in an atmosphere less pretentious and simply more convivial than the formal dining room. The menu at the Grill Room was the same as in the Pool Room, tableside preparation was standard, and the waitstaff of maître d', captain, waiters, and busboys replicated the service of formal dining.

James Beard (left), the "godfather of American cooking," had been one of the early menu developers at The Four Seasons and continued to be an éminence grise after Margittai and Kovi took over. Von Bidder is on the right.

It was James Beard who suggested they refine the Grill Room to resemble the Savoy and Connaught in London, Jack's in San Francisco, Chasen's in Los Angeles, Locke-Ober's in Boston, and the London Chop House in Detroit, all of which featured the kind of simple grilled and roast meats and seafood that appealed to conservative businessmen. It was an idea that was also attractive to literary agent Mort Janklow, who dined at the The Four Seasons almost daily and suggested to Kovi that something like London's Savoy Grill might click with those businessmen of the mid-1970s who were increasingly watching their calories and cholesterol. Kovi

Diana Ross came in to dine with her agent. When von Bidder tried to seat her at one of the prime tables in the Grill Room, she refused, saying, "I don't want to have lunch in the lobby."

took the idea under advisement and, with a menu sketchily suggested by Beard, brought Janklow a rough draft for inspection. The agent thought it was just about perfect.

The menu was abbreviated from that in the Pool Room, and the kitchen was told that everything on it had to be prepared in five minutes or less— grilled meats and fish, a good hamburger, and quickly sautéed vegetables would be featured each day, along with no more than one or two specials. This in itself was hardly revolutionary, but Kovi and Margittai further developed the idea by doing away with the pretensions of tableside carving and eliminating captains, waiters, and busboys. Instead there would be a manager and just two or three waiters.

On the menu were items like gravlax, broiled shrimp, poached salmon with dill sauce, grilled or sautéed paillards of veal, chicken, and beef, and stir-fried vegetables.

The grill concept was stripped to the bare essentials, but it also contained within it the seeds of a new sophistication that seemed to characterize New York business itself.

Philip Johnson's ascetic design for The Four Seasons Grill Room distanced it from the traditional clichés and raucous atmosphere of men's grills with their overstuffed red leather booths, caricatures of favored patrons, and brusque

APPETIZERS

Rillette of Salmon 9.50
Galantine of Capon 7.50
Seviche of Scallops 8.50
Shrimp Cocktail 10.00
Little Necks or Cherrystones 7.00
Pike and Salmon Pâté 8.00
Marinated Salmon 11.00
Vegetable Soup 6.50
A Cold Tomato
    and Red Pepper Bisque 6.50
Beefsteak Tomato
    with Mozzarella and Basil 8.50

COLD ENTRÉES

Sirloin Tartare 20.00
Bar Room Chef's Salad 17.00
Avocado and Shrimp Salad 20.00
Bundnerfleisch and Melon 19.00

ENTRÉES

GRILLED ON CHARCOAL

Today's Fish 22.50
Bar Room Burger with Creamed Spinach 15.00
A Skewer of Shrimp
    and Chipolata Sausages 21.50
Gravlax, Dill Mustard Sauce 22.00

THE BAR ROOM PAILLARDS:

Veal 23.00   Beef 22.00   Chicken 19.50

Thin Calf's Liver with Sage Butter 20.50
Entrecôte with Crisped Onions 21.00
Grilled Veal Kidney, Bearnaise 18.00
Devilled Baby Chicken 18.50

SPA CUISINE™
FOR THE HEALTH CONSCIOUS, THESE NEWLY CREATED
SPECIALTIES HAVE BEEN DEVELOPED BY
CHEF RENGGLI IN ACCORDANCE WITH THE LATEST
INSIGHTS FROM THE WORLD OF NUTRITION

Veal with Puree of Yellow and Red Pepper 19.50
Ginger Steamed Striped Bass 23.50
Lobster poached in Chablis with Green Noodles 24.00

SALADS

Four Seasons Slaw 5.00
Mixed Greens 4.50

DESSERTS

A Selection from the Dessert Wagon 4.00
Today's Sherbets 4.00
Berries with Crème Fraiche 7.50

Coffee or Espresso 2.00

THE FOUR SEASONS BAR ROOM

The new owners trimmed the menu but kept The Four Seasons' classics. Prices kept the restaurant among the most expensive in the United States. Pictured is an early menu from the Grill Room.

waiters whose English was confined to "Rare, medium, or well-done?" Instead, Kovi and Margittai promoted an atmosphere charged by the presence of well-dressed, well-mannered businessmen, the movers and shakers of New York, attended to by men who treated them as gentlemen, honored their whims, and got them in and out on time for their next appointments.

Despite their renewal of the grill concept, Kovi and Margittai believed the room was due for a name change in order to distinguish it from what had gone before. They turned to George Lois, who, with his typical macho instincts, responded, "Call it the Bar Room." However downscale that may have sounded, Lois knew—and Kovi and Margittai agreed—that

"Bar Room" had a certain swagger and implied this was a place where businessmen could drop in, have a couple of drinks, eat lunch or dinner, and get out in an hour. So the Bar Room it became, although most continued to call it the Grill.

Tentatively they debuted the new concept in October 1975, but it still didn't attract much of a crowd. On many days they were lucky to get twenty people for lunch, and at night they mostly took the overflow from the cocktail hour patrons, who somtimes found themselves three deep at the bar.

Kovi and Margittai decided that it was unlikely that the older customers at "21" would ever desert that watering hole for The Four Seasons, so they decided they must make their mark with a younger, more dynamic crowd, the kind of comers who were making their own headlines. Margittai and Kovi asked Dan Dorfman, then business columnist for *New York* magazine, if there was a way they might get some ink on the restaurant to show that there really was a new spirit at the old Grill Room. Dorfman responded by doing an article about coping with the recession and how Margittai and Kovi had made over the Grill Room into the Bar Room and begun to attract the new entrepreneurs of New York. As a result, some of them actually started to trickle in.

Esquire columnist Nora Ephron started bringing editors and writers to the Bar Room and dropped its name in the magazine's pages. Ephron found the place ideal for lunch because it was near the magazine's offices, had the kind of food she liked to eat, charged decent prices (by comparison with the Pool Room), and was usually deserted. She also found it always too cold, so Margittai arranged to have a white shawl ready for her at her usual banquette. Other journalists and publishing types soon followed. Mort Janklow brought over editor Michael Korda of Simon & Schuster, and soon Nelson Doubleday and Betty Prashker of Doubleday, Roger Straus Jr. of Farrar, Straus & Giroux, Jonathan Folger of Harper & Row, Richard Snyder of Simon & Schuster, Alexander Liberman of Condé Nast, and Leo Lerman of *Vogue* were finding the Bar Room very much to their liking and brought along their favorite authors to bask in the grandeur of that Miesian space.

While the Algonquin's Rose Room retained a hold on *New Yorker* editors and writers, The Four Seasons was soon hosting the young writers and journalists then making waves in New York and eating on their editors' expense accounts. By the late

When best-selling novelist Judith Krantz was asked to sign The Four Seasons' autograph book, she joked, "I only write for money." Von Bidder quickly proffered a dollar, which her agent Mort Janklow grabbed, saying, "I get fifteen percent of that!"

Julian Niccolini inspecting the day's seafood catch.

Julian Niccolini was put in charge of maintaining the eminence of The Four Seasons' wine cache.

After an assistant manager found two members of the crew engaged in sex in the projection room, Julian Niccolini unofficially christened it the Bunga Bunga Room.

1970s one might find Truman Capote, Louis Auchincloss, Gay Talese, Mario Puzo, and Tom Wolfe eating lunch in the Bar Room, while the Pool Room continued to attract captains of industry, celebrities, and out-of-towners.

Yet although Margittai and Kovi tried to personalize the Bar Room, they could not give their full time to the concept without compromising the increasing success of the Pool Room. They had a seasoned professional as maître d' for the Bar Room—an old-timer named François Rognoni—but he was ill attuned to the younger clientele they wished to attract. He was also, by his own estimate, tired out and lacked the verve the Bar Room needed to bring it back to life. Rognoni suggested Kovi and Margittai take a look at a young Italian named Julian Niccolini, who was working at the Palace—then the most expensive and extravagant restaurant in New York. He was said to be hardworking and indefatigable, coming in at six in the morning to receive provender, then serving as captain at dinnertime. And he was very Italian. Even more important, he was very Tuscan.

With a large, chiseled, angular face that could have served equally well as model for a courtier's portrait by Bronzino, a torturer by Mantegna, or, most appropriately, a Bacchus by Caravaggio, Niccolini exhibited a worldly demeanor buoyed by a knowledge and love of wine exceptional in someone only twenty-five years old. And, for him, The Four Seasons was the only restaurant in the United States that came up to his personal standards of refinement.

Niccolini had graduated from hotel school in Rome, moved to the United States and attended the New York City Technical College in hotel and restaurant administration, and worked at the Hotel de Paris in Monte Carlo. In those credentials Kovi and Margittai saw the kind of solid professionalism they needed to run the Bar Room, but in Niccolini's personality they saw something even more important. First, there was a kind of boyishness coupled with an exuberance and natural wit that sometimes manifested itself as irreverence. Next, Niccolini proved that he could show deference without obsequiousness. Last, he demonstrated that with customers he could get away with a lot more than Margittai, Kovi, or von Bidder simply because his eccentricities were shrugged off as mere Italianisms. In 1977 he took on the new position as "manager of the Bar Room."

Immediately Niccolini put his personal stamp on the restaurant, both in the dining room and the kitchen. Exuberant but volatile, he could turn to purple rage behind the swinging doors in the Bar Room, excoriating the staff for an impropriety, a lack of gentility, a small omission—all of which he invariably ascribed to "imbecility"—but he could go into the Bar Room and finesse the most powerful men in New York into ordering something they'd never eaten before and drinking a wine they'd never heard of. Even Philip Johnson allowed himself to be cowed by Niccolini's persuasiveness. "I don't dare tell him I don't like something," says Johnson, "because I'm afraid it might hurt his feelings and he wouldn't sleep at night."

He was also good at making everyone in the Bar Room feel as if they were part of a prestigious and exclusive club. He was a master at handling what came to be called the "negative reservation"—a call made by a Bar Room regular's secretary to tell Niccolini that the customer was *not* coming for lunch. "Some of the booths are always for the same people," he told a reporter for *GQ*, "and if they are not coming, we will give them to anybody who won't ask to be seated there the next time. No big fuss."

Any request—food cooked a certain way, theater tickets for that night, a table out of ear- and eyeshot for a man coming in with a woman not his wife—was always greeted with "No problem!" by Niccolini. On his way in on the train from his suburban home, he would skim the New York newspapers, *New York* magazine, *Women's Wear Daily, Publishers Weekly,* and any number of other journals to give him insight into the activities of his customers, so that he could engage in a little gossip, congratulate one or another on a new appointment, or show condolences for those who'd just suffered a setback. He found out what celebrities were in town, which politicians were staying at what hotels, and which people within the same industry to seat at a distance from others in the same industry.

Niccolini became known for his ability to joke with even the most powerful of his clientele; it was reported that he once told the hawkish Henry Kissinger and the more dovish Cyrus Vance, "We have a lovely breast of pheasant today. Will that be the right one for you, Dr. Kissinger, and the left one for you, Mr. Vance?"

My brother John Softness and I, after celebrating at a party, decided to go to The Four Seasons' bar for a nightcap. We began arguing over a trivial matter, as brothers are wont to do, and it soon escalated into an old-fashioned punch-up. There was no damage to the premises, but a potted palm was knocked over. Ancient barroom protocol clearly called for one of the combatants to be ejected. But which one?

I had patently started the fracas, but I was also a more regular customer. The decision was handed down: John had to take the rap. As he was led down the stairs by a phalanx of waiters, my brother complained in a loud voice: "I'd like to say I was thrown out of better places—but I can't."

—Donald G. Softness, Softness Enterprise

Although usually discreet, Niccolini sometimes crossed the line into a familiarity that got him in trouble, as when he passed an unflattering remark about clothes designer Perry Ellis to *Women's Wear Daily* publisher John Fairchild. Fairchild swore never to return to the restaurant again and stayed away for more than a year. Kovi once estimated that only one in ten thousand of Niccolini's wisecracks caused a problem for the restaurant.

Niccolini was, however, well aware that his customers were not his friends and, though often asked to do so, would not accept social invitations from any of The Four Seasons' patrons. In a rare moment of humility, he once said, "I realize that I'm not in their circle or at their level, so it would be foolish to hobnob with them."

With von Bidder making seating arrangements, Niccolini performing his ministrations, and Kovi and Margittai greeting guests every lunch and dinner hour, the Bar Room started to become popular with a regular clientele who helped focus and define its character so that, in 1978, The Four Seasons went into the black for the first time. The food press was getting on their side, too. In a review of restaurants entitled "Where Insiders Go to Dine and Wine," the *New York Times* awarded The Four Seasons three out of four stars, noting, "Quietly, with almost no promotion, this recent addition [the Bar Room] to one of the city's most famous restaurants has become a significant success in its own right," and reporting that the room was drawing an impressive number of people in the wine trade.

By the late 1970s the Bar Room had taken on a real cachet among New Yorkers, while the Pool Room was still the celebratory dining room for out-of-towners and what came to be called the "bridge-and-tunnel crowd" from the suburbs. It was a new era of fast-rising expectations in New York, even though the economy was still sluggish. Glamour industries like fashion, art, and publishing were gaining momentum, however, and American style was having enormous influence on the rest of the world. It was a time when new magazines were being born or remade according to a brash, irreverent form of "new journalism" pioneered by *Esquire* and *New York* magazine, both of which were run, at different

Many celebrities happily signed The Four Seasons' guest book, including couturier Yves Saint Laurent, who added one of his current designs.

Such a poignant picture to see now. It was taken at a great literary party in the fall of 1974 at The Four Seasons. We were toasting a book called *One Special Summer,* by Jacqueline Kennedy Onassis and Lee Radziwill, about the first trip the sisters took to Europe on their own, back in 1951. We ran it in the *[Ladies' Home] Journal,* and as editor in chief I spent some time with Lee learning about the joy and laughter that had gone into making the book. They had even done their own witty illustrations.

It was a smashing party. That's me, Jackie, Lee, and a gray-haired martini-swiller named Norman Mailer.

—Lenore Hershey,
    Former editor in chief,
    Ladies' Home Journal

times, by Clay Felker. Felker, who loved being first to pronounce a person, place, or thing as epitomizing a new trend in art, fashion, politics, or sports—especially if it involved money and power—had adopted The Four Seasons as his regular lunch spot. And, as he looked around him at his colleagues, competitors, and fellow achievers, he decided that this unique restaurant had become club to the most impressive talents in New York. Before long Felker took to calling the Bar Room "Publishing Central."

Felker and *Esquire* contributing editor Lee Eisenberg, who was also a Four Seasons regular, hatched an idea to write about the restaurant—not as a review of the food, but as an explanation of "How the books you read, the clothes you wear, the wines you drink, begin at The Four Seasons," complete with a diagram of what important people sat at what tables in the Bar Room. In a jaunty mix of hyperbole and New Yorkese, Eisenberg described how on any given day you'd find the likes of Philip Johnson; fashion designers Calvin Klein, Bill Blass, and Oscar de la Renta; TV personality Gene Shalit; *Vogue* editor Grace Mirabella; and real estate mogul Lew Rudin sitting at their favorite tables in the Bar Room. Eisenberg quoted Lois Wyse of Wyse Advertising as saying, "They call me the godmother of the Bar Room. The center banquette is always mine—even Jackie O. can't take it away from me. In it I extend my business life. . . . The tables are far apart, and there's no romance possible."

I remember the day when my daughter was celebrating her tenth birthday at home with the flu. To cheer her up and to substitute for the usual "Violets in the Snow" that The Four Seasons served her for her birthdays, I used the table phone and introduced her to the two young men with whom I was having lunch, Paul Simon and Art Garfunkel.

—Lenore Hershey

Alex von Bidder displaying a chicken pot pie. This was the cover photo for W *magazine's November 21, 1980 issue.*

The article contended that "it isn't the *head* of the company who lunches in the Bar Room; more likely it is the head *thinker* of a shop. Editors, creative directors, designers, wine aficionados—these are the lords and ladies who lunch."

The article, which appeared in October 1979, was titled "America's Most Powerful Lunch." Subtitles and captions inside read "The Taste and Glory of the Power Lunch," "Power Eaters," "Where the Power Eaters Eat," "Power Seasonings," and, at the head of the seating diagram, "The Field of Power."

What Margittai and Kovi had been trying for years to achieve, this article sealed. For before the *Esquire* piece appeared, The Four Seasons had been slowly building momentum, and the Bar Room in particular had taken on a distinct character of its own, built on the importance of the people who dined there every day at lunch. No matter that at night the Bar Room was still nearly empty. And no matter that it had taken Margittai and Kovi more than five years to start making any real money. What mattered and took hold was a new buzzword more tantalizing than all the George Lois ads and *New York Times* reviews put together—"power lunch."

Suddenly, to all the world The Four Seasons Bar Room was where everybody with aspirations to power, money, and glamour wanted to be between noon and three. This was where one could see the men and women who made New York hum, who made decisions that affected the money markets, the future of transportation, the elections of politicians, the furtherance of the arts, and next season's hemlines. By snaring a table at the Bar Room, one might absorb a little of the energy in such a place, overhear something that would change one's life or career, or, with money and time, even enter into the field of power itself and become part of something that seemed whole, unified, with its own rules and limits, its own dynamics, and a spirit embodied by those who nibbled at their chicken paillard and poached salmon with a degree of sophistication possessed only by aristocrats and those author Tom Wolfe would later call "Masters of the Universe."

"Men, such as they are, very naturally seek money or power," wrote Ralph Waldo Emerson, "and power because it is as good as money." At the end of 1979, Paul Kovi and Margittai had finally acquired the former and were just about to make buckets of the latter.

Bar Room Chicken Pot Pie

For the vegetables
2 medium carrots
2 small turnips
2 medium kohlrabis
1 small celery root
4 small pearl onions
4 large mushroom caps

For the sauce
6 tablespoons lightly salted butter
6½ tablespoons all-purpose flour
3½ cups chicken stock
¾ teaspoon kosher salt
Pinch of freshly grated nutmeg
Pinch of mace
Freshly ground white pepper
½ cup heavy cream

For the chicken
1 whole chicken, 3½ to 5 pounds
2 tablespoons lightly salted butter
Kosher salt
Freshly ground black pepper
1 tablespoon brandy
¼ cup dry white wine

For assembling the dish
2½ pounds puff pastry (defrosted if frozen)
4 sprigs fresh tarragon
1 egg beaten well with 1 teaspoon water, for glaze

1. To prepare the vegetables, peel the carrots, turnips, kohlrabis, celery root, and pearl onions. Wipe the mushrooms clean. Cut the carrots, turnips, kohlrabis, and celery root into quarters that measure about 2 inches long. Trim all of the sharp edges with a small paring knife. Work from the top to the bottom of the vegetables in a quick, curving method, turning the vegetables slightly between each cut. The result should be uniformly shaped vegetables that resemble large olives.

(Continued on next page)

2. Bring a large pot of salted water to a boil. Add all of the vegetables except the turnips and mushroom caps. Cook until slightly tender, about 5 minutes. Add the turnips and cook 1 minute longer. Drain well and cool. Set aside.

3. To make the sauce, melt the butter in a medium saucepan over medium-high heat. Stir in the flour. Cook, stirring often, until the bubbling subsides and the mixture is lemon-colored, about 2 minutes. Do not brown. Whisk in 1 cup of the chicken stock. Increase the heat to medium-high and bring to a boil. Cook, stirring often, until thickened and smooth. Pour in the remaining stock, reduce the heat to medium, and simmer uncovered, stirring often, for 10 minutes. Stir in the salt and season to taste with nutmeg, mace, and pepper. Stir in the cream and set aside.

4. Skin and bone the chicken. Remove the breast and thigh for this dish. Reserve the drumsticks, wings, and back for another use. Cut the breast and thigh of the boned chicken into chunks that measure about 2 inches.

5. In a large skillet, melt the butter over medium-high heat. Add the chunks of chicken, season to taste with salt and pepper, and cook, turning often, until lightly browned on all sides, about 3 minutes. Pour in the brandy and wine. Bring to a boil, turning the chicken to coat. Transfer the browned chicken to a plate or platter and cover. Stir the pan juices into the reserved cream sauce.

6. To assemble the pie, preheat the oven to 425° F. Butter four 2-cups capacity gratin dishes about seven inches long. Roll the pastry out into a ¼-inch-thick rectangle. Cut the pastry into 4 pieces the size of the gratin dishes. Place the pastry on a cookie sheet and keep refrigerated while preparing the dishes.

7. In each of the dishes, place equal portions of dark and white chicken meat. Add two turned carrots, two turned turnips, two turned kohlrabis, two turned celery roots, one onion, and one mushroom cap to each dish. Spoon about 1 cup of the sauce over each serving. Top each with a sprig of tarragon. Let cool if the sauce is hot.

8. Fit the pastry snugly over the filling. Lightly brush the top of the pastry with a small amount of the egg glaze. Place the pies on a large baking sheet and bake for 12 to 15 minutes or until the pastry is lightly browned. Reduce the oven temperature to 350° F. and cook for 20 to 25 minutes longer or until a skewer inserted in the center of the pies comes out hot and the pastry is golden brown. Serve hot.

Serves 4

Bar Room Slaw

You will need about
4 cups of finely julienne
vegetables for the
amount of dressing this
recipe makes. Choose
according to season and
availability from the
following list.

Black radish
Carrot
Celery
Chayote
Chinese cabbage
Cucumber
Daikon

Green bell pepper
Red bell pepper
Red cabbage
Summer squash
Tomato
White cabbage
Zucchini

For the garnish
Romaine lettuce
Belgian endive
Watercress
Alfalfa sprouts

For the dressing
2 large egg yolks
½ teaspoon Dijon mustard
1 tablespoon lemon juice
Kosher salt
Freshly ground black pepper
1 to 1½ cups olive oil
1½ teaspoons red wine vinegar

1. Place the julienne vegetables in a large mixing bowl. Line four serving plates with lettuce, endive, and watercress.

2. To prepare the dressing, combine the egg yolks, mustard, lemon juice, salt, and pepper in a mixing bowl. Stir briskly until well blended. Slowly add the olive oil, drop by drop, beating without stopping. When the mixture is thick, add the remaining oil in a slow, steady stream. Stir in the vinegar.

3. Pour the dressing over the vegetables. Toss or stir to coat. Spoon the dressed vegetables over the greens and sprinkle alfalfa sprouts on top.

Serves 4

Our 10th annual love letter:

This is the 10th holiday season for the two-of-us and The Four Seasons—
a decade that has given us more joy than we ever imagined possible.

For that we thank all our friends and loyal customers as well as Chefs Seppi Renggli
and Christian Albin, Pastry Chef Bruno Comin, Alex, Oreste, Julian and the nearly
200 other dedicated professionals who love this restaurant as much as we do.

Especially pleasing to us this year is the addition to the menu of our new
Spa Cuisine, which reflects the latest insights from the world of health
and nutrition. We're also most gratified by the outstanding success
of the Bar Room at night. This is truly New York at its best!

Our thanks to the media for the numerous stories on The Four Seasons this year.
The generous praise has touched us deeply, especially one simple sentence in an
article by James Villas in Town & Country: "Returning to The Four Seasons is like
going home." For the two-of-us, there can be no finer compliment.

From the heart, to you and yours, our best wishes
for a happy, healthy, prosperous New Year.

Tom Margittai

Paul Kovi

THE FOUR SEASONS

Populist president that he was, Jimmy Carter was fond of inveighing against tax-deductible debaucheries like the legendary "three-martini lunch." More legend than it ever was common custom, this relic of the 1950s had pretty much been discarded by the time Carter entered office in 1977, for the American way of doing business had changed greatly from the days when executives drank their lunch in restaurants with red leather booths and timbered ceilings, subsisting on steak tartare and broiled lobster.

An odd outcropping of the 1960s protest movement was the way young Americans had come to regard food, alcohol, and nutrition. The counterculture had originally used food as a weapon with which to goad the establishment. However sophomoric the rhetoric of the time sounded, those who feasted on two-inch steaks and three-martini lunches were vilified as the ones sending young men to their death in Vietnam. Establishment food companies were poisoning crops with DDT, shooting cattle full of hormones, allowing strontium-90 into milk, and coercing parents in Third World countries to switch from mother's milk to baby formula.

By instilling guilt in Americans over what they consumed—a tactic used by the nineteenth-century temperance advocates to achieve twentieth-century Prohibition—the counterculturists politicized food and transformed nutrition into a pop science that

Chapter Nine

Food, Wine, and Spa Cuisine

America's Tastes Change, and The Four Seasons Leads the Way

PAGE 114, Top left:
Tom Margittai, chef Hitsch
Albin, and James Beard.
Top right: The tempera-
ture-controlled wine cache
was restocked in the 1970s
to reflect more American
and international bottlings.
Bottom left: After taking
over the restaurant in 1973,
Margittai and Kovi took
out ads in the form of
"love letters" to New York,
reporting on news of the
restaurant and how it fit
into the city's state of
affairs. Bottom right: Kovi
(left) and Margittai (right)
enlisted chef Seppi Renggli
to create an entirely new
kind of low-fat, nutrition-
ally balanced menu for The
Four Seasons' customer.
It was called "Spa Cuisine,"
and recipes for it appeared
in a cookbook published
in 1986.

condemned the eating of red meat, white bread, white sugar, and processed foods in favor of organic or "natural" foods free of nitrites, nitrates, dyes, and preservatives.

What Americans ate—even where they ate it—became both a moral and philosophical issue, with strong religious overtones. Many in the counterculture turned to macrobiotics and strict vegetarianism based on Buddhist or Hindu principles or opened commune kitchens that served the kinds of food consumed in Third World countries like Bangladesh, Ethiopia, and Vietnam. In the early 1970s, the "soul food" of African Americans took on a faddish appeal and soared in popularity, as did all manner of ethnic restaurants, especially Chinese after Richard Nixon "opened up" China to American commerce.

The traditional American diet was assailed as unhealthy, wasteful, and based on too much fat, sugar, and salt. Fast food was renamed "junk food," and once-beloved products like whole milk, cheese, beef, pork, chicken, ice cream, and chocolate, all of which Americans consumed in abundance, were said to be killing us off with high cholesterol and cancer-causing agents of doom. Swordfish were discovered to have high levels of mercury. Dolphins were found dying in nets cast for tuna. Cattle were pumped full of antibiotics, calves shackled and force-fed into anemia, and chickens penned by the millions in claustrophobic cages.

No matter how inflated the accusations flung at the mighty capitalist food establishment, there was much truth to the fact that most Americans had a pretty poor diet and were dying not from a lack of good food, but from eating too much bad food. Thus, by the time the volatile issues of civil rights, Vietnam, and Watergate died down in the mid-1970s, many in the counterculture had turned their energies to the study, growth, prepara-tion, and cooking of an incredible new variety of foods Americans had never before considered eating, except for those among the newly emerg-ing immigrant and lower classes.

Beans, starches, pastas, and herbs began to find their way onto American tables, at first on ethnic menus at storefront eateries, then in full-service, tablecloth restaurants. Less fatty meats, more seafood, lighter sauces, and fewer dairy products were used than in the past, and dieting for slimness became a national passion. Affluence became tainted with guilt, and gluttony became a capital sin in the age of Aquarius.

More important, the American restaurant itself began a transformation in the 1970s as more and more people became more and more sophisti-cated about food and began demanding better, healthier products that had not been frozen, adulterated, or processed into a uniform blandness of a kind that had once characterized American food service. Restaurants like Chez Panisse in Berkeley, California, which had grown from a hippy commune kitchen into a dining room of national prominence, had extraordinary influence on the industry, especially in the use of fresh, local products prepared with integrity and the kind of dedication to detail once found only in Europe.

On a far more erudite level, rules of classicism had loosened up enough in France to encourage young chefs to experiment with new products, foreign spices, and dramatic presentation techniques, all based on the "Ten Commandments" of nouvelle cuisine as promulgated by Parisian-based food critics Henri Gault and Christian Millau:

1. Avoid unnecessary complications.
2. Shorten cooking times.
3. Shop regularly at the market.
4. Shorten the menu.
5. Don't hang or marinate game.
6. Avoid too rich sauces.
7. Return to regional cooking.
8. Investigate the latest techniques.
9. Consider diet and health.
10. Invent constantly.

Adhering to these rules sometimes led the chefs to create eccentric dishes unlike anything seen on a plate before—lobster with vanilla sauce, purees of vegetables in tiny dots on a plate, sorbets made from kiwi fruit, and seafood cooked bloody rare. Nouvelle cuisine was duly reported on in the American press, as much in the fashion and style sections as in the food sections. The way a dish looked became as important as what it tasted like, and a few French chefs became international celebrities—an idea unheard of in kitchen circles prior to the 1970s—as well known as Italian tenors or orchestra conductors. Names like Paul Bocuse, Roger Vergé, Michel Guérard (who pioneered a lighter form of French cooking called *cuisine minceur* for customers on a diet), the Troisgros brothers, and Alain Chapel became as recognizable to traveling Americans as to the inspectors for the *Guides Michelin*.

None of this came as a surprise at The Four Seasons, which had since its inception built its reputation on using the finest ingredients and by

France's revolutionary nouvelle cuisine was introduced to America when The Four Seasons began a series of dinners in the 1970s featuring some of France's great master chefs, including Jean Troisgros, Paul Bocuse, and Gaston Lenôtre (seated left to right in front row next to Seppi Renggli, who is seated at far left).

constantly creating new dishes. In fact, in January of 1973, nine months before Gault and Millau proclaimed their Ten Commandments of nouvelle cuisine, The Four Seasons had held an event that *New York* magazine called the "Dinner of the Century" (and twenty years later included in an issue entitled "The 25 Greatest Moments of the Last 25 Years"). Of that grand evening, the magazine's restaurant critic, Gael Greene, wrote, "In all of American history, there was perhaps only one meal that could rival it for portent—that first Thanksgiving potluck of venison, eels, roast duck, leeks, watercress, wild plums, homemade wine, and departing gift of popped corn from a brave named Quadenquina."

Hyperbole aside, the Four Seasons dinner of January 18, 1973 did prefigure much that was to develop in American gastronomy over the next decade.

At the time, The Four Seasons was still under RA's control, although negotiations for the transfer of ownership to Margittai and Kovi were well under way. The idea for the dinner began when wine merchant Bill Sokolin sought to create a media event out of his introduction to America of wines chosen by celebrity chef Paul Bocuse. The wines, actually made by producer Georges Deboeuf but selected by Bocuse with Sokolin's help to appeal to the American market, were all Beaujolais, a light red that went well with Bocuse's lighter-style nouvelle cuisine. The Four Seasons was chosen mainly because its kitchen facilities enabled it to serve so many people at once.

Paul Bocuse—known as the "lion of Lyon," where he ran a Michelin three-star restaurant that represented the highest standards of nouvelle cuisine—was about to celebrate his fortieth birthday, so Sokolin invited him to cook at The Four Seasons for New York's gastronomes. From the moment Sokolin mentioned the upcoming event in a customer newsletter, the phone rang off the hook, with more than 1,400 people pleading for a seat.

As Greene reported (in an article entitled "Trial by Pig's Bladder"), it was an evening of fabulous food, wines, and epiphany. Having heard of the inferiority of American ingredients, Bocuse brought his own from France, arriving at JFK Airport with foie gras, truffles, cream, butter, and tomatoes. Knowing his luggage would face the scrutiny of U.S. Customs, Bocuse chose the line with the stoutest customs inspector, believing such a man would appreciate good food and pass him through without confiscating anything. After telling the official that the truffles were only after-dinner chocolates, Bocuse sailed through, his larder pretty much intact.

On the evening of the dinner, The Four Seasons hosted a tasting of Bocuse's foods and wines for 250 people who had paid $25 each for the event. That event, which lasted from six to eight P.M., was followed by a sit-down dinner in the private dining room above the Bar Room, attended by thirteen chosen guests who had paid $75 each. The guest list included Greene, Kovi, wine maker and importer Alexis Lichine, wine merchant Melvin Master, gourmet businessman Ed Benenson, investment banker and head of the Chaîne des Rôtisseurs Roger Yaseen, lawyer Dan Kaplan, head of the Commanderie de Bordeaux Gregory Thomas, *New York Times* restaurant critic Raymond Sokolov and his wife, Gloria, Pat Buckley (wife of columnist William F. Buckley), and the Sokolins.

As the courses were served that evening, beginning with sautéed foie gras of a richness unimaginable—and unavailable—in America and followed by Bocuse's famous truffle soup with a pastry dome, the attendees were astounded at the refinement, taste, and creativity of the cuisine; they gave Bocuse a standing ovation, applauding and shouting, *"Vive Lyon!"* Sokolin himself realized that despite the existence of outstanding New York City French restaurants like Lutèce, La Grenouille, and La Côte Basque, no one there or anywhere else in America was doing the kind of food and presentation Bocuse had shown that stellar evening.

Behind the scenes, back in the kitchen, there was a stunned silence. Chefs Seppi Renggli and Hitsch Albin and their staff had never tasted food so wonderful, so blissful, so attuned to the modern era. As the last of the foie gras, truffles, and wine was cleared away, Albin looked at Renggli, shook his head, and said, much like Henri Soulé a generation before them, "If only we had ingredients like that, think what we might do!" Everyone at The Four Seasons knew they were in the presence of greatness and felt inspired to go farther than had been possible before.

The seed had been planted. The success of the Bocuse dinner initiated a series of invitations proffered to the leading exponents of nouvelle cuisine, which resulted in an Alsatian festival with the Haeberlin brothers from L'Auberge de L'Ill and a three-week celebration of the cuisine of Alain Chapel. And, in response to criticism that no women had been invited to the first Bocuse dinner (although Pat Buckley filled in for her husband, William F., and a couple of wives had accompanied their husbands), Margittai and Kovi threw a "Women of Accomplishment" dinner a year later for twelve of New York's most illustrious women—including Lillian Hellman, Louise Nevelson, Bess Meyerson, Charlotte Curtis, and Julia Child. Dishes for this extravaganza were cooked not only by Bocuse, but by other French star chefs like Michel Guérard, Jean Troisgros, and Gaston Lenôtre.

More lavish dinners were designed to catch the media's attention and were usually tied to a specific winery or famous restaurant in Europe. One of the first featured the foods of France's St.-Émilion region and the wines of Château Monbousquet; another series showed off the cuisine of Paris's great seafood restaurant Le Duc, inviting over owner Jean Minchelli to use American seafood to cook French dishes, like raw striped bass, lobster with bourbon sauce, porgy with thyme, and red snapper and Long Island bay scallops with green peppers. As classically structured as such gourmet extravaganzas were, The Four Seasons tried not to take any of it too seriously, as when the restaurant mounted a "Cyrano Festival" built around foods mentioned in Edmond Rostand's play *Cyrano de Bergerac* and held a "Full of Bologna Festival" to feature the foods of that sumptuous Italian city.

After Kovi and Margittai took over the restaurant in October 1973, The Four

José Ferrer signed The Four Seasons' guest book with a drawing incorporating two of his most famous roles— Cyrano de Bergerac and Toulouse-Lautrec.

Seasons instituted a series of seasonal dinners to honor friends and professionals and, at the same time, use them as guinea pigs for the kinds of menus Renggli was trying to develop: unusual nouvelle conceits like calf's brains flan, rosemary sherbet, and a tangerine stuffed with duck cracklings. But most of the dishes served at such dinners were wonderfully simple, refined, and based on the finest ingredients available. Ingredients were rarely so exotic as to shock anyone; indeed, they seemed to make perfect sense and made the guests wonder why no one had previously brought them together on a plate.

A dinner held to honor George Lang in 1977 began with foie gras and marinated scallops with pink pepper, then followed with a mousse of shad with crayfish tails, an essence of red snapper with *vesiga,* baby lamb with an *émincé* of its liver and kidney, spinach and mushroom *mille-feuille,* breast of pigeon salad, cheeses, and an array of desserts. That same year James Beard was treated to oysters in Champagne *velouté,* filet of striped bass in pastry, crabmeat mousse with caviar, essence of pheasant, calf's brains with mustard crumbs, *côte de bœuf,* and breast of pheasant salad. A winter menu for *New York Times*

The most powerful restaurant critic and food editor of the 1960s and 1970s was Craig Claiborne (left) of the New York Times, *seen here with von Bidder.*

food writers Craig Claiborne and Pierre Franey was an exercise in hearty but beautifully composed food—partridge and sweetbread terrine, salmon and oysters in court bouillon, crabmeat flan with crayfish tails, essence of fennel, confit of goose, a medallion of venison with root vegetables, and winter greens with calf's brains. For a 1979 Joe Baum dinner, sugar snap peas—a staple of Chinese restaurants but rarely seen on American menus—were paired beautifully with a filet of perfect veal and accompanied by Savigny-les-Beaune, Capron-Manieux '76.

Pastas had become a staple of Four Seasons menus. At a winter meal for Roger Yaseen, then head of the Chaîne des Rôtisseurs, risotto with wild mushrooms—a dish not easy to find in 1979, even in New York's finest Italian restaurants—was prepared with fresh American morels and chanterelles. Fettuccine was served with June peas for Michael Korda's fete and tortelloni with snow hare for Jerry Berns of the "21" Club; cornmeal polenta was often the accompaniment to the entrées.

Given the need to build business without alienating those who continued to patronize the restaurant after the change of ownership, Kovi and Margittai began subtly to modify the menus they inherited. The success of the Bar Room's simplified menu signaled that people wanted to eat somewhat lighter and with more concern for fat and cholesterol content. By the same token, this *was* The Four Seasons, and its preeminence as a place to splurge and dine extravagantly could not be discounted or compromised in any way.

The key, then, was to continue to expand the possibilities and to encourage creativity in the kitchen without going to the extremes of nouvelle cuisine then showing itself in France. Although the daily menu was still very American in its offerings, Renggli and Albin reveled in preparing the foods of Italy, and The Four Seasons held a two-week festival of

James Beard, Paul Kovi, and Roger Yaseen.

the cooking of Bologna, created with Italian cooking authorities Marcella and Victor Hazan. The menu included fresh egg noodles made with an authentic bolognese meat-and-vegetable sauce, macaroni with prosciutto and asparagus, quail cooked with sage, lamb chops done in parmesan butter, and the kinds of Italian desserts not to be found on any New York Italian restaurant menu at the time—rice torte, noodle torte, strawberries in balsamic vinegar, and melon marinated in Emiglia-Romagna wines.

The Four Seasons' kitchen could be playful—in the nouvelle style—but had to be correct, as when they piled tiny new potato skins with caviar and served them as canapés at parties. And the chefs could enrich a dish to the point of Lucullan excess, as when they served sautéed perch with a red wine sauce infused with beef marrow and butter.

By the end of the decade The Four Seasons had become as well known for its commitment to fine foods and wine as it had for its power lunch, its architectural grandeur, and its historic place in New York's social life. Twenty years after The Four Seasons opened, the *New York Times* architecture critic, Paul Goldberger, called the restaurant "as stunning as ever" and wrote, "It is the modern dining room that inspired all the others, and it is still far and away the finest—the only public room our time has produced to equal in quality the great dining rooms of another age in New York." In the same issue, *Times* restaurant critic Mimi Sheraton, who had once been a menu researcher for The Four Seasons, noted that "80 seasons later, the menu remains as innovative as the setting." In 1980 *Playboy* magazine announced that The Four Seasons ranked third among the twenty-five greatest restaurants in America in a poll conducted of international food authorities and chefs. Four years later it came in second (behind Lutèce) in the same poll. *Forbes* magazine upped its rating of The Four Seasons to four stars. And in 1981 the two French critics who christened nouvelle cuisine, Henri Gault and Christian Millau, awarded The Four Seasons three toques—a rating signifying "excellent."

Purely from a gastronomic point of view, the restaurant had achieved a tremendous reputation for innovation and refinement at a time when connoisseurship was fast becoming a form of elitism and one-upmanship among Americans who could afford to dine at such places. The knowledge of fine food and wine (based upon frequent trips to the temples of haute cuisine in Europe and regular visits to the deluxe restaurants of New York, Washington, Chicago, Los Angeles, and other cities) had led to a new form of elitist aberration that came to be called "Foodism." Ann Barr and Paul Levy, who had originally coined the term in 1982 in a satiric article in the English fashion magazine *Harpers & Queen,* explained in *The Official Foodie Handbook* that a "foodie" was "a person who is very, very interested in food. . . . They don't think they are being trivial—foodies consider food to be an art, on a level with painting or drama.

"Foodies are pleased with the state of their art. It has made them into an elite, an international elite, with branches in every country. Foodism is a good ism—it is helpful to the planet rather than doing any harm. Foodism is glamourous; Foodism is fun. 'I am a foodie' is as proud a boast as the old Roman citizen's '*Civis Romanus sum.*' 'I am a Roman citizen,' 'I am a Foodie'; what they both mean is 'I am a winner.'"

Barr and Levy cited The Four Seasons (along with An American Place, Huberts, La Tulipe, the Quilted Giraffe, and the River Café in New York) as a major stop on the foodie circuit, noting that "New York foodies must not only eat in the best places, they must be seen at the best tables." "Only midwestern tourists sit in the main dining room of The Four Seasons at lunch, drinking diet Pepsi with their étouffée of crayfish tails," sniffed the authors. "The smart publishers and power brokers are in the tastefully paneled and cheaper grill room, drinking Perrier with broiled fish."

There was much about Foodism and foodies that was snobbish, obnoxious, and just plain dull, but the movement was, in an ironic way, an inevitable outgrowth of the counterculture food movement of the 1960s

Chicken tycoon Frank Perdue visited The Four Seasons' kitchen one night and asked Hitsch Albin what species of fish he was cooking. Although the fish obviously were trout, Albin told Perdue they were baby sharks, and Perdue went back to his guests raving that they were going to eat baby shark that evening.

When former mayor
Ed Koch dined at The Four
Seasons, he demanded to
be served Slim-Fast
chocolate shakes, which
he was then being paid to
promote.

and 1970s. Actually there was a shared philosophy in both groups that food should be natural and untainted, include abundant grains, vegetables, and starches, and depend largely on seasonal availability.

Much of what The Four Seasons was already doing on its menus fit easily into this new style of gastronomy, so it seemed a capital idea to create a new Four Seasons cookbook reflecting all the changes at the restaurant since the first cookbook was published a decade earlier. The new book, put together with the help of food consultant Barbara Kafka, contained more than 250 recipes showing the full range of the restaurant's kitchen. Though not nearly as lavish as the first book, the new volume was quietly revolutionary in its inclusion of unorthodox recipes like sweetbreads with saffron and melon, lobster ragout, pureed white beans with confit of goose, ramp soufflé, avocado soup with avocado sorbet, fillet of pompano with citrus fruits and pistachio nuts, tournedos of veal with oyster puree, chopped lamb steak with pine nuts, hazelnut cake with chocolate chunks, and cream cheese and Riesling soufflé. Exotic ingredients like arugula, black Russian radish, Chinese cabbage, calabaza, chayotes, chipolata sausage, coriander, daikon, gado-gado, jicama, kohlrabi, mango, pancetta, pepita seeds, squash blossoms, Swiss chard, and wasabi powder were used throughout. Home cooks were discouraged from using canned or frozen ingredients and were advised on the best time of the year to try a dish, buy a particular wild mushroom, or use up the best ingredients in the marketplace.

If none of this now sounds particularly radical, one must realize that most of these ingredients and ideas were completely unknown and generally unavailable to the home cook, and that the recipes were examples of what soon came to be called the "new American cuisine."

Although many of the recipes were remarkably simple and easily made at home, others required a master chef and several assistants to bring them off successfully: the recipe for The Four Seasons' renowned crisp duck read "Begin the preparation three days before serving," then went on for five more pages.

The title of the book was not *The Four Seasons Cookbook, Part II,* but the simpler and more self-aggrandizing *The Four Seasons.* The subtitle proclaimed it "The Ultimate Book of Food, Wine, and Elegant Dining [with] 250 Original Recipes from One of the World's Great Restaurants." The book was supposed to express all that the restaurant had come to stand for and mean to Margittai and Kovi and to its regular customers, who could bask in the reflected light of a page that announced, "This is a famous dish in the Bar Room, the summer bread-and-butter of the advertising and editorial world as well as of the movers and shakers who meet there and wish to eat lightly." In his foreword, James Beard zeroed in on the way The Four Seasons had always been a manifestation of New York itself, underscoring the genteel tastes of its clientele: "You will find dishes that have earned their place in this collection because they have been accepted, loved, and gently cared for by the discriminating people who frequent The Four Seasons."

In their introduction, Margittai and Kovi summed up the history of The Four Seasons and explained its new directions, noting that "many people thought we were foolish" to take over the failing restaurant in 1973. "But we saw it as a challenge. We also knew that there were many positive things we felt about the restaurant and what we could do with it. We believe in New York City and in its life, present and future. We saw The Four Seasons as the quintessential restaurant of New York."

They went on to describe the importance of The Four Seasons in a way that went well beyond food, wine, service, architecture, and power lunches. "Indeed, we view food and restaurants as a part of general culture. They change and develop as other elements of the culture do. We felt that there was an enormous and growing interest in food and wine on the part of New Yorkers as well as the rest of the country; and from this group of seriously interested people— the same people who are interested in ballet, opera, and literature—would come an audience that would *understand* what we wanted to do with the restaurant."

The second Four Seasons cookbook indicating the new culinary direction of the kitchen was published a decade after the first cookbook.

Such a statement not only crystallized the original concept of The Four Seasons—and Margittai and Kovi were generous in their praise of Joe Baum's original vision for the restaurant—but also allied restaurants with the arts as indicative of a culture's highest standards of civilization. The idea that restaurants were more than mere eateries, more than dining rooms where people simply met to relax, more than places where business was conducted over food and drink, was as novel as the design and theme of The Four Seasons itself.

The Four Seasons was also one of the first books to make a serious attempt to go beyond the formulaic when it came to matching wines with foods. At a time when most Americans were highly unsophisticated about wines, The Four Seasons was suggesting they drink a California sparkling wine like Schramsberg Blanc de Noir with a duck liver salad, a New York

Margittai (left) and Kovi worked hard to put The Four Seasons in the vanguard of American cuisine and wine. In 1976 they instituted the California Barrel Tasting dinners, which featured many of the best wineries of the state.

State Seyval blanc with baked striped bass on sea salt with black pepper, or a Sonoma County merlot with veal kidney and mushrooms.

Great restaurants had, of course, always been expected to have fine wine lists, by which was meant a screed of French Champagnes, Bordeaux, and Burgundies. (Le Pavillon in its heyday carried 161 different Champagnes in 56 vintages.) But few restaurants of any kind stocked or promoted American wines, preferring to carry only a few standard—and largely undistinguished—labels like New York's Gold Seal and Taylor, California's Gallo and Sebastiani, and very little else. Not until the late 1960s did American wines have much credibility with connoisseurs, and not until persuasive personalities like Napa Valley's Robert Mondavi entered the scene were American wines regarded with anything but condescension.

It was also a fact of restaurant life that few owners or chefs knew much about wine, preferring to stock the famous French labels and requisite house wines without much thought. Wine was simply not a beverage of choice with dinner in most restaurants, and in the 1970s patrons were still more likely to order a single glass of insipid white house wine than a whole bottle from an individual winery. To many Americans wine was an affectation, unless it was sweet and fizzy, like cold duck, Lambrusco, or Lancer's Rosé (whose empty bottle could also double as a candleholder).

The Four Seasons' involvement with wine had been one of its principal virtues right from the start, when Johnson and Pahlmann designed the magnificent wine storage area one sees just before entering the Pool Room. The wine list had always been one of the best in the United States, and under Baum and RA the restaurant courted gourmet societies like the Commanderie de Bordeaux and Chaîne des Rôtisseurs for special wine dinners. After Margittai and Kovi took over, The Four Seasons became more of a force for change and a showcase for American viticulture than any other restaurant in the country.

Kovi in particular had developed a convert's zeal about California wines and knew personally many of the state's leading wine makers. By the middle of the 1970s men like Robert Mondavi, Louis M. Martini, Mike Grgich, Joseph Phelps, and Warren Winiarski were being touted as the new leaders of a viticultural revolution. Gradually the image of California wines as unrefined jug wines was being transformed—indeed, in subsequent blind tastings of California and French wines, several American varietals scored higher ratings than some of the finest wines from France's great vineyards.

Kovi had already been involved in wine education as a guest lecturer on the subject at City College of New York, and in the mid-1970s he began writing a wine column for *Sphere-Cuisine* magazine. As business slowly improved at The Four Seasons and interest in fine wines grew among their clientele, Kovi and Margittai tried to come up with ideas that would underscore their restaurant's devotion to all the fine things of life, which obviously included wine.

While in Paris on vacation, Margittai chanced to dine at the renowned Taillevent restaurant, which had had considerable success showcasing Bordeaux wine makers' new wines from the last vintage at an annual dinner for merchants, connoisseurs, and discerning clientele. Margittai returned to New York and told Kovi about the idea and, in discussion with California wine merchant and writer Gerald Asher, decided that featuring California wines had even more potential for publicity. The California wine makers were delirious over the prospect of displaying their wines at such a prestigious arena as The Four Seasons. Here was a chance to show the eastern media, restaurateurs, connoisseurs, and merchants how far California viticulture had come in a decade. Eighteen wineries were invited to bring a barrel sample from the latest vintage (1975) along with a mature bottle of the same wine. Asher and the wine makers would comment on each wine, and Renggli and his staff turned out a multicourse dinner that showed off the restaurant's new American style.

British news magnate Robert Maxwell would often dine alone at The Four Seasons, where he could barely fit his girth onto the Miesian chairs. He was known as a slovenly eater, for while he ate little (and drank a great deal), the food would invariably be found dropped and scattered all over the floor.

When word went out that The Four Seasons would hold such a dinner, requests for invitations poured in. With only 230 seats available, Kovi and Margittai faced an immediate crisis of good faith. On the one hand, they didn't expect to make any money from the event (although most guests paid $85 to get in, many close friends and media were invited with The Four Seasons' compliments), but they certainly didn't want to alienate regular customers who insisted on being accommodated. In the end they simply accepted reservations on a first-come-first-served basis for what promised to be a momentous evening.

It was. The establishment in 1976 of the first Four Seasons Barrel Tasting was a watershed event for California wines. The fact that The Four Seasons was holding this event gave the wines and wine makers a credibility they had previously lacked, and interest in the particular wineries sampled that night soared immediately afterward.

"Even though the wines were too rough and young, the wine maker had reason to taste and comment on them and wine writers to write about them," says Kovi. "It was an instant success, celebrities interested in wine came, like Burgess Meredith and Danny Kaye, and we established very close relationships with the wine makers." Thereafter, Kovi and Margittai could bank on getting anything they wanted from California, including special bottlings no one else in New York had.

The event was as much a social occasion as a night of raging oenophilia, and by midway in the evening few people were still listening to the running commentary about pH values, Brix levels, and use of Limousin oak barrels. With thirty-six wines to taste (in more than six thousand glasses) along with nine courses, the revelers became louder and more boisterous as the evening wore on. TV producer David Susskind was feeling little pain as he rose to give a speech late in the evening. Magazine editor Barbara Tober remembers him lumbering to the stage and "delivering a rambling discourse in stentorian tones, then falling back into his chair at the table," where he proceeded to line up eight glasses of the remaining wines, mixed them all together in one large goblet, sloshed it all down in a few gulps, and went weaving off into the night. The dinner finally ended at two in the morning.

Those still standing at this and subsequent dinners agreed they were among the greatest parties ever held in gastronomic circles in the United States, and the publicity value for California vintners and The Four Seasons was immeasurable.

In the years to follow, the annual event became grander but more refined. The number of wineries was reduced to fourteen, and the evening was orchestrated to end by midnight, with two fifteen-minute intermissions for those who needed a break or a cigarette (smoking was forbidden in the dining room). To have one's wines featured at the Barrel Tasting was to enter an exclusive club of those assumed to be the best, and to be invited to the event proved conclusively that you were among the most discerning and sophisticated connoisseurs in New York. As Warren Winiarksi of Stag's Leap Vineyard in the Napa Valley put it, "When Paul first invited us back in 1975, it was the first time we were taken seriously outside of California. It was a gesture that gave us all enormous confidence. I think sometimes that our maturity as wine makers grew out of that first acceptance in [New York]."

Given the finite number of seats in the Pool Room, where the event was held, the guest list could not grow, except in prestige. By the 1980s the event was a measure of one's social or professional standing, and more than a few egos were bruised as the event gained social stature.

The menus were extraordinary in both scope and complexity, especially since the courses had to be served efficiently to more than two hundred people at once. The menu for the March 20, 1978, Four Seasons Barrel Tasting Dinner was typical:

Red snapper and salmon tartare
Mousse of trout and leeks
Fillet of striped bass in phyllo
Sweetbreads with saffron and melon
Oyster broth
Quail eggs with chopped sirloin
Lobster ragout
Confit of goose
Calf's brains with mustard crumbs
Tournedos of beef with six peppers
Grapefruit and tequila sorbet
Game bird terrine
Medallions of lamb with coriander butter
Chèvre d'Authon
Cappuccino soufflé
Chocolate truffles and fig strip
Demitasse
Mignardises

There have been many pleasant and productive moments for me over the years at The Four Seasons, but there is one particular moment that remains vivid. It was the occasion when we took over the Pool Room for a Creamer Dickson Basford client, Ocean Spray. Editors from all over the world were invited to this unique press event. The pool was full of bubbling ruby-red cranberries, making a sharp, beautiful contrast to the cool white marble apron surrounding the pool. Chefs in full regalia came marching down the steps from the private dining room to the right, one at a time, and placed their cranberry creations on the marble apron. It was an incredible setting and it worked magnificently in every way. *The moment, however, was defined when one journalist tried to squeeze by several others, causing one of the cranberry desserts to tumble into the pool. Of course, it had to be one of the triple-decker jobs. As it submerged, fluffy remnants of whipped cream surfaced,*

So successful—at least from a public relations point of view—were these events that they were soon being copied around the United States; wine makers' dinners became a standard marketing technique for both wineries and restaurants. Thus, when the Italian wine producer Ceretto sought to introduce a $100-per-bottle Barolo called Briccho Rocche Briccho Rocche, it did so at The Four Seasons and was thereby able to corral the best wine writers and merchants in the New York area to attend.

The Barrel Tasting went on for a decade before falling victim to its own success. For despite raising the price of the dinner to $175 per person, The Four Seasons was losing money on the event. "It had just outlived its usefulness," said Margittai. "There were so many wine makers' dinners being given around the country that ours was no longer unique. More important, there was just so much pressure from our friends for more seats—which we simply couldn't create—that we started making enemies. And that was the kiss of death." For those 230 seats, Margittai and Kovi were getting more than 2,000 requests—all of them from people they knew well and had served for years.

Thus, Kovi and Margittai planned to bring the New York event to a close in its tenth year. That night in March 1986, there was a palpable sense in the Pool Room that something out of the ordinary was about to occur, though the two owners had not told anyone of their decision and had saved the announcement for the end of the evening so as not to throw a damper on the festivities. The dishes came out in impeccable order with the parade of wines—Dover sole with lobster served with Wente Bros. and Robert Mondavi sauvignon blancs; seafood risotto with Acacia and Iron Horse chardonnays; oxtail soup to clear the palate; salmon braised in red wine and served with Clos du Val and Firestone merlots; peppered breast of duck with Felton Empire and Trefethen pinot noirs; wild boar in puff pastry with Burgess Cellars and Louis M. Martini zinfandel; juniper sorbet; medallion of venison with Jordan, Joseph Phelps, Ridge, and Stag's Leap Wine Cellars cabernet sauvignons; and cheese and fruits.

As the evening drew to a close, Kovi and Margittai stood up, thanked everyone for coming, and told the guests that this would be the last Barrel Tasting dinner in New York—an announcement that hit the assembled audience like a bomb blast. "The Barrel Tasting is not leaving," Kovi said nervously. "It is going home." Plans had already been made for the event to move to San Francisco's Stanford Court Hotel, which had the capacity for twice the number of guests.

Gerald Asher tried to put a positive spin on the decision, telling people, "It *needs* to be in California. These pearls need to ornament the shoulders of California," to which vintner Bill Jekel of Jekel Vineyards in Monterey County snapped back, "It was never the purpose of the barrel tasting dinner to ornament the shoulders of California. The whole purpose was to bring these wines to the attention of the East. The barrel tasting ending in New York is a sad occasion."

The news certainly hit the papers on both coasts, with elegies for the event making it sound as if someone had canceled Christmas and the Fourth of July. Indeed, California wineries and writers scrambled immediately to create a similar event to take place in New York the following spring, to be called a "View from the Vineyards" and held in a series of banquet rooms in the Pierre Hotel on Fifth Avenue. The publisher of *The Wine Spectator*, Marvin Shanken, also started up the "California Wine Experience" to promote California wines in New York. Both events could handle hundreds more paying guests than could The Four Seasons' Pool Room.

In order to keep their wine profile strong, Kovi and Margittai debuted an annual dinner featuring the most recently imported vintage of Bordeaux, not as barrel samples but as finished wines. This became an event almost equal in status to the Barrel Tasting and maintained The Four Seasons' link with the great traditions of European wine making. And more often than not something happened that made the papers the next day. In 1989 the event made headlines when wine merchant Bill Sokolin (who had helped mount the Bocuse dinner in 1973) brought in a bottle of 1787 Château Margaux supposedly owned and signed by Thomas Jefferson and said to be worth $519,000. Sokolin contended that he simply wanted to show that the Founding Fathers had had an abiding interest in Bordeaux and that the bottle (which he had on consignment from an unknown seller) was a great historic rarity. Unfortunately, to everyone's horror, Sokolin let the bottle slip out of his hands and crash to the floor. Julian Niccolini bent down, dipped his finger into the wine as it soaked into The Four Seasons' carpet, shrugged, and said, "This is a piece of history? This is mud."

Margittai and Kovi had also been careful to cultivate friendships with a new phenomenon of the 1970s—the wine writer. Though the traditions of singing the praises of wine date back to Homer and the Bible, the idea of writing regularly about wine was more an avocation among European gentlemen who came by their income in other ways. Foremost among these were the British, men like George Saintsbury and Evelyn Waugh, for whom wine writing was a hobby and adjunct to other pleasures in their lives. A few American men of letters like Clifton Fadiman contributed to the arcana of the subject, joined in the 1960s by specialists in the trade,

mixing with the cranberries in the pool. Except for a dismayed pastry chef, everyone found it quite amusing.

—Donald E. Creamer, Partner, Creamer, Inc.

The accidental destruction at a 1989 Four Seasons wine dinner of a rare, $519,000 bottle of wine said to have come from the cellars of Thomas Jefferson made the headlines of every newspaper in New York the day after it occurred.

A homeless woman once got past the maître d' and sat at a table in the Grill Room, ordering a very expensive bottle of Veuve Clicquot Champagne. When the captain demanded payment, she barked, "The government will take care of it," and stormed out. Amazingly, she returned a week later, ordered another bottle of Veuve Clicquot, and tried to pay for it with someone else's signed traveler's check. When refused and threatened with arrest, she reached into a shopping bag and pulled out the exact amount of the bill in cash. But she did not leave a tip and was never seen again.

like Frank Schoonmaker, Alexis Bespaloff, and Leon Adams, who began chronicling the rapid changes then occurring in the world of viticulture. The field was expanded in the 1970s when a generation of young, well-traveled journalists began to take up the subject of wine with a characteristic American scholarliness that led to abstruse discussions of everything from the effect of Slovenian oak on the tannins in a wine to the trellising techniques of certain Napa Valley viticulturists.

A loose organization called the New York Wine Writers' Circle was formed in the mid-1970s to bring together a group of journalists—most of whom made their living writing about other subjects—for the purpose of tasting the new releases of wine makers and thereafter writing about them in the increasing number of wine columns being added to newspapers. Much of this writing fell somewhere between the academic and the romantic, filled with endless descriptions of "cassis overtones and high acids" and "Mozartian structure and sumptuous chewiness," adding words like "corkiness" and "barnyard odor" to the new vocabulary of oenophilia.

Kovi and Margittai saw that such writers were well worth cultivating, and what better place to hold their monthly wine tastings than at The Four Seasons? Thus, by offering the circle a four-course lunch in a private room for the astoundingly low price of $25, The Four Seasons became the most important forum in the United States for vintners to show off their wines to the media.

At Christmastime the circle would hold its annual champagne luncheon at the restaurant, where a dozen of France's finest new releases were served.

Renggli enjoyed making menus for these monthly luncheons because it gave him a chance to experiment with old and new concepts. At the same time, he was careful never to compromise the focus of such luncheons, which was to show off the wines to best advantage. Never was a menu repeated, though dishes were kept simple. Throughout the 1970s and into the 1990s, new dishes were created and traditional ones refined and geared to the characters of the wines served. Thus, a German wine lunch might include smoked trout with apple horseradish to go with a Baden Halbtrocken, follow with a lamb curry and Spätlese Riesling, and end with a butterscotch mousse to go with a sweet Eiswein. If a California vintner brought in a series of California reds, lunch would begin with beef consommé and a Petite Syrah, move on to venison cooked with the pinot noir under discussion, and end with a fine St. André cheese to go with a massive older cabernet sauvignon.

The menu for the 1982 Champagne Christmas luncheon began with breast of quail en croûte, then filet of salmon in Champagne sauce, lobster risotto with white truffles, medallions of veal with wild mushrooms, and, for dessert, the traditional Christmas cake, a bûche de Noël.

If such gastronomic luxury seemed the very antithesis of the stripped-down cookery advocated by health food faddists and nutritionists, there was certainly no disagreement on either side that the best food should be made with the best ingredients, and that they should be unadulterated in any way and as pure and seasonal as was possible to obtain—such was the guiding principle of The Four Seasons' kitchen.

By the same token, the simple grill cuisine of the Bar Room menu was very much attuned to customers' new concerns for lower fat and cholesterol in food. It seemed perfectly natural, therefore, for Rodale Press, a Pennsylvania-based publisher and advocate of healthy eating and organic foods, to consult with The Four Seasons in 1981 about holding a luncheon to introduce the Madison Avenue crowd to Rodale's kind of food and attract advertising to their magazine *Organic Gardening.*

Rodale's manager of special projects, Tom Stonebeck, saw the event as a "coming out party in New York," where "Madison Avenue and Main Street in Emmaus, Pennsylvania, intersect." *Organic Gardening's* 1.4 million readers were not just a bunch of weekend farmers but part of a whole new generation of Americans for whom ecology and healthy eating went hand in hand with the kinds of food products and kitchen technologies Madison Avenue was advertising in the slick magazines.

Yet when Stonebeck told Alex von Bidder that Rodale wanted to serve bean sprouts, the banquet manager winced. "I don't recall ever serving bean sprouts at The Four Seasons," he said glumly. "Our customers go to California to eat that kind of thing." Seppi Renggli also had reservations about serving tabbouleh, a Lebanese salad concoction he had no idea how to cook, much less make palatable. And another thing: no alcohol would be served with the meal. Rodale suggested serving blueberry juice—an idea that curdled von Bidder's Swiss blood.

"We didn't want to alter what The Four Seasons stood for," said Stonebeck, "but we challenged them, and they rose to the challenge. . . . We're having an unconventional menu, but we're sure it will be good."

In the end, The Four Seasons agreed to work with Rodale, especially after one of their PR people reminded von Bidder that "fine French cooking uses natural foods anyway, and its vegetables are not overcooked." That hit home and also made good sense. The Four Seasons kitchen could work within those guidelines and perhaps even make some news.

The Four Seasons is definitely the best restaurant in the world. In my life, I have been there two times. I went for my tenth birthday and then for my fifteenth birthday. We sat in the Pool Room, which is beautiful, and I ordered a Caesar Salad and Châteaubriand, which I shared with my mother.

It seems like every detail is taken care of at The Four Seasons. While you're waiting for your meal, you're given a variety of breads. My favorite kind was the croissants. They also gave us black olives. Your food is sliced by the waiters so that you can watch. For dessert there is a dessert tray with lots of delicious-looking pastries. I had a wonderful time at The Four Seasons and I can't wait to go back.

—Loren Kannry, age 15

The New Yorker magazine considered this eccentric accommodation worth a "Talk of the Town" piece, reporting that many in the Madison Avenue crowd were wary of the idea, to say the least. "When I got into advertising, they promised me all these crazy perks in the wild and wonderful world of advertising," moaned Gene Falk of Doyle Dane Bernbach, "and this [luncheon] was my first perk. We admen were supposed to be three-martini-lunched to death, but actually everybody has to get back to work in the afternoon."

The menu was revelatory, based on many ingredients Rodale brought in from its farms. Renggli and his crew baked whole-wheat rolls with herbs and served a refreshing cucumber soup made with yogurt instead of heavy cream. Salmon was poached in court bouillon with crisp vegetables sliced in the Japanese manner. The dandelion salad contained radish sprouts. And everyone drank iced tea (which was to become a beverage of choice among power lunchers in the years to come). For dessert there was cantaloupe and strawberries with a dollop of rich crème fraîche. Rodale and the Four Seasons exchanged cookbooks.

Not only was the luncheon a success, it was an event that excited and motivated the Four Seasons personnel. Von Bidder thought the food was terrific and told Rodale he'd like to drive out to their dining room and try the food there.

Sensitive to changes in the American diet, The Four Seasons had decided to forge a new style of cooking based not just on the kinds of fresh, seasonal provender it had always prided itself on using, but on modern concepts of nutrition and healthfulness that transcended the proverbial "rabbit food" served at most health food eateries run by ponytailed men with bad skin. The Four Seasons' version would be more along the lines of the cuisine prepared by Michel Guérard, who had developed low-calorie dishes under the sobriquet *cuisine minceur* as part of a spa regimen at his restaurant in Eugénie-les-Bains.

If The Four Seasons was to try such an approach, it would have to apply its signature style and high standards. Merely adding some lighter items on the menu, along with pronouncements on how good such things were for a person to eat, would be insufficient. They decided to make sure that what they said on the menu was true to the concept, and there would be no fudging in the menu lingo.

Margittai and Kovi had looked out their window and seen the future. "For each jogger on Park Avenue, clad in stylish running apparel and Nike footwear," they said, "there was a diner at The Four Seasons requesting a mite less salt, a touch less sauce, a shade less meunière, and more and more of our customers were ordering Perrier and lime before dinner."

In early 1983, the two of them sat down with Seppi Renggli and drafted a memorandum describing their new concept:

> *TO INCLUDE IN BOTH OUR BAR ROOM AND POOL ROOM:*
> *low-calorie, low-sodium, low-cholesterol courses that are*
> *gastronomically pleasing for*
> > *a. composition of flavors*
> > *b. texture*
> > *c. presentation*
>
> *REASONS:*
> > *a. future trends of health and diet*
> > *b. our customers' awareness of nutrition*
>
> *RECOGNIZED NUTRITION EXPERT:*
> *Food preparation to be done with controlled and documented*
> *quantities and ingredients and with the consultation and approval*
> *of a well-known and respected authority on nutrition.*

They assiduously avoided using the word *diet* in their conceptual meetings, believing it had a negative, guilt-ridden association in most people's minds. They then consulted with George Lois and his partner, Bill Pitts, as to what they should call this new concept, and the two men came up with the name "Spa Cuisine," which Kovi and Margittai promptly registered as a trademark.

Pitts also suggested they get in contact with a Four Seasons regular, Dr. Myron Winnick, director of the Institute for Human Nutrition at Columbia University's College of Physicians & Surgeons. Winnick loved the idea and signed on as consultant, recommending that a full-time nutritionist on his staff, Joyce Leung, work on recipe development with Renggli. Leung would provide reams of information on iron content, grams of fat, and so on, and Renggli would adapt them according to the following guidelines:

1. Use foods with high nutrient density per calories, especially folic acid, vitamin B_6, vitamin C, iron, calcium, and zinc.
2. Use foods low in fat, saturated fat, and cholesterol.
3. Use foods low in sodium (not sodium free).
4. Add fiber through vegetables and cereals.

5. Use complementing proteins like corn, rice, and beans to create balanced protein content.

Difficult as it was at first to work with Leung, who once said quite soberly, "I always see straight through taste and presentation to nutritional components," Renggli became "a chef possessed" with the idea of Spa Cuisine, which was different from all previous conceptions of what low-calorie, low-fat dishes should taste like. He worked hard to provide as much flavor as possible to dishes that had been robbed by necessity of most fat. Satisfaction had to be built into the recipes, based on the use of strong herbs and seasonings. Salt was not used, though low-salt soy sauce was. Fats were cut down by trimming meats, offering smaller portions, and sautéeing in a nonstick pan with only a gloss of vegetable oil. Loin of lamb would be wrapped in cabbage leaves and steamed in plastic wrap, resulting in a meat entrée of only 315 calories.

The number of grams of fat and milligrams of sodium in Spa Cuisine dishes were supposed to total one-third of the daily consumption for someone restricted to 2,100 calories—far from a starvation diet—with each appetizer and main course totaling between 700 and 750 calories.

Renggli decided that desserts would not be part of the Spa Cuisine menus because, except for fresh fruits, desserts that fit the nutritional guidelines would require the use of ersatz cream, fake eggs, and substitute sugar—vile-tasting, chemically engineered products he could neither enjoy nor approve.

The first Spa Cuisine items appeared on The Four Seasons' menu in January 1984—three appetizers and two main courses—sandwiched in with the crisp duck, the rack of lamb, and the chocolate velvet cake. According to Margittai and Kovi, "At first little or no fanfare ushered in this inspired innovation. Spa Cuisine appeared discreetly on our menu as simply another category of dishes." But before long, Spa Cuisine became one of The Four Seasons' most effective and identifying marketing ideas, with at least 25 percent of the restaurant's customers ordering such items each day.

Many of the dishes were not just innovative but remarkably flavorful, like whole-wheat fettuccine with lobster, grilled veal with tuna sauce, and striped bass with eggplant. The absence of salt was certainly noticeable, but for those on a restricted diet, most of the food had amazing depth of flavor. Some dishes, like the paillard of turkey quickly sautéed and served with crunchy strips of pepper, were just plain bland and not really much better than most diet food.

It is against the policy of The Four Seasons to allow patrons to photograph other patrons. One night actor Yul Brynner was in the Pool Room and a man got up to take a Polaroid snapshot. Immediately a captain ran over and snatched the camera away from the man.

But when the Polaroid developed, it turned out the man had only tried to take a picture of the chocolate velvet cake.

The food press, increasingly infatuated with healthy food and diets, picked up on Spa Cuisine with incredible applause, from the *New York Times* food pages to the life-style section of *Women's Wear Daily* and *Metropolitan Home*. No matter that the food service industry ripped off the "Spa Cuisine" name with impunity (Kovi and Margittai hadn't the resources to fight it), because the term became synonymous with The Four Seasons in a very positive sense, and by the mid-1980s Kovi and Margittai had the best of both worlds at their door—the free-spending high livers and those who were watching their waistlines *and* their livers. *American Health* even declared Spa Cuisine to be "menus for the alert mind—the real power lunch."

The success and promotional value of Spa Cuisine gave Kovi and Margittai the opportunity to do a third cookbook. In fact, their contract with Simon & Schuster (who Margittai felt had botched the sale of the second book by cutting the print run just before Christmas) offered the publisher an option on another book, so Kovi and Margittai suggested the topic of Spa Cuisine. Working with recipe consultant Susan Grodnick, Renggli created more than a hundred recipes, arranged in forty-six menus, according to the strict guidelines of Dr. Winnick and Leung, and the result was published in a format (without the celebrity autographs) similar to that of the second book. The title of the new volume was *The Four Seasons Spa Cuisine,* and it sold much better than the first two.

In almost every recipe Renggli and Grodnick gave good instructions on how to prepare a dish and why certain ingredients were used. The recipes were eclectic and exciting— pepper pot soup, chicken gumbo, squid salad with black beans, pork-stuffed artichoke, boiled beef, steamed leeks with crayfish vinaigrette, grilled breast of pigeon with red wine sauce, and medallions of buffalo with wild mushrooms—a far cry from the usual cottage-cheese-and-lettuce diet dishes found elsewhere. And though some found the accompanying breakdown of dishes into grams and milligrams of fat, sodium, and so forth to resemble a hospital kitchen handbook, several other cookbook authors followed suit. It was ironic that a restaurant that had once represented the very excesses opposed by the counterculture now found itself at the vanguard of a movement advocating healthful, healing cuisine.

By the time the book appeared in 1986, The Four Seasons was once again in the forefront of American gastronomy. By then the restaurant was more than a quarter century old, and it was just hitting its stride.

Despite many rave reviews of The Four Seasons' cuisine in *Gourmet* magazine, former editor in chief Jane Montand never ate anything but chicken paillard there and told the staff the food was boring anyway.

The cover of The Four Seasons' spa cuisine cookbook, published in 1986.

A Skewer of Shrimp and Chipolatas

24 large shrimp, about 2½ pounds, shelled and deveined
½ cup chopped fresh parsley
2 garlic cloves, minced
Juice of 1 lemon
¼ cup olive oil
¼ cup fresh bread crumbs
¼ teaspoon ground mace
¼ teaspoon dried oregano
1 teaspoon Hungarian sweet paprika
1 teaspoon kosher salt
Freshly ground black pepper
24 chipolata sausages, 2 to 3 inches each

1. In a large bowl, combine the shrimp with the parsley, garlic, lemon juice, olive oil, bread crumbs, mace, oregano, paprika, and salt. Season with pepper to taste. Toss to thoroughly mix and coat. Cover and marinate, refrigerated, for at least 8 hours or overnight.

2. Bring a large amount of salted water to a boil. Add the chipolatas and bring back to a boil. Cook until plumped and almost done, 4 to 5 minutes. Drain well.

3. Preheat the broiler. Alternate four shrimp and four chipolatas on 6 large metal skewers, piercing each one crosswise through the middle. Arrange the skewers on an oiled broiling pan and set the pan 4 to 6 inches from the source of heat. Broil until the shrimp are pink and firm on one side, about 2 minutes. Turn and broil on the other side about 1 minute longer. Serve hot.

Serves 6

Tournedos of Beef with Six Peppers

1 teaspoon white peppercorns
1 teaspoon black peppercorns
¾ teaspoon Szechwan peppercorns (available in Oriental specialty markets)
1 teaspoon grains-of-paradise peppercorns (available in Oriental specialty markets)
¼ teaspoon crushed red pepper flakes
1 teaspoon green peppercorns, packed in brine, drained and crushed
1 teaspoon kosher salt
12 beef tournedos, about 3½ ounces each
4 tablespoons lightly salted butter
¼ cup dry red wine
¼ cup *glace de viande* (see Note, page 54)
1½ tablespoons olive oil
2 red bell peppers, peeled, seeded, and cut into long, thin julienne strips

1. Place the white, black, Szechwan, and grains-of-paradise peppercorns on a large work surface. Crush the peppercorns with the bottom of a heavy saucepan or skillet. Transfer to a small bowl. Mix in the pepper flakes, crushed green peppercorns, and salt.

2. Sprinkle both sides of the tournedos very lightly with some of the pepper mixture. (There will be some mixture left. Store for another use in a dry, cool area, tightly covered.)

3. Divide the butter between two large, heavy skillets. Heat over medium-high heat until the butter foams and then begins to subside and turn light brown. Add the tournedos and cook for 2 minutes per side for rare meat and longer for medium or well-done. Remove the tournedos to a side dish and cover with foil to keep warm.

4. Pour off the excess fat from both skillets. Add 2 tablespoons of wine to each skillet and stir with a whisk over high heat to pick up any bits in the bottom. Add 2 tablespoons *glace de viande* to each skillet and melt. Whisk to combine the juices. Return the meat to the skillets and coat each piece with some of the syrupy pan juices.

5. In a separate skillet, heat the olive oil over high heat. Add the pepper strips and cook, stirring constantly, until heated through, about 1 minute. Serve the tournedos on heated plates garnished with a few strips of the red peppers.

Serves 6

Red Snapper and Salmon Tartare with Anchovy Butter

Serve the Tartare with warm fresh toasts. Let guests help themselves to spread on some of the butter and top with the fish mixture.

For the olive oil dressing

½ cup olive oil
¼ cup Cognac
2 garlic cloves, minced
12 whole cloves
1 tablespoon freshly crushed black peppercorns
1 sprig fresh tarragon
1 sprig fresh lemon thyme

For the fish tartare

9 ounces salmon fillet, skin removed
9 ounces red snapper fillet, skin removed
Kosher salt
Freshly ground white pepper
2 tablespoons Olive Oil Dressing

For the anchovy butter

2 anchovy fillets
Pinch of Hungarian sweet paprika
4 tablespoons lightly salted butter, softened
Freshly ground black pepper
1 tablespoon Olive Oil Dressing

1. To make the dressing, combine the olive oil, Cognac, garlic, cloves, pepper, tarragon, and lemon thyme in a clear jar with a tight-fitting lid. Close tightly and shake to blend. Let the dressing rest for several hours or overnight. Line a strainer with several layers of rinsed cheesecloth. Set the strainer over a small bowl and pour over the dressing. Strain well and discard the solids. Makes about ¾ cup dressing.

2. To make the tartare, cut both fillets into slices that measure about ⅛ inch thick. Stack the slices and cut them into ⅛-inch-wide strips. Cut across the strips to make ⅛-inch cubes.

3. Place the fish in a serving bowl and season lightly with salt and pepper to taste. Add the dressing and mix well. Keep cold until ready to serve.

4. To prepare the anchovy butter, place the anchovies in a large bowl. Use the back of a large spoon to smash the anchovies against the side of the bowl to form a thick paste. Whisk in the paprika, butter, and pepper to taste. Stir in the dressing and whisk until smooth and thick. Cover and chill for at least 1 hour before serving.

Serves 6

Calf's Brains in Mustard Crumbs

3 pairs calf's brains, about 12 ounces each
Kosher salt
Freshly ground black pepper
1 cup all-purpose flour for dusting
1 cup fresh bread crumbs for dusting
3 egg yolks
6 tablespoons Dijon mustard, preferably imported and green-herb
    flavored
12 tablespoons lightly salted butter
Fried Capers, optional (recipe follows)

1. Soak the brains in cold water to cover for 2 hours to help loosen the membrane. Slip your fingers under the membrane and carefully peel off the filaments. Rinse the brains thoroughly 2 or 3 times in cold water to remove all traces of blood. Pat them dry with paper towels.

2. Season the brains with salt and pepper to taste. Place the flour and the bread crumbs in separate large, shallow bowls. Mix the egg yolks and mustard in a small bowl. Roll the brains in flour and then use a pastry brush to apply a thick coating of the mustard mixture. Next roll the brains in the bread crumbs to coat. Pat into an oval shape and set aside.

3. Preheat the oven to 350° F. Melt the butter in a well-seasoned, oven-proof skillet. Add the brains and cook over medium-high heat until golden brown on one side, about 2 minutes. Carefully turn and brown on the other side. Place the skillet in the oven and cook until slightly firm to the touch, about 8 minutes.

4. Serve the brains hot with any accumulated butter from the skillet spooned over the top. Sprinkle with Fried Capers if desired.

Serves 6

Fried Capers

3 tablespoons large capers, packed in vinegar
Vegetable oil for frying

1. Strain the capers and rinse under cold running water. Pat dry with paper towels.

2. In a deep-fryer or electric skillet, heat 2 to 3 cups oil to 350° F. Add the capers and cook, stirring, until opened, about 35 seconds. Remove from the oil and drain briefly on paper towels. Serve at once.

Cappuccino Soufflé with Cappuccino Sauce

4½ tablespoons unsalted butter plus 2 tablespoons for buttering dish
⅓ cup sugar
4½ tablespoons all-purpose flour
1½ cups milk
1 tablespoon instant coffee, preferably instant espresso
6 egg yolks
⅓ cup coffee liqueur
½ teaspoon ground cinnamon
8 egg whites, at room temperature
Pinch of salt
Confectioners' sugar
Additional ground cinnamon for dusting
Cappuccino Sauce (recipe follows)

1. Preheat the oven to 400° F. Heavily butter an 8-cup soufflé dish. Pour in the sugar and tilt the dish to coat. Make a collar for the dish. Cut a piece of aluminum foil or wax paper about 2 inches longer than the circumference of the soufflé dish. Fold it lengthwise to double. Butter on one side and wrap the collar, buttered side facing inward, around the mold to extend about 2 inches higher than the rim. Secure the collar with a paper clip or loose-fitting piece of string. Set the prepared dish aside.

2. Melt the remaining butter in a medium-heavy saucepan over medium-high heat. Stir in the flour and cook, stirring often, until the foam subsides and the mixture is lemon-colored, about 2 minutes. Do not brown.

3. Meanwhile, combine the milk and the instant coffee in a medium saucepan. Warm over medium-high heat until tiny bubbles appear around the edges.

4. Stir the hot milk and coffee into the butter and flour mixture. Whisk over medium heat until smooth and thickened. Remove from the heat and stir in the egg yolks, two at a time, beating well after each addition. Stir in the coffee liqueur and the cinnamon. Set aside to cool.

5. Beat the egg whites with a pinch of salt until stiff peaks form. Stir about one fourth of the whites into the base mixture to lighten. Gently fold in the remaining whites.

6. Spoon the mixture into the prepared mold. Bake for 35 to 40 minutes or until puffed and slightly firm in the center. Immediately sprinkle over enough confectioners' sugar and cinnamon to cover the top. Carefully remove the collar. Serve at once with Cappuccino Sauce.

Serves 6

Cappuccino Sauce

1 cup milk
2 teaspoons instant coffee, preferably instant espresso
¼ cup sugar
2 egg yolks
¼ cup coffee liqueur

1. Combine the milk, coffee, and sugar in a small, heavy saucepan. Place over medium heat and stir until dissolved. In a medium bowl, lightly beat the egg yolks.

2. Remove the hot milk mixture from the heat and gradually stir about one fourth of the mixture into the egg yolks to raise the temperature of the yolks. Pour the yolk mixture into the milk in the saucepan. Cook over low heat, stirring constantly, until the mixture thickens. Do not boil.

3. Remove the sauce from the heat and stir in the coffee liqueur. Cool to room temperature. Chill for several hours or overnight before serving.

Makes about 1¼ cups

Great rooms, great meals, memorable moments. I recall a certain Tuesday in June when lunching in the Grill Room of The Four Seasons was somehow like having been in St. Petersburg in 1917 when Lenin arrived in a sealed railroad car at the Finland Station. But we were waiting not for Lenin but for Tina.

First news of the coup came from London. That's how these things are done: a transatlantic phone call to the managers of The Four Seasons from the *Times* of London asking comment on the astonishing news that the *New Yorker* magazine had just named its fourth editor, Tina Brown of *Vanity Fair*. Not that they got any information, the managers of The Four Seasons being gentlemen. But salute the Brits. For they knew that on the day Robert Gottlieb was axed as editor of the *New Yorker* and Tina Brown anointed, it would be in the Grill Room of The Four Seasons that the entrails would be pawed over and scrutinized for omens. And so it was.

One of the first to arrive was *New Yorker* president and C.E.O Steve Florio (later to ascend even more dizzyingly at Condé Nast), who had employed Mr. Gottlieb for five years. And now, as he entered, instantly about the room ran the legend: Steve had only recently, they whispered, raised fists to the sky and wailed aloud, "If only I can get this woman . . ." The woman, I need not tell you, was Tina Brown.

Lunching with Mr. Florio, fresh from a motorcycling trip, suntanned and luxuriating in a pussycat grin, was Jann Wenner of *Rolling Stone*, who seemed mightily to be enjoying a meal with a man who had just won the lottery. I was across the room, unable to read lips. Next to me, Ed Kosner, then editor of *New York* magazine, was lunching with that indefatigable coroner of magazine cadavers, Michael Gross. Alexandra Penney of *Self* magazine then arrived, accompanied by Ellen Straus of both the Macy's and the *New York Times* families. By now Arthur Cooper was among us, editor of *GQ*. Michael Korda arrived. Only Si Newhouse, who had caused all these changes to come about, was absent.

All of this sort of thing used to happen a few blocks away, at the round table of the Hotel Algonquin on West Forty-fourth Street. It was there that Harold Ross, cofounder with Raoul Fleischman of the *New Yorker* back in 1925, and his chums used to meet, to dine, to drink, to talk. To cut up rivals and seduce the beautiful. In James Thurber's marvelous essay "The Years with Ross," he wrote about young Truman Capote, then a child of seventeen or so and looking thirteen, who worked in the art department of the *New Yorker*, running errands and such. According to Thurber, one of those gofer tasks was to go across the street to the Algonquin and lead back to their typewriters drunken *New Yorker* writers. I asked Truman once if that were true.

"Yes," Mr. Capote said, and then, wickedly, "And one of those drunken writers I was sent to bring back was mister . . . James Thurber!"

These days Ross probably would send Capote to the Grill Room of The Four Seasons.

—James Brady, columnist for *Parade* magazine and for *Advertising Age*

William Steinberg's father once told him that to be a success, a man should eat at the same restaurant every day—a notion the young barter and trade broker took to heart. In fact, when Steinberg was looking for office space in Manhattan, he stipulated to the realtor that the building had to be within four blocks of The Four Seasons, which for hundreds of businessmen and -women had become an extension of their office.

Having dined at the restaurant at least six times a week for more than fifteen years, Steinberg had learned the truth of his father's advice. By making himself a regular—and by spending tens of thousands of dollars at The Four Seasons—Steinberg had become more than a mere customer; he was a good friend of the house. He never saw or even signed a bill, could count on pretty much any table he wanted in the Pool Room, which he preferred to the Grill (once again the more commonly used name for the Bar Room by the 1980s), and could ask the kitchen to make just about anything he or his guests felt like eating. He could count on a warm greeting from everyone in the restaurant, expect a certain deference shown to his guests, and know that he would never be disturbed or inconvenienced in any way. The maître d' knew his likes and dislikes, his foibles and idiosyncrasies; and the entire staff could be counted on to be discreet from the moment he

Chapter Ten

Elephant May Take a Little Longer

The Customer Is Always Right

entered the front door till the moment he left it hours later. And, most important of all, none of this would be lost on the business clients Steinberg took to lunch or dinner at The Four Seasons.

"When I have an important client to deal with," he explains, "all I have to do is tell him we're having lunch at The Four Seasons and he'd know this was something serious." Steinberg happily points to tables in the Pool Room where some of his biggest deals were sealed. "Last week I closed a forty-million-dollar contract at that table over there," he says, pointing. In addition, most of the important events of Steinberg's adult life have been held at The Four Seasons, including his first date with the woman who would become his wife, his midnight wedding reception, and the annual Christmas party he throws for three hundred friends and colleagues.

Although Steinberg sounds like an amazingly faithful customer, he is actually only one of many house accounts for whom The Four Seasons has become part workplace, prestigious club, communications forum, celebration hall, and intimate dining room. As insurance broker Jules Epstein observes, "The Four Seasons is totally reflective of you the individual: whatever you want to get out of the restaurant, you will."

According to wine investor Paul Schlem, "Clients are impressed with being taken to The Four Seasons. It's become sort of a trademark with me. I guess I could make a deal somewhere else, but it's helpful to do it at The Four Seasons. Besides, it makes the other guy feel better."

It would be impossible to assess the importance of The Four Seasons' setting, food, and service to successful deal making, but its effect is undeniable. Michael Whiteman, an associate of Joe Baum's, describes how the magic works: "Joe and I were summoned by a famous real-estatenik to a business chat with six other people, none of whom we knew, but one of whom was considering retaining us as consultants on some arcane project. We had lunch at The Four Seasons, and, of course, we were all immediately seduced and diverted by splendid food and grand wines. The social chitchat flowed as naturally as the burgundy until, after four courses and two hours, the real estate magnate glanced at his watch and abruptly shoved back his chair. 'Dammit!' he shouted over his shoulder as he headed for the exit. 'I'm late for my sauna. I'm not sure what this lunch was all about, but everyone seems so nice that you can count me in for a million dollars.'"

According to writer Dominick Dunne, an important scene in his novel *A Season in Purgatory* about a business deal between a powerful older man and a reluctant younger colleague simply wouldn't work until he set it in the Grill Room, where the powerful man "tries to impress the younger man with his familiarity with the occupants of the various tables in his vicinity of the restaurant."

Some habitués credit The Four Seasons with changing their lives or careers. Men's fashion designer Alan Flusser recalls how, when he worked for Pierre Cardin, they'd hold fashion shows in the Pool Room. "It was quite unusual to hold a fashion show in a restaurant," he says. "But if you held a show at The Four Seasons in those days, you'd get a much more positive response from the press than if you said, say, the Drake Hotel. The first time we did it my wife was modeling, and they'd put a walkway across the pool, and she fell in. This caused a big splash, of course, and made the erroneous headline: CARDIN'S WIFE FALLS IN THE POOL AT FASHION SHOW. It was great publicity but strictly unintentional, I assure you. Anyway, my name became known to the press through those shows, and on one occasion when Cardin actually showed up, he sought to take all the credit for the show, and the press got so incensed that they started to refer to the collection as 'Alan Flusser for Pierre Cardin.' As a result, my name was catapulted into the media, and I was soon able to go out on my own and start my own business."

Some years later Flusser was having an important lunch with Steve Florio, publisher of the men's fashion magazine *GQ*, which was then about to undergo a design change with the help of Condé Nast's legendary creative director, Alexander Liberman. "Liberman refused to eat with fashion people," recalls Flusser, "but Florio got him to have lunch with me. So, we're sitting at one of the 'power tables' in the Grill Room, and I'm nervous as hell. We never even mention *GQ* until dessert. I'm fumbling around for something to say, and I order a piece of chocolate velvet cake, which I'd never tasted before. Well, it was so rich, I got an immediate sugar rush and started giving a fifteen-minute treatise about how I thought a man could only learn about the newest fashions from reading *GQ*, but not really how to dress well. Well, I thought I'd completely blown it with Liberman. He and Florio left in silence in their limo, while I walked back to my office. But by the time I got there, Florio was on the phone to tell me Liberman agreed with everything I said and was going to institute some changes. So, I suppose The Four Seasons' chocolate velvet cake had a radical effect on both me and *GQ*."

Other regulars will only take friends and colleagues to The Four Seasons if they think them worthy of the experience. "I don't invite just anyone to The Four Seasons," says Al Teller, head of MCA Entertainment Group, who books his huge annual Grammy Awards party at the restaurant. "Only those who I think will truly appreciate the environment and the food."

Currently, The Four Seasons lists 2,500 house accounts, and although

One night a man paid his girlfriend to strip down to her underwear and jump into the pool. She did so, to the applause of the entire dining room.

When Al Teller took a date to The Four Seasons for the first time, he was shocked to find the bill equaled a week and a half's salary. Twenty years later, as head of MCA Entertainment Group, Teller booked his Grammy Awards party at the restaurant and ran up a bill for service for more than a thousand people.

Despite her vehement objections, Citibank officer Jane Heller was given an upstairs table in the Grill Room the first time she made reservations at The Four Seasons. After lunch, she vowed never to return. A few months later Tom Margittai went to Citibank for a mortgage loan and was embarrassed to find that Heller was to be the loan officer. Nevertheless, The Four Seasons got the loan, and Heller, who became a regular, was never again seated upstairs at the Grill Room.

not all of them come in with the regularity of Bill Steinberg, many do, and some wouldn't think of eating anywhere else. For some, there *is* nowhere else to eat in New York—these are the people who form the basis of the "negative reservation." One New York banker has eaten lunch every day at The Four Seasons since Kovi and Margittai took over, and at least five times a week a curmudgeonly insulation salesman named Al Kevelson shows up flanked by at least three attractive young women, whom he treats to his own specially made low-calorie egg salad.

In this The Four Seasons is not unique, for there are other restaurants around the United States whose owners can boast of customers who frequent their dining rooms with the same fidelity an English gentleman shows to his London club. But throughout the 1980s none could claim the number of such powerful regulars as The Four Seasons, and it was clear why.

Having weathered a decade of insolvency, recession, and stifling inflation, The Four Seasons had emerged in the 1980s as the quintessential New York restaurant, as much for its social importance as for its service of food and wine. By trial and error, the restaurant had finally forged a synthesis of power, glory, and exquisite taste at a time when the city of New York itself, having come back from the brink of bankruptcy, was emerging as the world's most important metropolis.

Indeed, the 1980s was clearly the "New York Decade," with a booming economy, a soaring stock market, and the kind of dynamism that seemed to increase and inflate with no end in sight. Clearly New York had emerged as the world's financial center. Money flowed freely from Wall Street, real estate, and investment. The sale of risky junk bonds made millionaires of men not yet out of their twenties.

Pockets of new wealth and novel style sprouted all over town. Madison Avenue became encrusted with outrageously expensive boutiques. Park Avenue south of Grand Central attracted the publishing and advertising crowd. The neighborhood around the Flatiron Building at Fifth Avenue and Twenty-second Street was fast becoming gentrified. The bohemian soul of Greenwich Village moved farther downtown to SoHo (South of Houston Street) and TriBeCa (Triangle Below Canal Street) as artists moved into lofts, galleries into ironbound buildings, and retro restaurants into former warehouses on the edge of Chinatown.

Out-of-towners had always been dazzled by New York's money, greed, and lasciviousness, all of which seemed deliciously on the increase in the 1980s, so that New York became the very symbol of unbridled entrepreneurship. Traditional liberal politics had turned more and more conservative and intolerant, it seemed, just as it had throughout the rest of the country. One of the best-selling novels of the decade was a scorching satire of New York life called *Bonfire of the Vanities,* by Tom Wolfe, and a movie entitled *Wall Street,* which glamorized the amoral greed of the 1980s, might just as well have been called *New York.*

Despite inroads made by women, the world of corporate power was still dominated largely by men who continued to show off their success in public displays of wealth and influence. An ostentatious developer like Donald Trump might be vilified in the press on a daily basis, then honored publicly for repairing the Central Park skating rink so neglected by New York City's Parks Department. Wheeler-dealers (and later convicted felons) like

Tableside preparation has always been a distinguishing mark of the Pool Room.

Ivan Boesky and Michael Milken made hundreds of millions of dollars selling junk bonds. Salaries of New York baseball players seemed based more on their media value than on their talents, and the losing New York Mets became known as "the worst team that money could buy."

There was so much money to go around and so many ways to spend it at the company's expense. Nowhere was this more evident than in New York's restaurants, which enjoyed an unprecedented golden age in the early 1980s. Expensive "dining establishments" popped up on every corner in every neighborhood, and menu prices went through the roof. As long as one's expense account was unchecked, the idea of spending $75 per person for a three-course meal (without wine, tax, or tip) at a nouvelle cuisine establishment like the Quilted Giraffe in the AT&T Building seemed completely justified. Pasta dishes at high-class Italian restaurants like Felidia, Primavera, and Il Nido topped the $20 mark—up to $60 in some places if you wanted a few shavings of white truffles on a dollar's worth of fettuccine. By accepting such prices, the dining public gave the go-ahead to a whole slew of less-than-deluxe new restaurants whose neighborhood, decor, and service did not begin to justify such high tabs. Chanterelle, a barren room in scruffy SoHo with waiters in white aprons and no decor whatsoever, defended its $55-per-person menu by convincing customers and the media that the exquisiteness of such personalized cuisine demanded the price. It worked: in the

Simon & Schuster editor in chief Michael Korda, who dines nearly every day at The Four Seasons, told a reporter, "The authors [I bring here] always eat a lot, because they're afraid they'll never get another meal, and they want to get something back from the publisher."

The first and only time notorious lawyer Roy Cohn came to The Four Seasons, Niccolini seated him in the back of the Grill Room, "where he belonged." Cohn was furious, but Niccolini refused to move him. Then Cohn tried to sign the check. Niccolini told him he had no account. Now apoplectic, Cohn screamed, "Do you know who I am? I'm a friend of the President." Niccolini would not budge. Cohn paid with a credit card he'd had all along and stormed out. Ever after, whenever he'd try to make a reservation, he was refused a table.

mid-1980s Chanterelle usually had a three-week wait list for a table most nights of the week.

Such was happily endured by businessmen and -women on lavish expense accounts, and the celebration of signing a new contract was always good reason to pop the cork on another $200 bottle of Dom Pérignon or a $300 vintage Port. More and more, the need to be seen in the company of one's most powerful peers as a self-defining moment was part of doing business, especially among those who came to be called the "yuppies" of the era. The reward for a job well done was not mere money—that was easy to come by—but access to the best tennis and social clubs, box seats at the U.S. Open, and preferred tables at New York's most exclusive restaurants. Food in such an atmosphere was often way down the list of priorities, so that a cover story in *Manhattan, Inc.* on egomaniacal lawyer Roy Cohn, who often brought his own can of tuna and glass of iced tea to Le Cirque, was entitled "Roy Cohn: All Power, No Lunch."

To get a table on a moment's notice at deluxe dining rooms like Lutèce, La Côte Basque, Le Cirque, Parioli Romanissimo, or the River Café was tough enough; but to get a "good" table in an "A" section of such a restaurant was to demonstrate one's clout. To be able to sign for it all—complete with lavish tips to captains and Rolex watches at Christmas to maître d's—was to show a cavalier attitude toward money. Probably the favorite line among yuppies who drove BMWs and ate out six nights a week was John Jacob Astor's famous put-down of a man who asked him how much Astor had paid for his yacht: "If you have to ask, you can't afford it." Among restaurateurs in the 1990s, the 1980s became known as "the good old days."

Throughout the 1980s The Four Seasons was, arguably, the most famous restaurant in the United States and one of the most expensive in the world. Entrée prices at dinner in the Pool Room easily topped $30 (with vegetables extra), and appetizers might be $15 or more. Baby lamb in tarragon cream was $35, crabmeat mousse $14, liver steak $29, gravlax $23, and desserts $6.50. Ad executive Ned Doyle once cautioned von Bidder, "Don't ever show me a check, because I would never eat in this goddamn place if I knew what it cost."

But unlike other New York restaurants charging such prices, The Four Seasons also delivered Mies van der Rohe, Philip Johnson (who could still be seen every day at table 32 in the Grill Room at lunch), art by Picasso, Miró, and Stella, a pool where any other restaurateur would have set six tables, and a ratio of service and kitchen staff to customers that humbled that of any other restaurant in America. It was one thing to pay $20 for pappardelle noodles with wild mushrooms at a cramped trattoria on the Upper East Side, but it was quite another to pay the same price for the same dish amid the splendor of The Four Seasons, whose day-to-day maintenance probably cost more than that of any other restaurant in the United States. In 1984 Kovi and Margittai were paying $3 million a year for foodstuffs, $175,000 for laundry, $100,000 for uniforms, and $100,00 for flowers. Fortunately, they also sold 195,000 meals that year and grossed $12 million.

The Four Seasons also guaranteed newcomers a panorama of celebrities who dined there day in and day out. Of course, no one ever actually "rubbed elbows" with celebrities at The Four Seasons, because the tables were deliberately and widely separated from one another to ensure privacy, and the sound level in both the Grill Room and the Pool Room was kept at a low hum. An article in *New York* magazine actually tested noisiness in Manhattan restaurants and found The Four Seasons to have the lowest decibel level of them all—described as being just a bit above that of the main reading room of the New York Public Library. Fashion designer John Weitz once told *Cosmopolitan* magazine, "[The Grill] is one of the very few rooms in which you can divorce your wife, fire somebody, or *get* fired without anyone overhearing."

Visual contact with such celebrities was exciting enough to most Four Seasons patrons, but among those who dined there on a regular basis, there were other benefits. Business clients of regular Paul Schlem, a wine distributor, would gape and be duly impressed when celebrities nodded to Schlem as he entered The Four Seasons. "Kissinger and Jackie Onassis probably don't have the foggiest idea who I am," Schlem explains, "but they smile and say hello to me on the street because they know my face from the Grill Room."

In the Pool Room it would be rare not to find a visiting celebrity in one's midst—Elizabeth Taylor and her lawyer at table 36, Luciano Pavarotti and his entourage at table 52, and Orson Welles taking up most of table 61 while regaling friends with stories of his life. The Pool Room always seemed dotted with several celebrities on any given evening. Travel writer Jan Morris recalls the time she took her daughter to The Four Seasons and immediately spotted an impec-

Orson Welles's entry in The Four Seasons' guestbook was this self-portrait.

At a Christmas party a group of Wall Streeters negotiated with a tipsy woman to remove articles of her clothing in the Pool Room. Only after she'd collected $10,000 and was half-naked did she cut off negotiations and put her clothes back on.

cably tanned Douglas Fairbanks Jr., who came over to say hello. The girl was obviously star-struck by Douglas's appearance at her elbow but practically fainted when the actor told her to "give a wave across the pool." When the girl did so, she saw Laurence Olivier waving back.

One afternoon von Bidder got a frantic call from the Pool Room. "We got trouble, Alex," said the maître d'.

"I rushed down to the Pool Room and saw two women and ten men running furiously around the pool and screaming at each other," recalls the usually unflappable von Bidder. "I had no idea what was going on, so, with the help of a couple of my bigger waiters, I tried to position myself between the men and women as they came around the turn. The only thing I could think of to do was to yell, 'Everybody shut up and sit down!'

David Frost with Alex von Bidder.

Which, I was amazed to see, they all did, wherever they happened to be in the dining room. Apparently what had happened was that a Middle Eastern fellow and his two sons were having lunch, when in comes the man's wife on the arm of his own brother. They went nuts. The man jumps up, attacks the woman and his brother, other guests jump into the fray to help out the woman, everybody's screaming, and the husband is shouting, 'He's kidnapping my wife!' The brother is telling the woman, 'I'll take you to Paris,' and the sons are telling their father to stay away from his brother. By now our customers have taken sides and are cheering on one side or another. We called the cops, but they were nowhere in sight, so I grabbed the arm of the woman and dashed off through Picasso Alley toward the Fifty-second Street entrance, with the husband and two sons tearing after us. When they got outside the restaurant, they hail a cab, but the two sons block the cabdriver from going anywhere. The cabdriver opens the door and sprays the guys with Mace. Then the cops pull up, grab the brothers, who continue to struggle with them, so one cop hits one of the brothers right in the face. Bam! Well, that calmed things down, and they started to sort things out. But just when I think everything's getting back to some kind of normalcy, the husband comes back into the restaurant to find me and threatens to sue me for allowing his wife to be kidnapped. Somehow I took it all calmly, the man left, and we never heard from them again. But while I'm standing there trying to get a grip on myself, two ladies from Texas come up to me and say, 'You sure know how to entertain your guests!'"

Celebrities felt comfortable dining at The Four Seasons, not coddled or pampered, and they were assured that no stranger or autograph seeker would ever approach their table. After one visit they felt that every need would be taken care of without having to ask for it. When Grace Kelly arrived, she would nonchalantly undo her wrap, pull it back to her shoulders, and move forward, ever confident that someone was behind her to take it.

Occasionally celebrities themselves caused a bit of a stir. One day composer Stephen Sondheim was having lunch on the balcony of the Grill Room, when suddenly actress Maureen Stapleton appeared below him and started belting out a Sondheim show tune in the hope that he might cast her for his upcoming musical. He didn't.

The incessant presence of bodyguards for famous people caused no end of annoyance to The Four Seasons' staff, who had to keep them at a discreet but secure distance and try to deter them from making the whole place jumpy. During United Nations sessions, a large percentage of the seats at the restaurant were taken up with security men. On one particularly busy afternoon, the Turkish ambassador exited the restaurant to find so many Secret Service cars

Walter Cronkite, Jean Stapleton, and Arthur Godfrey.

parked along Fifty-second Street that his own motorcade had had nowhere to park, so he had to walk back to the Waldorf-Astoria, where he was staying. On another occasion someone accidentally left his briefcase on the stairway, causing the entire restaurant to be evacuated until the bomb squad could check it out for explosives. They found only an absent-minded businessman's papers.

Once, at a press conference for a blue-jeans manufacturer, spokeswoman and sometimes actress Marla Maples, then having an affair with developer Donald Trump, was served with a summons by Trump's estranged wife, Ivana. A process server waited till Maples had sat down to lunch, then came over and asked, "Are you Marla Maples?" and tried to hand her the summons. Instantly her bodyguard snatched away the summons, shoved it back into the server's pocket, and told him firmly but quietly, "You never served this summons, understand?" Then he whisked Maples out the back door.

When arms dealer Adnan Khashoggi was placed under federal house arrest, he still took his meals at The Four Seasons, wearing a special ankle bracelet that let the FBI know where he was at all times. He would show up at the Pool Room, then order one of the most expensive Bordeaux on the menu for his lawyers, although he never touched a drop himself because he was a Muslim.

Unlike other restaurants, where the chef might have been offended at customers with odd dietary habits, the staff at The Four Seasons never lifted an eyebrow at even the quirkiest request. Actress Gloria Swanson used to bring her own salad dressing with her, and ad exec Ned Doyle would carry his own tomatoes in his pockets, hand them to Niccolini, and have them prepared for him. On one occasion Doyle forgot they were in his pocket, ruined his suit, and tried to get Niccolini to pay for a new one. The wife of screenwriter James Goldman was fond of ordering littleneck clams for dessert, and President Jimmy Carter's brother Billy wanted his beer served in a can (a request the bar was unable to fulfill!).

Few such "menu adjustments" were refused, and most were carried out without the slightest hint of effort or condescension. Wine writer Charles Rubinstein recalls a lunch at The Four Seasons with an important out-of-town business associate who insisted the kitchen make him a salad dressing according to his own peculiar instructions. The kitchen complied, and the man offered his concoction for others at the table to taste. "It was horrible," remembers Rubinstein. "But the captain told the guy, 'The kitchen thinks that's a very interesting dressing, sir. Could we possibly have the recipe?' The guy was so floored and so flattered that he gave them the recipe and left a *huge* tip to Oreste. I always thought that if you asked the kitchen to cook an elephant, they'd do it on a moment's notice."

Perhaps elephant would take a little longer, but switching gears with less exotic fare was as easy as agreeing to do it. One evening the chairman of Doyle Dane Bernbach International, Bob Levenson, arrived at The Four Seasons to go over a menu for a party he'd planned for one hundred guests at eight o'clock. "I got to the restaurant at seven," says Levenson. "And I noticed that the entrée was to be lamb—which is what many of us had had two nights running at other restaurants. I mentioned this to Alex with a shrug. Now, remember, this was thirty minutes before a hundred people were going to sit down. But Alex said it would be no problem to change everything. 'How about veal?' he asked. I blinked and said, sure.

'And we should probably change the wine, too,' said Alex. Well, everybody that night sat down to a spectacular veal dinner with appropriate wine, and it all went off without a hitch. That was pretty amazing to me. To this day, I don't think Alex knows why I order lamb as often as I do at The Four Seasons."

It was important to all at The Four Seasons that such an international clientele be made to feel at ease upon being greeted and served. Kovi and Margittai boasted they knew at least 80 percent of the customers in the Grill on any given day and felt perfectly at ease calling them by their first names. The staff had always been composed of a good number of Europeans who could speak several languages, and, over the years, employees were added who could intercede in Greek, Czech, Korean, Vietnamese, Dutch, Thai, Portuguese, and Spanish. In an effort to make an increasing number of Japanese customers feel at home, von Bidder visited Japan and took Japanese lessons, once testing out a prospective employee whose résumé listed residency in Japan by conducting the interview in Japanese.

Anticipating a customer's needs, both gastronomic and emotional, was key to The Four Seasons' success in the early 1980s. A woman named Dahlia Carmel, who was confined to a wheelchair, remembers how, on her arrival before the formidable staircase, the staff escorted her to a freight elevator that opened onto the kitchen. "I was treated like royalty," she says. "After dinner they served me the chocolate velvet cake and then escorted me out to a waiting limo."

Kovi, Margittai, von Bidder, and Niccolini all knew that the smallest slight, an offhand remark, an indiscreet whisper, or a fallen soufflé could cause a temperamental guest to storm out the glass doors never to return, only to tell others—including everyone in his corporation with a large expense account—how The Four Seasons had gone into irreversible decline. In his book *Chic Savages, Women's Wear Daily* publisher John Fairchild described the Grill as looking like "a paneled basketball court with a striped rug" and told *New York* magazine, "The women you see there don't dress very well."

Even though the staff of The Four Seasons insisted everyone was to be treated equally, deference was obviously shown to regulars and other important people, and a judicious amount of flattery was used to buoy up the clientele, especially for the edification of a regular's guest. Pamela Fiori, editor in chief of *Travel & Leisure* magazine in the 1980s, remembers the time she was dining with her mother in the Grill and Oreste Carnevali

Despite the fluency of The Four Seasons' staff in several languages, mixups do occur. On one occasion two Spanish customers who spoke little English tried to order two martinis. The waiter misunderstood and brought them two glasses of ice water. The Spaniards looked down at their drinks and said, "But we asked for olives with our martinis."

When *New Yorker* editor William Shawn ate at The Four Seasons, his meal was usually cornflakes and milk.

came over. "You know, Mrs. Fiori," he told her mother, "your daughter is a very famous lady." And when Ellen Levine, editor of *Woman's Day,* noticed a particularly thick passel of security men outside the restaurant and inquired of Margittai, "Is somebody very important here today?" the smooth Transylvanian cooed (probably not for the first time in his career), "Yes, you."

The staff went to extraordinary lengths to guarantee a steady clientele, sending flowers when a regular was taken ill, sending notes to ask why one had not been in to dine recently, and sending all kinds of favorite bonbons to customers too long away from The Four Seasons' comfort foods.

Power seating in the Grill Room, 1986, as rendered by illustrator Julian Allen: Henry Kissinger stands in the forefront; other notables at their favored tables include S. I. Newhouse, Pete Peterson, John Loeb, John Fairchild, Bill Blass, Michael Korda, Mort Janklow, Alexander Liberman, Nelson Doubleday, Philip Johnson, Larry Tisch, and Bob Tisch.

When Fred Adler, venture capitalist and one of the founders of Data General Corporation, had to have his hips replaced in 1983, he did so in a Boston hospital. "I never told Tom and Paul which hospital I was in," says Adler, "but I was there less than three days when in comes one of their people laden down with champagne, hors d'oeuvres and the nicest note in the world from Alex, Paul, Julian, and Tom. Over the next two months I must have received at least six phone calls from them to see how I was doing, and after my second operation one of their waiters showed up in full dress with champagne, a Bordeaux I loved, cold veal, salads, gravlax, and dessert enough for four people. My surgeon came in, and we all had a party."

In an article entitled "My Favorite Restaurant," Simon & Schuster's editor in chief and author of the book *Power!,* Michael Korda (who dines in the Grill every day—often wearing jodhpurs and boots after a horseback ride—and estimates he spent about $24,000 a year there in the mid-1980s), described how the staff of The Four Seasons would act at the slightest hint of a guest's inconvenience: "An appointment with Doctor So-and-so, who is booked up for months ahead? It's done. The best way to hook up a VCR to a new cable box? Margittai sends for a pad of paper and does a wiring diagram. A hotel room in Venice, the name of the best tailor in Rome, the name of the attractive young woman sitting at the far banquette?" For Korda the food is of no importance; he prefers to subsist on creamed spinach, baked potato, and nonalcoholic beer, explaining that not ordering from the menu "eliminates one other thing to think about." For Korda's birthday, Simon & Schuster's Richard Snyder arranged for his gift of a motorcycle to be displayed in the Pool Room as Korda entered.

While von Bidder made the seating of powerful egos seem like the most natural thing in the world, the seating game played at The Four Seasons and other deluxe restaurants in fact became more and more problematic. Many customers simply assumed that such-and-such a table was theirs whenever they wanted it, and when such an assumption could be accommodated, it was. The horror of not having one's table was more than some customers could bear; some actually pleaded on the phone that they *had* to have a certain table or be humiliated in front of their colleagues. Marvin Sloves, chairman of the Scali-McCabe-Sloves ad agency, once told a reporter, "If I lost my table at The Four Seasons, I'd feel as if I had lost my club. I'd leave New York and move to London immediately."

On any weekday, one was more likely than not to find entertainment lawyer Robert Montgomery at table 42; Betty Prashker, by then Crown Publishing's editor in chief, at table 16; and any number of other editors from the publishing industry. One day Prashker noticed Barry Diller of 20th Century–Fox at a table with Howard Squadron, a lawyer for communications titan Rupert Murdoch. "I put two and two together and figured out that Murdoch might be buying Fox, which turned out to be true. That's valuable information in the communications business."

Condé Nast owner and publisher S.I. Newhouse always commands a table in the Grill and is usually able to nod hello to one of his editors from *Vogue, Vanity Fair, Condé Nast Traveler,* or *GQ* at another. The first time Tina Brown, then the new editor of *Vanity Fair,* arrived, she was seated on the upper level of the Grill—for the first and only time. And when Newhouse bought the *New Yorker,* he was even able to extract editor William Shawn from his sacred table at the Algonquin Hotel to dine occasionally at The Four Seasons.

A man who wanted to propose to his girlfriend at The Four Seasons signaled the staff to come to his table, then told them, "Move the table away." But the staff thought he said, "Move away," which they did. Everyone stared at each other for thirty seconds until the frustrated man just reached into his pocket and gave her the ring without kneeling down, as he had hoped he might if the table had been moved.

Ad exec Dave Kreinik once remarked to Paul Kovi that some people felt intimidated by his restaurant. Kovi just shrugged, smiled, and said, "That's fine with me."

So identified had the Grill become with New York's elite that Barry Diller once tried to interest novelist Dominick Dunne in creating a television series using the Grill as a takeoff point. According to Dunne, each episode would depict "the adventures or misadventures of the occupant of a particular table or banquette. [Diller] saw it as a series about the people who control New York and make it run. It was a good idea. I could have done it, but the timing was wrong, so it didn't come to pass. Besides, I didn't want to become a pariah at a restaurant I enjoy so much."

Long before the Grill became a success, however, Margittai and Kovi had vowed never to become slaves to their clientele and agreed to part company with anyone who crossed the line from expecting reasonable deference to making unreasonable demands. "We simply ignore anyone who snaps his fingers to get attention," says Margittai, "and once, when an international financier went straight to what he presumed was *his* table without checking at the desk, I told him the table had been reserved for someone else. He got up and left and canceled six house accounts, and we lost thousands of dollars that way. Another regular stormed out when we gave his table away, but he came back when it started to snow that winter. His office was across the street." Ever protective of his personnel, Margittai refused to tolerate those who showed disrespect to a staff member. When one unconscionable boor spit at a captain in the Grill Room, Margittai went to the table and asked the man to leave the restaurant at once.

No one was amused—though the staff tried to be understanding—when a New York comedian couldn't make it to the downstairs men's room and resorting to pissing into a wastebasket in the upstairs checkroom. On a rare night when the insecurities of one customer demanding a table by the pool became all too ridiculous, Kovi responded, "My dear sir, if the only purpose in your coming here is to sit at a poolside table and we don't happen to have one, then perhaps you must find another restaurant in New York that does."

The same has applied for gentlemen who kick up a fuss over The Four Seasons' dress requirements.

The pop singing group Frankie Valli and the Four Seasons standing slightly underdressed outside the restaurant of the same name.

Since the coatroom carries blue blazers in every size, including for boys, those ignorant of the rules usually shrug and put one on. On occasion, however, a man has put up a fight, only to find himself on the losing end. When a very wealthy Texan sat down and neglected to remove his Stetson hat, Kovi went over to him and said gently, "Sir, we are gentlemen here, and gentlemen take off their hats in restaurants." When another fellow who'd just ordered a $200 bottle of champagne protested that he was a producer in Hollywood, where no restaurants demanded a jacket, Tom Margittai reminded him,

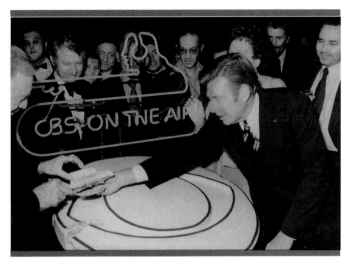

Walter Cronkite and Arthur Godfrey celebrating the tenth anniversary of 60 Minutes.

with the demeanor of a man explaining that the world was not flat, "This isn't Hollywood." When the man further protested, Margittai came up with a compromise: the producer and his companion could have their champagne in a private room.

On one notorious occasion, a Pool Room busboy, working close to a table where Elizabeth Taylor and her party sat, accidentally set fire to his sleeve while refilling a heating lamp with alcohol. In the ensuing confusion, Taylor's assistant's arm was singed. Immediately Taylor's South American lawyer, who was dining with them, demanded to see von Bidder, informing him that Miss Taylor had been badly burned and probably scarred for life both physically and mentally, but that a $10,000 payment on the spot might head off a nasty, costly law suit. Von Bidder apologized and said he'd take it under advisement. The next day The Four Seasons' attorney called Taylor's lawyer and asked him if he was licensed to practice law in the State of New York, and if not, was he familiar with New York's extortion laws? Von Bidder never heard from Taylor or the lawyer again.

When President Jimmy Carter's brother Billy came to the restaurant dressed like a truck driver, Kovi had to refuse him access unless he put on a jacket. After some give and take, Carter gave in, grumbled, "What kind of place is this?" then ordered a steak and a beer in a can. When he was told the bar carried beer only in bottle or draft, Carter was convinced this was the worst restaurant in the world. Meanwhile his nephew Chip Carter asked to make a telephone call from the front desk. "I'm at The Four Seasons," he told the person on the line. "You know, the one on Park Street."

Baked Whole Sea Bass with Peppers, Garlic, and Saffron Vinaigrette Sauce

For the saffron vinaigrette

1 $1/2$ cups olive oil
2 small shallots, finely chopped
$1/2$ small jalapeño pepper, seeded, finely chopped (about 1 tablespoon)
Pinch of saffron threads or $1/2$ teaspoon powdered saffron
$1/4$ cup chicken broth
2 tablespoons Pommery mustard
1 tablespoon balsamic vinegar
2 tablespoons rice vinegar
Salt and pepper
3 tablespoons finely chopped chives

For the sea bass

1 large sea bass, about 3 pounds, cleaned and trimmed for baking
Salt and pepper
1 bouquet garni (see Note)
1 large all-purpose potato, about $1/4$ pound
$1/4$ cup extra-virgin olive oil
10 medium garlic cloves, peeled
2 tablespoons unsalted butter
1 large red pepper, roasted, peeled, seeded, and cut into thin strips
1 large yellow pepper, roasted, peeled, seeded, and cut into thin strips
1 tablespoon balsamic vinegar

1. To prepare the Saffron Vinaigrette Sauce, place 2 tablespoons of the olive oil in a small sauté pan over low heat. Add the shallots and jalapeño pepper. Cook, stirring often, until the shallots are translucent, 4 to 6 minutes. Remove from the heat and cool.

2. In a small saucepan over low heat, combine the saffron and chicken broth. Warm, stirring often, until the saffron is dissolved, about 5 minutes. Do not boil. Remove from the heat, cover, and cool to room temperature.

3. In a medium mixing bowl, combine the saffron infusion, the mustard, the balsamic vinegar, the rice vinegar, and salt and pepper to taste. Whisk to dissolve. Add the remaining olive oil gradually, in droplets, whisking constantly until thick and emulsified. Whisk in the cooked shallots and jalapeño pepper. Season to taste with additional salt and pepper. Add the chives just before serving.

4. To prepare the fish, preheat the oven to 375° F. Season the outside and cavity of the bass with salt and pepper. Place the bouquet garni in the cavity. Peel the potato and square off the ends to make a firm support and

NOTE: To make a bouquet garni, combine 3 parsley stems, 2 bay leaves, 2 sprigs fresh thyme, and 2 whole black peppercorns in a piece of cheesecloth and tie together with kitchen string. Remove after cooking.

place in the cavity to keep the shape of the fish. Place the fish on its side in a lightly oiled baking dish and pour 2 tablespoons of the olive oil over the top. Bake for 40 minutes or until the fish flakes easily with a fork. Discard the potato.

5. Meanwhile, prepare the garnish. Bring 2 small pots of water to a boil. Add a pinch of salt to one of the pots. Plunge the garlic cloves into the unsalted pot and bring back to a boil. Drain and plunge the garlic into the second pot of salted water. Bring back to a boil and cook rapidly until tender, 4 to 5 minutes. Drain and rinse under cold running water to cool. Transfer to paper towels and pat dry.

6. Melt the butter in a medium sauté pan over low heat. Place the garlic in the butter and cook, stirring often, until golden brown and "roasted," about 10 minutes. With a slotted spoon, transfer the garlic to drain on paper towels. Season with salt and pepper.

7. In a small bowl, combine the peppers with the remaining 2 tablespoons of olive oil, the balsamic vinegar, and salt and pepper. Stir well and set aside in a small sauté pan.

8. Use a long spatula to transfer the fish to a large serving platter. Cover with foil to keep warm. Gently heat the peppers over low heat for about 2 minutes to warm through. Surround the fish with the peppers and sprinkle the roasted garlic around and on top of the fish. Serve at once with some of the Saffron Vinaigrette Sauce spooned over the top. Serve the remaining sauce on the side.

Serves 2

Blackened Tuna

For the blackening spices

    2 tablespoons sea salt
    1 teaspoon dried thyme
    2 teaspoons dried fennel seeds
    2 teaspoons celery seeds
    1 tablespoon whole black peppercorns
    1 tablespoon coriander seeds
    1 tablespoon ground cumin
    1 teaspoon cayenne pepper
    ½ teaspoon ground mace
    1 teaspoon ground white pepper

(Continued on next page)

3 tablespoons sweet paprika
1 tablespoon curry powder

For the salsa fría
2 large tomatoes, peeled, seeded, and diced
½ cucumber, peeled, seeded, and diced
½ small onion, finely chopped
1 small jalapeño pepper, seeded and finely chopped
1 tablespoon chopped fresh cilantro
½ teaspoon minced garlic
¼ cup extra virgin olive oil
2 tablespoons red wine vinegar
Salt and pepper

For the blackened tuna
4 large tuna steaks, about 8 ounces each
1 recipe blackening spices
6 tablespoons clarified butter

1. To prepare the spices, combine the salt, thyme, fennel seeds, celery seeds, peppercorns, coriander seeds, cumin, and cayenne in a spice grinder. Grind to a fine powder. Empty into a small bowl. Add the mace, white pepper, paprika, and curry powder and mix well. Store in a glass jar with a tight-fitting lid. Makes about ¾ cup.

2. For the salsa fría, combine the tomatoes, cucumber, onion, jalapeño, cilantro, garlic, and olive oil in a large nonreactive bowl. Season to taste with vinegar, salt, and pepper. Cover and refrigerate for several hours or overnight before using. Makes about 1½ cups.

3. To blacken the tuna, dust the steaks with a fine layer of the spices. (Reserve the leftover spices for later use.) Place the butter in a large bowl. Use your hands to dip and coat the tuna in the butter.

4. Preheat a large cast-iron skillet over high heat. When very hot, place the steaks directly on the bottom with no additional butter or oil. Cook until blackened and crusty, about 2 minutes per side. (The result will be a tuna steak that is rare in the center. If additional cooking is desired, transfer the blackened tuna to a preheated 375° F. oven and cook about 5 minutes longer.)

5. Transfer the tuna to warmed plates. Serve with salsa fría on the side and snow peas sautéed in butter.

Serves 4

A Paillard of Turkey with Peppers and Pineapple

4 slices turkey breast, about 4 ounces each, cut 1/2-inch thick
1 tablespoon peeled, chopped fresh ginger
1 tablespoon chopped fresh lemongrass
1 small jalapeño pepper, cored, seeded, and finely chopped
1 garlic clove, minced
1 tablespoon olive oil
1 large scallion, thinly sliced on the diagonal
6 ounces savoy cabbage, cut into ¼-inch-wide strips
½ large red bell pepper, peeled, seeded, and cut into ¼-inch-thick strips
½ large yellow bell pepper, peeled, seeded, and cut into ¼-inch-thick strips
½ large green bell pepper, peeled, seeded, and cut into ¼-inch-thick strips
¾ pound fresh pineapple, cut into small cubes
2 cups turkey or chicken stock, reduced to ½ cup
2 tablespoons reduced-sodium soy sauce

1. Place the turkey slices in a medium glass baking dish. Sprinkle over the ginger, lemongrass, jalapeño, and garlic. Cover and marinate at room temperature, turning once or twice, for 1 hour.

2. Preheat the broiler or a grill. In a 10-inch nonstick skillet, heat the olive oil over medium-high heat. Add the scallion and cook, stirring often, until lightly browned, about 2 minutes. Add the cabbage and cook, stirring only once or twice, until browned, about 3 minutes. Place the strips of pepper on top and cook 2 minutes longer. Add the pineapple and the reduced stock. Stir briefly to mix and set aside, covered, while preparing the turkey.

3. Place the turkey on an oiled broiling pan or hot grill set 4 to 6 inches from the source of heat. Broil about 2 minutes on each side. Transfer to heated plates and sprinkle each paillard with soy sauce. Spoon the vegetables on top and around the turkey. Serve hot.

Serves 4

Curried Swordfish with Pickled Vegetables

For the best blend of flavors, the pickled vegetables should be prepared three days in advance.

For the pickled vegetables
1½ cups white wine vinegar
½ tablespoon salt
½ cup sugar
½ teaspoon caraway seeds
½ cup ¼-inch diced carrots
½ cup ¼-inch diced daikon
½ cup ¼-inch diced red bell pepper
½ cup ¼-inch diced yellow bell pepper

For the sauce
4 tablespoons olive oil
1 small onion, finely chopped
3 red bell peppers, cored, seeded, and finely chopped
½ cup dry white wine
½ cup chicken broth
1 tablespoon finely chopped shallots
1 small garlic clove, minced
1 teaspoon chopped lemongrass
2 tablespoons peeled, chopped fresh ginger
1 teaspoon red curry paste (available in specialty food markets)
½ cup unsweetened coconut milk
1 tablespoon curry powder
Salt and freshly ground black pepper
2 tablespoons chopped fresh basil
1 tablespoon chopped fresh cilantro

For the fish
4 large swordfish steaks, about 7 ounces each
Salt and freshly ground black pepper
1–2 tablespoons mild curry powder, or to taste
12 stems fresh chives, for garnish

1. To prepare the vegetables, combine the vinegar, salt, sugar, caraway seeds, and 1 cup cold water in a small, heavy saucepan. Bring to a boil over high heat. Stir to dissolve, remove from the heat, and pass through a fine-mesh sieve. Add the diced carrots and daikon to the hot liquid. Cool to room temperature and add the diced peppers. Cover and refrigerate for 3 days before using.

2. To make the sauce, heat 2 tablespoons of the olive oil in a medium saucepan. Add the onion and cook over medium-high heat, stirring often, until softened, about 2 minutes. Stir in the peppers. Add the wine and increase the heat to high. Bring to a boil and stir often until the wine has evaporated. Pour in the chicken broth, reduce heat to low, and cook, stirring often, until the peppers are very soft. Transfer to a blender or food processor and purée until smooth. Set aside.

3. Heat the remaining 2 tablespoons of olive oil in a medium saucepan. Add the shallots, garlic, lemongrass, ginger, and the red curry paste. Cook over medium-high heat, stirring often, until the shallots are softened, about 2 minutes. Add the coconut milk and the curry powder. Increase the heat to high and bring to a boil. Boil until the mixture has reduced by half. Stir in the puréed pepper mixture, season with salt and pepper to taste, reduce the heat to medium-low, and simmer, stirring often, for 15 minutes. Remove the sauce from the heat and stir in the basil and cilantro. Set aside, covered to keep warm.

4. To prepare the fish, preheat a grill to hot and preheat the oven to 375° F. Season the swordfish with salt and pepper to taste. Dust evenly on both sides with curry powder. Place the fish on the hot grill and cook for about 1 minute on one side to make decorative marks. Carefully turn to make a crosshatch effect on the same side. Repeat this procedure on the other side. Transfer the marked swordfish to an oiled baking dish and place in the oven. Cook until slightly firm to the touch when pressed in the center, about 8 minutes.

5. Meanwhile, use a slotted spoon to remove the pickled vegetables from their liquid. Place the vegetables in an ovenproof dish. Cook in the oven with the swordfish, stirring often, until warmed through, about 4 minutes.

6. Gently reheat the sauce and spoon equal amounts over the bottom of four warmed serving plates. Place a swordfish steak on top of the sauce. Surround with the warmed vegetables. Garnish with chives and serve at once.

Serves 4

In 1984 The Four Seasons turned twenty-five, having become perhaps the most famous restaurant in the world—the kind of place guidebooks called a "New York institution," a "once-in-a-lifetime" experience, and a place to which gourmets needed to "pay homage."

The publicity surrounding the "power lunch," the promotional success of Spa Cuisine, the lavish mountings of wine events like the Barrel Tasting, and the now classic status of the architecture had all worked to make The Four Seasons what it was intended to be— *the* exemplary New York restaurant that kept evolving right along with the city itself. In 1981 the industry newspaper *Nation's Restaurant News* voted the restaurant into its Fine Dining Hall of Fame. *Restaurant Business* magazine summed up the importance of the restaurant by saying, "In the greatest sense of the word, The Four Seasons is a classic—one whose architectural vision laid the foundation for a restaurant that remains ahead of its time, and probably will for many years to come."

The kitchen had also achieved a critical reputation for fine food that had long eluded it. The *New York Times*, whose critics had never raved about the food, finally awarded it three stars, with reviewer Bryan Miller praising Seppi Renggli's "stunning dishes using native provender," the "unqualified successes" of the

Chapter Eleven

A Public Trust

The Landmarking of an Institution

*Johnson designed new car-
peting, the pattern of which
was set by computer to
match perfectly.*

hot appetizers, and the "justly renowned" desserts. Miller wrote of the restaurant's quarter century in business, "Such longevity alone in this volatile business merits at least a silver spoon award; even more impressive, though, is how this grand vessel of luxury has managed to stay right on course during its long voyage, maintaining standards of food quality and service that are paragons of the industry."

It seemed an appropriate time, therefore, for Kovi and Margittai to pat each other on the back and celebrate their achievements on a grand scale. They were, after all, survivors in the great New York tradition of those who took an absurd gamble on a good idea and, despite awesome odds, finally won. It would have been easier, of course, to allow The Four Seasons to roll through the rest of the twentieth century merely by maintaining the status quo its current clientele had come to love. But Margittai and Kovi, and the new generation of management under von Bidder and Niccolini, knew that such complacency would destroy the ideal of The Four Seasons as it had been conceived a quarter century earlier: change was a good thing not for its own sake, but to keep things fresh and vital in an ever-mutating metropolis. The new goal was to prevent coveted titles like "classic" and "institution" from hardening the arteries of a thriving organism that might easily slip into middle age.

Kovi and Margittai therefore decided to celebrate The Four Seasons' well-earned status by shaking things up a bit and forcing the world to look upon the twenty-five-year-old restaurant as a dynamic, exciting place to dine. For starters, they asked Philip Johnson and his partner, John Burgee, to spruce up the decor, which included the installation of a dazzling shattered-glass divider edged in bronze between the Grill and the bar—an addition that remedied an omission that had long bothered Johnson. "We just plain overlooked the necessity of providing visual privacy from the bar for people sitting at the grill tables," he told *Interiors* magazine. Of course, in the early years, very few people were sitting at those grill tables, but with the success of the "power lunch," the need for "visual privacy" became obvious. Johnson also designed an $80,000 rug, with a pattern that had to be set by computer so that every diamond shape fell on precisely the same spot on every stairway step.

Kovi and Margittai also set into motion the plans for a yearlong birthday party for The Four Seasons, punctuated with an extravagant anniversary feast on June 16,

1984, for 650 of their "nearest and dearest friends and guests." To com-memorate the event, the owners produced a beautifully composed booklet entitled "One Hundred Seasons," whose endpapers were filled with celebrity autographs taken from *The Four Seasons* cookbook. There were gorgeous two-page color spreads of the dining rooms, a patrician-looking photo of Kovi and Margittai in front of the Picasso, a shot of Seppi Renggli being embraced by a Manhattan socialite, and a portrait of the restaurant's principals, maître d's, and bartenders. Also included was a witty minihistory of the past twenty-five years of world events, which irrev-erently sandwiched achievements such as astronaut John Glenn's space orbit around the earth with the victory dinner given for Sophia Loren at The Four Seasons after she won the Oscar in 1962 for her role in the film *Two Women*. A Hungarian Goose festival at the restaurant was given equal billing with the winning of the NBA championship by the New York Knicks in 1970, and the Rolling Stones' 1981 rock tour was commemo-rated right along with the historic "Down Coat Cloakroom Controversy" at The Four Seasons (an unfortunate media flub caused when Tom Margittai made an offhand remark to a *New York Times* reporter to the effect that only secretaries wore bulky down coats to dine at restaurants like The Four Seasons).

In their foreword to the booklet, Margittai and Kovi pulled out all the stops and dashed any false modesty, unblushingly placing The Four Seasons and New York into context the way a court poet might extol the omnipotence of imperial Rome:

> Over the span of 100 seasons our restaurant has evolved as the glitter-ing centerpiece of western civilization's premier metropolis. Here, at Manhattan's heart, the leaders of our creative society, men and women from every frontier of our dynamic culture, gather to dine. Amid grandeur, they shape bold ventures, consider abstractions, decide con-cretely. At The Four Seasons our guests reflect upon the arts, ascertain priorities, speak of great expectations, celebrate victories, find solace during stress, rebound from loss, toast the triumphs and bliss of being alive. Our restaurant offers culinary splendor in a setting of supreme elegance. Our restaurant is a vital evolving experience. The Four Seasons changes with each season as our gracious world within harmo-nizes with the changing natural world outside. For each new season there is a new menu. For each new season there are new plantings. For each new season there are new hues to match the changing leaves or the green, sprouting grass. Experimentation flourishes here as the

freshness of our seasonal variations parallels the freshness of an inventive society. The Four Seasons is a restaurant and more than a restaurant. Mies van der Rohe's glorious building is our home. Philip Johnson's exquisite design exalts our interior. Picasso greets our guests. The immutable creations of Lippold, Wegner, Stella, Blatas, Huxtable, Saarinen, and, now, Rosenquist make The Four Seasons an ornament of the quintessential civility of our grand city. The vitality of The Four Seasons, its restless creativity, its reverence for perfection in each nuance, are celebrations of the preciousness of life itself. May we always change.

We thank you for celebrating our joyous evolution, our 100 seasons.

The commissioning of a $100,000 painting by James Rosenquist for the private dining room continued The Four Seasons' commitment to fine art amid fine food. Standing left to right are Margittai, Johnson, Rosenquist, and Kovi.

The reference to "Rosenquist" was Kovi and Margittai's biggest surprise of the evening. In the middle of the booklet was a foldout picturing an original work of art by James Rosenquist specially commissioned by Margittai and Kovi at a cost of $100,000. The twenty-three-by-seven-and-a-half-foot canvas by one of the most celebrated artists of the New York School was striking, even startling when seen displayed against the wall of the upper private dining room (thereafter called the Rosenquist Room)—a blast of striated colors flanked by two seductive women's faces and crammed with red, pink, and white flowers underneath which swam two silvery trout. Seen from down below in the Pool Room, the enormous painting drew the eye upward, as in a cathedral one looks up at the altar.

Rosenquist was notorious for ignoring or not accepting commissions, but he was eager to take on The Four Seasons' project because he liked the company it would keep amid Mies's space and artwork by Picasso and Stella. According to Judith Goldman's study of the artist, Rosenquist told Margittai and Kovi, "I wanted to do fish, flowers, and ladies wrapped in

Saran Wrap, like the precious things you keep in the refrigerator. At the meeting I mentioned this to the owners; one of them looked a little worried, but no one said anything."

While Margittai and Kovi anxiously waited for the work to be done, Rosenquist was in Florida examining fish in a fish store, telling the restaurateurs he was "waiting for the fish to come in." He wanted the painting to have something of the spirit of Howard Chandler Christy's murals at New York's Café des Artistes—flirtatious nudes romping in a forest that strongly resembled Central Park. "I wanted to show happy ladies being happy about eating," said Rosenquist.

Working from photographs of fish and flowers, Rosenquist finished the oil painting in March and invited Margittai, Kovi, Philip Johnson (who had originally suggested Rosenquist), David Whitney, and artist Jasper Johns to see it at his studio. Everyone loved the work, then discussed what to call it. Johns got bored with the banter and interrupted, "Why should it have a title if the artist doesn't want to give it one?" Gallery owner Leo Castelli then arrived, applauded the work, and won over Rosenquist to the title *Flowers, Fish, and Females for The Four Seasons* to which the artist replied, "Not bad, Leo, not bad." The name stuck.

The evening of the birthday party was spectacular, even by the standards of The Four Seasons. It was to be a grand buffet for 650 guests, who would feast on raw shellfish, sweetbread and crayfish pâtés, lobster and capon, salmon and trout, and duck and goose. There was the famous salmon rillettes; tartare of snapper, salmon, and sturgeon; baby artichokes with calf's brains; four kinds of sushi; crisp roast duck; ravioli stuffed with lobster; roast saddle of lamb in salt crust; a gratin of frogs' legs and rabbit;

The painting was entitled "Flowers, Fish, and Females for The Four Seasons." It measured 23 by 7.5 feet in length.

double sirloin of beef with peppers; shrimp and chicken curry; sambals of aromatic rice; striped bass with fennel; cold roast loin of veal with tuna sauce; zucchini; and buckwheat noodles. Three tables were set just for desserts. The liquors served were from fine houses—Chivas Regal, Beefeater's gin, Grand Marnier, Stolichnaya vodka, and a good sampling of Seagram's products. The wines were first rate, including three vintage Champagnes, Mayacamus Cabernet Sauvignon, and Château Mouton-Rothschild '78.

The guest list that night included friends of the house like Mayor Ed Koch; art dealer Leo Castelli; editors and publishers Jacqueline Onassis of Viking Press, Tina Brown of *Vanity Fair*, Helen Gurley Brown of *Cosmopolitan*, Lee Eisenberg of *Esquire*, Michael Korda of Simon & Schuster, Cathleen Black of *USA Today*, Andrew Heiskell of *Time*, and Abe Rosenthal of the *New York Times*; novelist Tom Wolfe; wine maker Robert Mondavi; fashion designers Bill Blass, Oscar de la Renta, Perry Ellis, Calvin Klein, Ralph Lauren, and Pauline Trigere; media personalities Tom Brokaw, Diane Sawyer, and David Susskind; and actor Gregory Peck. James Rosenquist was on hand to unveil his new painting. Perhaps most important of all, the party reunited many of those who had been there at the beginning, the men and women who had dreamed up The Four Seasons and seen it through its germination, birth, and growth over various periods in its history—Joe Baum, Phyllis Lambert, Philip Johnson, James Beard, Richard Lippold, Garth Huxtable, George Lang, Stuart Levin, Alan Lewis, George Lois, Alan Reyburn, and Fred Rufe. It was a good opportunity to thank those special people who had made The Four Seasons the world's most famous restaurant and then gone on to other grandiose projects.

Although he never did another restaurant after The Four Seasons, Philip Johnson went on to design many of the most important and influential buildings in America, including the New York State Theater at Lincoln Center for the Performing Arts, the Kline Science Tower at Yale University, Pennzoil Place in Houston, and the AT&T Building in New York, whose style harked back to a more classic skyscraper that had enormous influence on subsequent urban architecture. In 1978 Johnson received the American Institute of Architecture's highest award, the gold medal.

After overseeing the creation of the Seagram Building and The Four Seasons, the indefatigable Phyllis Lambert went on to study architecture at Yale and earned a master's degree under Mies at the Illinois Institute of

An invitation to The Four Seasons' twenty-fifth anniversary party was among the most sought-after prizes of New York's social whirl in 1984.

Technology. For her work on the Los Angeles Biltmore Hotel she received a National Honor Award from the American Institute of Architects, and the Massey Medal of the Royal Architectural Institute of Canada was awarded to the Saidye Bronfman Centre for Jewish culture which she designed.

Lambert eventually moved back to Montreal, where she was in the forefront of the fight to save historic sections of the city and went on to build the Canadian Centre for Architecture there.

Within months of leaving RA in 1970, Joe Baum had recovered his health and bounced back with a project that dwarfed anything he had ever done—the creation of Windows on the World, a restaurant on the 107th floor of what was then the tallest building in the world, New York's World Trade Center.

Baum would go on to develop other restaurants in the World Trade Center and, later, several more in the World Financial Center next door. Ten years after opening Windows, Baum announced that he and his partners, Michael Whiteman and Dennis Sweeney, would build their own restaurant called Aurora in midtown Manhattan. Believing that the executives he had once courted at The Four Seasons had finally come around to appreciating fine cuisine, Baum brought over a Michelin two-star chef from France, Gerard Pangaud, to man the kitchens and stole away a master wine steward named Ray Wellington from Windows on the World.

As the New York economy soured, so did Aurora, which closed three years after opening. Shrugging off the failure and loss, Baum threw himself into an even bigger project he'd already been working on—the $25 million renovation of the grand Rainbow Room on the sixty-fifth floor of Rockefeller Center.

With its marvelous art deco appointments, its twenty-foot windows looking out over all five boroughs, and its revolving dance floor with two bands, the room was returned by Baum and Whiteman to a level of glamour many believed had faded from New York nightlife. Baum even brought back some of the dishes from the old days—*pigeon en cocotte* the way it had been done at the Colony, oysters Rockefeller, tournedos Rossini, and, since he could never resist a flame, baked Alaska for dessert.

In the years after leaving RA, Jerry Brody acquired two of New York's most historic institutions—a Broadway speakeasy-turned-steakhouse named Gallagher's and the magnificent Grand Central Oyster Bar, opened in 1913 in Grand Central Terminal. At the Oyster Bar he scraped away decades of grime and ugly aquamarine-blue paint that covered the glori-

Actor Gregory Peck would always call to make his own reservations by saying, "Hello, this is Gregory Peck, and I'd like a table at eight o'clock," then hang up, certain he would not be disappointed.

ous tiled archways (done by Rafael Guastavino, who later did similar work at the Ellis Island Terminal), and made the place over into one of America's great seafood restaurants. Brody also ran the Rainbow Room for more than a decade.

After departing from RA, George Lang became one of the most respected innovators in the restaurant world. He wrote the authoritative *Cuisine of Hungary* (1971) and took on a long-running restaurant column for *Travel & Leisure* magazine. Lang developed scores of new restaurants in countries around the world, including Canada, Germany, the Philippines, and Greece. But, like other RA veterans of the 1950s and 1960s, he had an abiding nostalgia for restaurants that once seemed to symbolize the soul of a city, opulent places where money flowed as freely as champagne and the discussion of art, music, and literature.

When asked if he'd be interested in buying the famous but tatty Café des Artistes on West Sixty-seventh Street, Lang, who lived on the same block, took on the challenge of renovating the restaurant's reputation out of love rather than horse sense. He restored the notorious nude paintings by Howard Chandler Christy and made the Café over into one of New York's most celebrated and celebratory restaurants, a stone's throw from Lincoln Center for the Performing Arts, from which it drew many of its patrons. Eventually Lang would return to his home country, Hungary, and do for Budapest's famous Gundel restaurant what he'd done for Café des Artistes in New York.

Meanwhile, Stuart Levin, after his tenure at The Four Seasons, tried to keep another legend alive—the late Henri Soulé's Le Pavillon; but he could never maintain the spirit of the place without Soulé, and the restaurant was finally shuttered in 1972. Levin later ran the Top of the Park restaurant above Central Park. Crippled by a muscular disease in the 1980s, Levin was bound to a wheelchair, but today he continues to teach classes on restaurant management.

Restaurant Associates itself had come a long way since its tailspin in the late 1960s. Under president and C.E.O. Max Pine, RA divested itself of unprofitable properties and emerged from the 1970s a much stronger company. Never again, however, would RA go after the deluxe restaurant market. The company continued to own and run the Brasserie in the Seagram Building, Mamma Leone's (relocated to a site on West Forty-fourth Street), Trattoria and other eateries in the Pan Am Building, and, right under the gazes of Joe Baum at the Rainbow Room and the statue of Prometheus, the American Festival Cafe and the Sea Grill, flanking the

OPPOSITE PAGE: The glass divider in the Grill Room affords privacy between the dining area and the bar.

skating rink at Rockefeller Circle. RA also ran the food concessions at the U.S. Open and the Publick House in Old Sturbridge Village, Massachusetts and had numerous service contracts to operate eateries in museums and the United Nations. (In April 1990, Restaurant Associates was taken over by a Japanese food company named Kyotaru, and today it grosses more than a quarter of a billion dollars annually.)

Thus, while the glory days of RA had long passed, many of its alumni were doing better than ever in their careers, tending to the care and feeding of the very people they had been courting for more than two decades.

As Kovi and Margittai had hoped, their anniversary party ignited a whole new burst of media attention, from the architecture and shelter magazines that assessed how well Mies's and Johnson's design had worn over a quarter century to those in the food press who used the restaurant as a signpost of all that had occurred in American gastronomy over the past three decades. *Interiors* magazine called it a "glistening model of enduring design integrity" and praised Johnson's addition of the glass panels and Rosenquist's new painting. *New York* magazine's restaurant critic, Gael Greene, in a breathless paean (complete with knuckle rappings about some of the food), summed up the what the restaurant had come to mean to New York: "Like New York, the Four Seasons can seem awesome, stark, and intimidating. Like New York, it is sentimental, brashly affectionate, and a pushover for any sad tale. This is the Four Seasons at 25. The obsessed, gifted, flamboyant, tyrannical, generous visionaries who shaped its form and style dreamed it would become precisely what it is today."

Ironically, the twenty-fifth anniversary also goosed the management of The Four Seasons into the realization that their work had just begun. Having pronounced their workplace a restaurant of unwavering and timeless classical standards as well as a restaurant for the future, they now had to maintain that balance ad infinitum. That meant enormous expenditures of money just to keep things running in peak condition and at a minimum of discomfort to their guests. When Kovi and Margittai spent a half million dollars in 1988 to "spruce up" the place, the *Wall Street Journal* reported that despite the new glass divider and rugs, new table settings, and a Rosenquist mural, the patrons of the restaurant hadn't noticed much change at all, much to their common satisfaction. Kovi and Margittai couldn't have been happier.

Two of the original creative personalities of The Four Seasons—Philip Johnson (left) and James Beard (right), with von Bidder in the center—celebrate the restaurant's twenty-fifth anniversary in 1984.

The commitment to subtle change and correction was crucial to the survival of The Four Seasons, but Margittai and Kovi realized their own energies were beginning to flag. By the mid-1980s the two men were nearing sixty, trying to slow down, turning over much of the day-to-day operations of The Four Seasons to von Bidder and Niccolini. Von Bidder still planned the banquets, oversaw labor negotiations, and handled the business side. Niccolini had become increasingly impassioned about wine and soon made himself master of the thirty-thousand-bottle wine cellar. There was talk that, little by little, if everything went well, von Bidder and Niccolini would become the heirs apparent by receiving enough stock eventually to take over The Four Seasons.

There was no question that Kovi and Margittai, as éminences grises, were crucial to the perpetuation of The Four Seasons' image. Yet when asked about their continuing presence in the dining rooms, Margittai seemed resigned to admit, "There comes a point when people who go out to dine at places like The Four Seasons don't want to see two old men hobbling around. It's simply not very appealing." Regulars had come to depend on von Bidder and Niccolini for their care and feeding, but Kovi and Margittai represented the unchanging face of genteel grace, and despite The Four Seasons' New York swagger, they were a definite link to a kind of Old World hospitality that was fast on the wane in the so-called go-go eighties.

But other changes were occurring around them that spelled potential trouble, primarily the fact that in 1980 Seagram had sold the Seagram Building for $70.5 million (and the land for another $15 million) to the Teachers Insurance and Annuity Association/College Retirement Equities Fund (TIAA/CREF). And despite a cordial landlord-tenant relationship with The Four Seasons, nothing in the lease (which ends in 1999) guaranteed the restaurant's survival. Indeed, if Kovi and Margittai left The Four Seasons or could not renew their lease, nothing could prevent their landlord from completely gutting The Four Seasons and turning it into an appliance store or yuppie gym.

TIAA/CREF did see the value in protecting the integrity of the Seagram Building and had agreed as part of the sale to propose the building for landmark status when it turned the requisite thirty years old. But no such guarantees were made to Margittai and Kovi. The New York Landmarks Preservation Commission, which had been formed in the 1960s to save the city's great buildings from the same sad fate suffered by Pennsylvania Station (demolished in 1962) and the disgraceful desecration of Grand Central Terminal (by the emplacement of the Pan Am Building atop it), was quite anxious to award the Seagram Building and The Four Seasons landmark status, and TIAA/CREF had no problem with the former structure; it was the latter they opposed.

Landmark status is a double-edged sword. On the one hand, it seems to protect a beautiful or historic building from being razed or compromised architecturally; on the other, it prevents an owner or tenant from changing anything about the building. A 1973 amendment to the first landmark law in 1969 expanded the commission's jurisdiction by charging it with promoting the use of interior landmarks "for the education, pleasure, and welfare of the people of the city."

Simple maintenance of such buildings can be prohibitively expensive and improvements may take years to be approved, so many owners simply walk away from such structures, which may afterward fall into neglect and ruin. Thus, while landmark status protects an existing building from radical change, it does not protect it from the wrecker's ball.

Kovi and Margittai, therefore, were honored that The Four Seasons was being considered for landmark status but knew the pitfalls and expense involved merely in getting it. Only one other restaurant interior in New

One day Philip Johnson fell on the steps coming off Fifty-third Street and split open his eyebrow, which bled profusely. After being told by Margittai that he should have it looked at, Johnson went to the hospital, leaving his lunch guest alone. When Johnson returned half an hour later with a bandaged eye, he was upset that his guest had not waited for him.

York—Brooklyn's Gage & Tollner, built circa 1890—had landmark status. The 106-year-old German restaurant Lüchow's on Fourteenth Street had landmark status for its exterior, but since the former owners had closed the place, both the interior and the facade were left to decay, and no one was interested in taking over a very costly, outdated building.

While this seemed unlikely to happen to Mies van der Rohe's midtown masterpiece, there was nothing to prevent it. There had been serious talk about razing the famous Lever House, just across Park Avenue, because it was too small to realize the kinds of profits attainable from a taller, more massive skyscraper. The fact that Lever House was granted landmark status in 1983 made its destruction more difficult, but not impossible, in the future.

The process of landmarking is a lengthy and costly one, and Kovi and Margittai had to prepare an enormous amount of documentation and support, even though the landmark commission was squarely on their side. TIAA/CREF vice president Philip Di Gennaro opposed granting such status to the restaurant because, he argued, the space might be worth more if it were not forever designated a restaurant. Ironically, Seagram itself was queasy about seeing the artwork it had long lent to The Four Seasons locked into place there, even though Phyllis Lambert pleaded with the commission that "one just has to imagine the loss of presence were the restaurant not there, or it being a bank or private offices." Di Gennaro countered that without the artwork and furnishings, the space would be "a void, without any particular architectural character."

Many of New York's most powerful tastemakers and art historians were happy to testify on behalf of The Four Seasons' position, and a long, detailed description of the historic design and furnishings of the restaurant was presented to the commission, acknowledging the uniqueness of the restaurant. Finally, on October 3, 1989, the commission issued its decree, granting landmark status to the space but tying it exclusively to use as a restaurant. The final report asserted that The Four Seasons' interior "has a special character, special historical and aesthetic interest and value as part of the development, heritage, and cultural characteristics of New York City." It cited the accomplishments of Johnson and Restaurant Associates in creating an interior of extraordinary and refined beauty that had been impeccably maintained by Kovi and Margittai and noted that "the distinctive design of the interior spaces and the exceptional culinary reputation of the Four Seasons make it a cultural magnet for tourists as well as New York's elite."

The designation left open the question of the status of Seagram's loaned artwork and furnishings, and TIAA/CREF immediately appealed the decision to the New York City Board of Estimates, contending that the designation "effectively prevents future adaption of the space" and "unduly and unfairly enhanced the interest and position of the tenant, while at the same time effectively restricting TIAA's ownership rights."

The appeal meant more time, effort, money, and lawyers on Kovi and Margittai's part, but again, influential, longtime friends rallied to their support. One of the most impassioned and eloquent was Bill O'Shaughnessy, president of two radio stations in Westchester County, who in his plea before the board made a case for The Four Seasons as a public trust protected and overseen by the zeal of two immigrants from Eastern Europe. "I didn't come before you to plead for a watering spot for tycoons and titans," said O'Shaughnessy. "There are many of those abroad in the land—thousands of restaurants and hundreds of private clubs for them to do their deals and commerce. I'm here for Tom Margittai and for Paul Kovi, who have lovingly and relentlessly held this serene and special place in their enlightened care and keeping for thirty years. Margittai and Kovi fled from the oppression and tyranny of Hungary and Transylvania, one of them from a concentration camp. They came to our country as young men, carrying with them the creative and artistic souls that contributed so much to their stewardship of The Four Seasons. They started as apprentices, waiters. And now they are the permittees. But they know who they are—and where they came from. They want only to preserve that beauty, that great design, that art which was given to them. So, I'm here for *them*. And for what they would have you do. Looking beyond their own purse, they have created the *quintessential New York restaurant*. And with sensitivity, Old World grace, and an innate sense of hospitality they bring to everything they do, Margittai and Kovi have made it accessible and beckoning to hundreds of thousands of ordinary people—not alone to those tycoons and corporate chieftains who favor the place."

On October 15, 1993, a New York Court of Appeals unanimously dismissed the challenge of the Teachers Insurance Association, thereby protecting the "architectural style, design, general arrangement, and components" of The Four Seasons, noting in its decision that both the building's exterior and interior "have been acclaimed as quintessential expressions of the International Style" and that "no one disputes their special historical and aesthetic interest."

1991 CHARDONNAY
NAPA VALLEY
THE FOUR SEASONS
CELLARED AND BOTTLED BY THE FOUR SEASONS CELLARS
NAPA, CALIFORNIA • ALCOHOL 13.4% BY VOLUME

As any restaurateur will tell you, the perfect customer is a middle-aged New York Republican C.E.O. with a cholesterol count of 180 and a brand-new, second, wife. If he's Jewish and really likes to eat, so much the better.

Healthy, wealthy, and able to afford to eat anything he wants without guilt and with enormous pleasure, such a man likes nothing better than to bask in the spotlight a fine restaurant affords him, a place to show that he's a mensch, a pillar of the community for whom a good table, good food, good wine, and a good wife are manifestations of his refinement and place in the world. And—with the exception of the wife—fifty percent is tax deductible.

In the mid-1980s New York was full of such men and a growing number of women who had taken their place at the tables of power in restaurants like La Grenouille, Lutèce, and The Four Seasons. Whatever "Reaganomics" or "voodoo economics" meant for the future, an awful lot of people were getting rich by going along with the charade.

But despite the continued success of such old-line Manhattan restaurants, new, more casual restaurants started to make a dent in their polished veneers of impregnability. The experiments with nouvelle cuisine, the development of more healthful menus, the increased interest in American wines—all changes The Four Seasons had helped pioneer—seemed antithetical to the old way

Chapter Twelve

One Hundred Sixty Seasons and Counting

When former president Ronald Reagan was wined and dined by Christopher Forbes of *Forbes* magazine and several colleagues, they tried hard to get Reagan to comment on world affairs and politics. But Reagan merely ate his appetizer, main course, and two desserts and drank white wine, oblivious to their questions. He then exited, waved to a crowd outside the restaurant, and, when asked for autographs, handed out a stack of business cards with his signature and presidential seal on them.

of doing things. Young, energetic entrepreneurs who had no previous experience in running restaurants were garnering media attention for "retrochic" eating places that drew young, energetic style makers. A shabby converted luncheonette in SoHo with no name on a graffiti-scrawled door would have limos parked outside to disgorge the season's hottest German models, Hollywood actors, and British rock singers. Italian trattorias serving pizzas and pastas could do three hundred covers each night, and no one seemed to care if there was a two-hour wait for a table because the crowd was so glamorous, even while dressed in torn blue jeans and black T-shirts.

Being among the first to try out a new restaurant in a scruffy neighborhood became still another form of fashion one-upmanship; indeed, an article in *New York* magazine gave a name to people's ravenous appetite for eating out—"restaurant madness." "More and more people feel entitled to what was once the preserve of the wealthy," wrote author Patricia Morrisroe, "and in accommodating these people, restaurateurs have democratized dining."

The Old Guard restaurants that had for so long catered to a regular, faithful, and dressy clientele found many of their customers moving out of New York, retiring, or just plain dying off, while their sons and daughters headed to Chelsea, TriBeCa, and the Lower East Side for a night out. Suddenly restaurants that had not seen an empty table for decades noticed more and more expanses of white linen on unoccupied tables. Rooms once reserved for newcomers and nobodies were being closed off because there was no one to fill them. And chefs who had not kept up with the evolution of taste in America found their customers asking for foods and ingredients they'd never heard of, like carpaccio, extra-virgin olive oil, balsamic vinegar, portobello mushrooms, and tiramisù.

Many of the old-timers just couldn't survive because they simply couldn't—or wouldn't—change with the times. Once glamorous restaurants like Orsini's, Le Madrigal, San Marco, Trader Vic's, Perigord Park, and Quo Vadis—still serving the tired clichés of continental cuisine—floundered and then were gone by the end of the decade. Others struggled mightily to survive. For years the "21" Club had been losing customers and cachet, until the old jokes about bad food and outrageous prices were no longer funny and tables went begging for customers. In 1986 this dinosaur was bought by carpet magnate Marshall Cogan for $21 million. Cogan poured another $9 million into its renovation and brought in new management and chefs to revive the dreary kitchen. Aged waiters and captains were fired and a younger staff hired, causing the waiters' union to throw up a picket line outside the famous iron gates.

Yet despite Cogan's attempt to maintain the look and feel of the old "21," many of the restaurant's steady customers were disappointed by the clean, well-lighted, renovated look of the place; even more so, they hated the new food. Regulars were embarrassed and outraged when new chef Anne Rosenzweig made a snide remark to the press that she'd changed the beloved "21" chicken hash "by adding some chicken to the recipe." Eventually, with some major retooling and stroking by management, the old-timers came back and new faces tried the place out. The "21" Club did survive and thrive, but until it did, it was an expensive tightrope for Cogan to walk.

When Barbara Bush arrived for a lunch in her honor, von Bidder greeted her and asked the First Lady if this was her first time dining at The Four Seasons. She looked at him and replied, "Young man, I have no idea where I am."

Meanwhile The Four Seasons was doing just fine, enjoying the biggest profits in its history and an image of still being where the action was. The Grill Room was packed every day, parties filled the private dining rooms, and no one seemed to care that entrée prices had hit $40 and more in the Pool Room.

From its preeminent position as the power dining room of international business, The Four Seasons seemed immune to the vagaries of fad and fashion; as originally conceived, the change of decor, trees, and menus each season continued to give the thirty-year-old restaurant a freshness others couldn't match. As other posh eateries came and went, The Four Seasons sailed on, secure, profitable, and rather smug.

But in the late 1980s it was not gradual changes in taste or flash-in-the-pan fads and fashions that came to cripple the restaurant industry as a

Left: Mr. and Mrs. Herb Siegel, Mr. and Mrs. Arthur Liman, and Mr. John Veronis. Right: CC Kieselstein with Mary Tyler Moore and her husband, Dr. Robert Levine

whole. It was a single, defining moment that exploded the foil-thin skin that had enveloped the gaseous world economy.

Julian Niccolini sensed the depth of the crisis the moment he arrived at work on October 19, 1987. "It was extremely quiet in the Grill Room that day," he recalls, "as if a bomb had dropped. All our regular customers were there, but nobody was talking. The room was absolutely still, and people were going to the phone every fifteen minutes to find out how much the Dow Jones had fallen. Liquor sales were way up that afternoon."

What had happened that day? Merely what the chairman of the New York Stock Exchange described as "the nearest thing to a meltdown that I ever want to see." On that day, the stock market took a devastating plunge of 508 points.

The upstairs dining room with the newly-installed Rosenquist.

There had been ominous signs that something like this might happen: the economy had been so overheated and stocks so inflated (the Dow Jones had topped out at a record 2,722.42 in late August) that the market was due for a "correction." It came on Friday, October 16, when the Dow dropped precipitously by 108 points. But when Monday's markets opened, the real horror began. By the end of the day $500 billion in stock equity had been wiped out, and the Dow had plum-meted by 36 percent—almost three times the decline on the infamous Black Friday of 1929. At Shearson-Lehman Brothers, someone posted a sign reading "To the lifeboats!"

At The Four Seasons that day the order went out to carry on as if noth-ing had happened, to function as a kind of oasis of serenity in a world turned upside down. "I tried very hard that day to put up a tough screen," says Niccolini. "It was even tougher the next day, because by then every-body knew just how much they'd lost."

The party was over. With a $2 trillion debt, the United States had spent itself into impotency, and the failures of banks, the junk bond market, and real estate and brokerage houses were swift that fall and winter. No one felt the blow as immediately as the restaurateurs of New York, although the shock waves were felt soon afterward in restaurants around the coun-try. Business dropped by double digits all over town. House accounts were canceled overnight, expense accounts were cut, and with more than fifty thousand jobs lost on Wall Street alone, free-spending customers disappeared into the unemployment lines. That this happened in autumn meant a double whammy for restaurants, because companies began to cancel the kinds of lavish Christmas and New Year's parties that formed a major part of restaurant business.

Curiously, business at The Four Seasons did not go into an immediate tailspin. The regulars kept coming, the holiday parties held strong. So, in their "14th annual love letter to New Yorkers" printed in various magazines at year's end, Kovi and Margittai, still smiling from the steps of The Four Seasons, mentioned nothing unusual about the business climate in New York. The ad spoke of Philip Johnson and John Burgee's refinements of the Grill Room's decor, the success of the seventh annual Bordeaux dinner (celebrating the 1984 vintage), and the arrival of a new pastry chef, Alain Roby. They did mention that "late dinners appear to be more and more popular in Manhattan." Every-thing seemed to be going just fine.

"A day or two after the crash things seemed back to normal in the Grill," recalls von Bidder, "and relatively few people canceled their holiday party plans. But on the day after New Year's, you could have thrown a chair through the restaurant and not hit anyone."

Throughout the fall many regulars too ashamed not to show up two or three times a week for lunch continued to do so. But in the background accountants were sharpening their pencils: by the turn of the year, massive cuts began. Companies drew up lists of exactly how much might be spent for a business meal and at what restaurants it could be spent. At the top of many companies' no-no list was The Four Seasons, judged to epitomize the kind of conspicuous consumption fast becoming unfashionable. All of a sudden the idea of spending $40 on a piece of fish or meat and $8.50 for a slice of cake seemed unacceptable. As the leases on yuppies' BMWs ran out, so did their expense accounts, and The Four Seasons, among many restaurants of its ilk, never saw many of its faithful clientele again. One night soon after the turn of the year, Niccolini counted heads in the restau-

Joan and Sandy Weill celebrating his sixtieth birthday with former president Gerald Ford. The Pool Room was transformed into an Adirondack summer camp, complete with canoe, stuffed grizzly bear, and live trout in the pool.

It was the only Sunday in March in recent memory to record a two-foot snowfall—which further authenticated the theme.

rant and said with a sigh: "Tonight we had four hundred covers. To most people that sounds great, until you know that last year on this same evening we did five hundred. That's a twenty percent drop."

Overpriced restaurants that depended almost exclusively on expense account customers started dropping away—Le Cygne, Laurent, the Gloucester House, and Da Nanni closed their doors after long runs. Maxwell's Plum, one of the most profitable restaurants in American dining history, but one dependent largely on big spenders who arrived in limos and left with young ladies, went under. Régine's, a caviar-and-champagne disco for the jet set, locked its doors for renovation and never reopened. Pierre Cardin's garish reproduction of Maxim de Paris flopped. Even celebrated temples of gastronomy like Lutèce, Chanterelle, and Le Cirque

At The Four Seasons' annual Through-the-Kitchen Party: (From left to right) Ivana Trump with Riccardo Mazuchelli and Lauren Veronis; Henry Kissinger and Joe Armstrong.

no longer had three-week waiting lists, and lunch tables were no longer so difficult to come by. The most expensive restaurant in the United States— the Quilted Giraffe, in the Philip Johnson–designed AT&T Building— eventually closed, and its owners, Barry and Susan Wine, went to work for Sony, which had bought the building at the end of the 1980s.

There was another body blow to the restaurant industry in 1988, when Congress cut back the tax deductibility of business meals to 80 percent of the bill. Now those who once thought nothing of ordering a $150 bottle of Bordeaux made do with a glass of house wine. Those who could never resist caviar before now found self-discipline a virtue. Indeed, an antipleasure syndrome set in, so that it seemed that more and more chastened executives—at least those who still had a job—adapted a more ascetic diet, which usually boiled down to the cheaper items on the menu. After all, a slab of fat-rich foie gras at The Four Seasons cost $25 as an appetizer and chateaubriand with béarnaise went for $45, while a more monastic bowl of consommé cost only $9 and scallops wrapped in vegetables went for a mere $34.

The casual visitor, however, could hardly tell that anything had changed at The Four Seasons. True, you might get a reservation on short notice, even for lunch that afternoon if you called that morning. And you might be asked if you'd prefer the Pool Room or the Grill rather than be seated entirely at Alex von Bidder's discretion. Ironically, the whole place took on a more relaxed atmosphere, and the intimidation factor that had for so long compromised the genteel service at The Four Seasons seemed to dissipate. Access to the restaurant seemed easier, the doorman smiled more broadly, and at the top of the stairs everyone welcomed newcomers, if not

with open arms, at least with a friendly demeanor that put people at ease at once.

In their 1988 "15th annual love letter to New Yorkers," Margittai and Kovi began by proclaiming, "Oh, what a year it was!"—a seeming reference to the crash of the market and the onset of a long recession. But the copy picked up from there with nothing but upbeat news, such as the awarding of landmark status to The Four Seasons, the success of the eighth annual Bordeaux dinner, the hiring of another new pastry chef, Patrick Lemble, and the award by *M* magazine to Julian Niccolini as "best wine picker in New York." There was also notice that a local dining guide survey had named The Four Seasons "The Overall Most Popular Restaurant in New York City," something of an exaggeration if simple numbers of customers had been the criterion.

There was also the announcement—which would have raised eyebrows

Left: Vernon Jordan and Barbara Walters; Center: TV personalities Maury Povich and Connie Chung; Right: Beverly Sills and her husband, Peter Greenough.

My older son lives in Florida and when he comes to New York with his family, I like to share the best of New York with them. Some years ago they were visiting and I arranged to take them to The Four Seasons. The three children were young but not too young to enjoy fine dining. We were seated at a large table in the Pool Room and as the captain passed menus to the ladies, my daughter-in-law mentioned that no prices were listed. The captain said the menus with prices were only for the gentlemen. My nine-year-old grandson was suitably impressed at being handed a menu with prices. His eyes sparkled, and he sat up straight and began to read it.

Just then someone (I think it was my other son) remarked that he had never noticed that the ceilings were so high. My nine-year-old grandson, mindful of his very modest personal allowance, immediately said, "That's to make it harder for someone to hit the ceiling when they see these prices."
—Julia Schwartz,
   Park Tower Group

only among regulars and restaurant industry people—that the Grill Room now featured a pretheater dinner to complement the long-standing pretheater dinner in the Pool Room. The implementation of such a fixed-price meal ($41.50) in the Grill was not the result of overwhelming public demand, but a way to spark some kind of evening business in the Grill. Prices in the Pool Room remained as stratospheric as ever.

Behind the scenes, for the first time in more than a decade, the management of The Four Seasons was, like that of every other restaurant in New York, scrambling for every customer it could get. The staff at The Four Seasons had to get used to the occasional Japanese businessman who would have too much to drink and slump over into his dinner plate as the rest of his colleagues went on with their own meals and carousing.

The Four Seasons continued to get notice in the press, but increasingly the continuing, irresistible allure of the "power lunch" story far outweighed the food media's interest in the restaurant's food. Article after article read like guest lists of The Four Seasons' clientele, with nary a mention of the food. But there were rumblings among the food press that The Four Seasons was coasting in the kitchen.

On the occasion of the restaurant's twenty-fifth anniversary in 1984, *New York* magazine's Gael Greene wrote a memoir of the restaurant, noting that while The Four Seasons still "glows with a mythic vitality," the food was "wildly uneven. . . . I've slept through dinners without a stirring mouthful," she wrote, "and I've thrilled to dazzling savor," noting "occasional missteps and mediocrity."

While other food critics continued to pay the restaurant a certain homage, others began to complain of what clearly seemed to be a case of the emperor's new clothes syndrome developing in the kitchen. Mimi Sheraton, a consultant to The Four Seasons back in the RA days, harshly criticized the restaurant while she was food critic for the *New York Times* in the 1980s, and later in her own 1989 restaurant guide, she gave the food only one star out of four. A year later *New York Newsday*'s restaurant critic, Jane Freiman, blasted The Four Seasons for "greasy hazelnut crumbs," "hideously overcooked" veal, "rubberized grilled shrimp," and "sickeningly sweet desserts," dropping the restaurant from three stars to one, calling it "a sad state of affairs for one of New York's most enduring institutions—a culinary legend that is running the risk of becoming a myth."

Margittai and Kovi were of course stung by such reviews and characterizations, but behind the smiling, seemingly self-satisfied masks, the two

men knew that Freiman was right. Kovi even told a reporter, "The article was basically a correct one." The kitchen at The Four Seasons had become inconsistent, turning out breathtaking feasts on a special occasion, then serving up rather dull food during the day. More often than not, the regular customers couldn't have cared less, and Margittai and Kovi had never made a secret of catering to the plain, simple tastes of people who admitted that food was never really the point of going to The Four Seasons. After all, many regulars ate nothing but grilled fish with a bottle of Perrier on the side, while others consumed only cornflakes at lunch. Kovi and Margittai still spoke of serving only the finest beef, veal, and truffles money could buy, but the prepared food on the plate was not always exciting enough to justify the $40 customers paid. What Mark Twain had once said about a hotel seemed completely applicable to The Four Seasons in the late 1980s: "It used to be a good hotel, but that proves nothing—I used to be a good boy, for that matter."

It was also becoming increasingly obvious to the staff that chef Seppi Renggli, who had been making an astonishing $200,000 a year, had at fifty-

The kitchen and dining room staff of The Four Seasons on the stairway of The Pool Room. A survey of restaurant-goers voted The Four Seasons the number-one most popular restaurant in New York City for three years in a row beginning in 1989.

In 1986, my wife and I took my wife's sister to The Four Seasons to celebrate her twenty-fourth birthday. We were all looking forward to a quiet evening as well as a memorable meal. However, this was the night the New York Mets eventually beat the Houston Astros seven to six in a sixteen-inning baseball playoff game that had all New York following every pitch for nearly five hours. It was simply impossible for me to relax not knowing what was happening.

Luckily, our waiter was a baseball fan also, and he was listening to the game on the radio in the kitchen whenever he went to pick up food. Each time he'd walk by me I was handed a slip of paper with the game's current status. Things like "bottom of the 14th, still tie score, one out, Ray Knight is up."

To this day, I still think about that game every time I walk on Fifty-second Street between Park and Lexington.

—Steven Schragis,
  Publisher,
  Carol Publishing Group

eight become tired and lost much of his initiative and drive after seventeen years at The Four Seasons. In fact, he'd asked for less responsibility in the kitchen and was often away from the stoves. He still loved to cook: indeed, he was never happier than when cooking a special dish for a regular customer. But too often this intensity did not enliven a kitchen that needed new direction, and there was no doubt that The Four Seasons' culinary reputation had stagnated.

Bolstered by the urgings of von Bidder and Niccolini, who had taken on more and more responsibility at the restaurant, Kovi and Margittai asked Renggli to step down and consider a position as consultant to the restaurant until the end of the year. Renggli's removal in April 1990 made the newspapers, and Margittai and Kovi found themselves fielding questions from reporters after Renggli told of being summarily dismissed after seventeen years on the job. Kovi put the best face on a delicate situation, telling reporters, "We have great respect for Seppi, but the time came for the separation in a long marriage. Really, we just found that we have to go in a different direction, in a different style."

The executive chef's position was given over to two men, Hitsch Albin, who had worked side by side with Renggli since the RA days, and Stefano Battistini, an Italian most recently from New York's Sea Grill—ironically a Restaurant Associates property that immediately hired Renggli. Hedging his bets, Margittai gave an interview to *New York Newsday* about the changes in the kitchen, telling reporter Cara DeSilva, "It became necessary to change the guard in order to go back to where we were five years ago. That was when we started living on our old reputation instead of moving on. But I remember when we were always the first, the first to bring in crayfish, fiddlehead ferns, salsify, the first to start featuring American cuisine, the first to offer Spa Cuisine. But we stopped, and now we have to restore ourselves in the forefront of change."

Like Renggli, Albin was a very shy man with the public and press, despite the fact that he was a vocal practical joker in the kitchen. While expediting orders, he would slam a metal rod onto the counter to get attention, and he had a tremendous ability to put out hundreds of dinners each night with efficiency. He had never sought the top chef's job, nor had he in any way tried to undermine Renggli, with whom he was still friends. He also had no desire to turn The Four Seasons' traditions upside down in the name of novelty; instead he sought to modify the menu according to the seasons and to let it evolve.

Not wanting to make the same mistakes the "21" Club had—alienating regular customers with an entirely new culinary direction—Kovi and Margittai waited until summer before introducing new seasonal items onto The Four Seasons' menu. In a press release they announced to the world that

> The secret of The Four Seasons' success reflects uncompromising quality and personal supervision—together with a *vision*. Ours is *not* a restaurant like any other restaurant. It is an ever-changing cultural, social, and culinary experience—not just a clubhouse for the rich and famous. We present Chefs Albin, Battistini, and [pastry chef] Lemble's gastronomic glories in a sybaritic environment envisioned by Mies van der Rohe and designed by Philip Johnson. Reflecting the fast-paced lifestyle of New Yorkers, The Four Seasons changes with each season, so our world within harmonizes with nature's world without. For each new season there are new plantings and new culinary achievements. The vitality of The Four Seasons, its restless creativity, its reverence for perfection in each nuance, are celebrations of the preciousness of life itself. May we always change.

However familiar much of that rhetoric sounded to those who had followed the ups and downs of The Four Seasons' history since the days of Joe Baum, Jerry Brody, and Philip Johnson, by writing it down again in 1990, Margittai and Kovi were reminding themselves of the personal and professional necessity of rebirth and renewal. For while they were signaling a profound change in the way The Four Seasons would be run in the next decade, they were also returning it to the original vision set in motion back in 1959. They had been coasting for too long, buoyed by good times and full coffers.

Maybe it never was the food that brought customers to the restaurant. Maybe it didn't matter that the restaurant's seasonal changes had come to be expected rather than happily anticipated. And maybe it was The Four Seasons' fault that so few people ever complained anymore. Maybe success had made everyone too fat and contented. It was time for real change. Yet again.

More and more Margittai was spending his time

The 17th annual love letter was addressed not just to New Yorkers but to friends—and potential customers—all over the U.S.A.

at his home in Santa Fe, New Mexico, and Kovi caught up on travel plans delayed for the past three decades by his tenure at The Four Seasons. Regulars had come to depend on von Bidder and Niccolini for their care and feeding. After all, the two younger men had been at The Four Seasons for nearly twenty years, and they had certainly managed to bring in a younger, more handsome crowd of customers who took nothing for granted. While the old-timers brought gravitas to the proceedings, new faces brought vivacity.

It was revealing, then, that The Four Seasons' "17th annual love letter" was addressed not solely to New York, as had been the case for the first sixteen, but to "all our friends all over the USA." There was a change in the accompanying photograph, too, for 1990. Instead of repeating the old

Left (from left to right): Billy Joel, Ron Brown, Jann Wenner, and Christie Brinkley. Right (from left to right): Don Johnson, Melanie Griffith, Diane von Furstenberg, and Yoko Ono.

shot of Kovi and Margittai shaking hands atop the steps of the Park Avenue entrance, now there was a photo of Kovi and Margittai on the exact same spot, standing just above von Bidder and Niccolini—the kind of subtle but important photographic evidence Kremlinologists used to deconstruct who held power in Russia. The photo was telling the world that although the torch had not entirely passed to the younger men, von Bidder and Niccolini had taken their rightful place in the running of a landmark institution. Previous ads had featured von Bidder's and Niccolini's names and signatures, but this was the first time their faces had appeared.

The letter also made reference for the first time to events outside Manhattan's parochial boundaries—the breaking down of the Berlin Wall, troubles in the Middle East, and the sagging economy. With uncharacteristic concern for the future, the letter read, "In the face of uncertainty, we continue to place renewed emphasis on that master certitude we believe in, *quality*."

The commitment was not paper thin; it was real. Instead of retrenching and cutting back, as so many other New York restaurants did in 1990 and 1991, The Four Seasons spent a load of money to refurbish its luster. Since the premises had been redone only recently, effort was put mainly into the kitchen and service. New china designed by Tiffany & Co. was purchased, and The Four Seasons proudly cellared its own labels of chardonnay from Spring Mountain and pinot noir from the Napa Valley vineyard of Walter Schug. Albin and Battistini mounted lavish seasonal dinners four times a year, and Niccolini went after the top corporations in New York for their party business. Thus it was that *Rolling Stone* magazine, which in earlier

days might have thrown a party at a West Side disco or a downtown night-club, celebrated its twenty-fifth anniversary at The Four Seasons.

Left: Martin Scorcese (left), Eric Clapton, Jann Wenner, and an unidentified guest. Right: Fran Lebowitz (left) and John F. Kennedy Jr.

When the 1992 Democratic Convention came to New York, The Four Seasons, along with forty-nine other restaurants, invited delegates from every state for lunch with a celebrity and a New York power broker. The Wisconsin delegation walked up the stairs of The Four Seasons (some of the men were asked to put on a jacket over their plaid, short-sleeved shirts) and were graciously greeted by Julian Niccolini, who showed them to a table where he'd already seated Bianca Jagger.

Fully aware that the boom years of the big spenders had subsided—though those who were still around tended to dine at The Four Seasons as often as possible—Margittai, Kovi, von Bidder, and Niccolini lowered prices in the Grill Room to a bargain rate of $26.50 to $37.50 for a fixed-price, three-course meal, a tab less than the single price of an entrée fifty

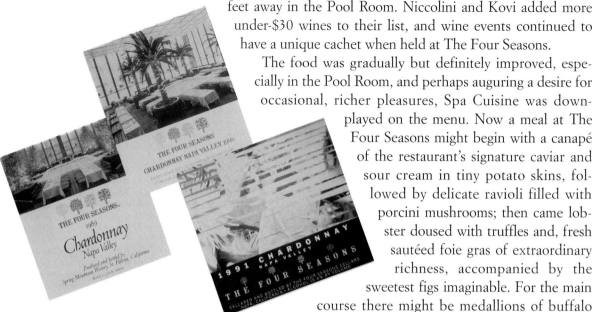

The Four Seasons had a California winery blend and bottle wines under the restaurant's own labels, one of which was designed by James Rosenquist.

feet away in the Pool Room. Niccolini and Kovi added more under-$30 wines to their list, and wine events continued to have a unique cachet when held at The Four Seasons.

The food was gradually but definitely improved, especially in the Pool Room, and perhaps auguring a desire for occasional, richer pleasures, Spa Cuisine was downplayed on the menu. Now a meal at The Four Seasons might begin with a canapé of the restaurant's signature caviar and sour cream in tiny potato skins, followed by delicate ravioli filled with porcini mushrooms; then came lobster doused with truffles and, fresh sautéed foie gras of extraordinary richness, accompanied by the sweetest figs imaginable. For the main course there might be medallions of buffalo with potatoes and roasted sun-dried tomatoes, wonderful French and Italian cheeses in peak condition with freshly baked raisin bread, and then a peach and black currant vacherin for dessert.

Some might even say, yes, The Four Seasons had returned to the way it had been in the old days. But in fact that was only partly true, for such ingredients had never been available in the old days—no fresh domestic foie gras, no porcini mushrooms, no buffalo, no cheeses of such flavor and texture. As had always been the plan, The Four Seasons had changed and moved inexorably upward, drawing to it the newest and best to be had in the market and preparing it with a simplicity only the finest chefs could master and only the most self-assured restaurants could serve.

As the recession ground on, The Four Seasons remained the same by changing each day. It remained fresh where other restaurants grew dim. It invested money where others cut back. And it continued to maintain standards in an industry that seemed to have lost sight of the social graces and the appeal of fine dining. Restaurants had, of necessity, become more casual, louder, and cheaper. So many of the gains in sophistication that had been pioneered by RA in the 1950s and refined by restaurateurs like Joe Baum, George Lang, Tom Margittai, and Paul Kovi had slipped into a tide of mediocrity that seemed to appeal to those less familiar with good manners, decorum, and the pleasures of a well-set, quiet table.

Medallions of Buffalo with Roasted Potatoes and Sun-dried Tomatoes

24 small new potatoes, about 1½ pounds, unpeeled
3 tablespoons vegetable oil
Salt and freshly ground black pepper
4 sprigs fresh rosemary, plus several more for garnish, if desired
4 buffalo medallions, about 6 ounces each
½ cup dry white wine
¼ cup sun-dried tomatoes, cut into thin julienne strips
¼ cup pitted olives, halved
1 cup *glace de viande* (see Note, page 54)
2 tablespoons chopped fresh parsley

1. Preheat the oven to 400° F. Wash and pat dry the potatoes. Place them in a medium baking dish and drizzle over 2 tablespoons of the oil. Shake the pan or stir the potatoes to coat in oil. Season with salt and pepper to taste. Add the rosemary. Bake, shaking the pan often to ensure even cooking, until the potatoes are tender, 30 to 35 minutes. Drain off any excess oil, remove the rosemary, and cover with foil to keep warm. Set aside.

2. Season the buffalo medallions on both sides with salt and pepper to taste. Add the remaining tablespoon of oil to a large skillet. Heat over medium-high heat. Add the buffalo and cook, turning once, until browned and slightly firm to the touch, 6 to 10 minutes. Remove to a large platter and cover with foil to keep warm.

3. Pour off any excess oil from the skillet. Add the wine and stir with a whisk over medium-high heat, picking up any bits from the bottom of the pan. Add the sun-dried tomatoes and olives. Boil until reduced by half. Add the *glace de viande* and return the buffalo to the sauce. Cook for 2 or 3 more minutes to warm through. Add the chopped parsley.

4. Place the buffalo on warm serving plates and surround with potatoes. Spoon over equal amounts of the sauce from the skillet. Serve at once, garnished with fresh sprigs of rosemary if desired.

Serves 4

Spring came late to New York in 1994, after the worst winter anyone could remember. There had been seventeen major snowstorms since Christmas, many of them on weekends, and all businesses had been hurt badly by the incessant, unstoppable blizzards that mounted inches of fresh snow upon inches of hardened ice, so that many New York streets were impassable for days on end.

Earlier in the autumn, The Four Seasons had taken measures to blunt the effects of the recession, which had just begun

to release its grip on the New York economy. The number of firings and loss of jobs by attrition had decimated Wall Street and other industries, but there were no layoffs at The Four Seasons. Instead, many in top management were asked to take a pay cut. "After a rough '92 and '93, we were predicting the worst for '94," said von Bidder, "but when not one single person balked at the pay cut, it was a sign of solidarity and commitment to The Four Seasons as we had always run it, and it had the effect of making us all work harder to maintain what we had worked so hard to build."

To everyone's surprise, however, the year-end holidays brought a flurry of business, large parties, and full reservations books throughout Christmas and New Year's. Miraculously, despite the pounding New York took from the winter storms of January and February, the restaurant managed to have a tremendously gratifying first quarter. The ship had been rocked and battered, and it not only survived, but continued on an even keel.

Tom and Paul spent as much time as possible looking in on their friends, but they had increasingly been enjoying semiretirement. The old-timers missed seeing them in the dining room but were happy that the two master restaurateurs were enjoying themselves after so many decades at a backbreaking job.

There were several other changes during those months. Chef Stefano Battistini left to open his own restaurant, and maître d' Oreste Carnevale, who had been at The Four Seasons since the 1960s, parted company with its management and went to work for the "21" Club.

In his place, The Four Seasons hired a young woman who had not even been born when The Four Seasons opened in 1959. She was not only the first woman to be Pool Room manager; she was the first person in over thirty years to take over the job, period. Her name was Karen Klein, and she had worked her way up from waitress to manager at a chic West Side restaurant named Remi.

"We had been considering change for some time," says Niccolini, "and we saw in Karen the kind of ebullience, *joie de vivre*, and beaming personality that was missing in the Pool Room. We didn't really even consider the fact that she was a female, although I know there was some initial resentment at our having such a young person—she was thirty at the time—taking over such a predominantly male dining room."

Klein had long dreamed of such a position at The Four Seasons. "For me, The Four Seasons is the pinnacle of New York restaurants. I love the theater of it all, meeting people from all over the world, yet treating them all as if they were special, whether they're spending forty or four hundred dollars here. From the moment they make their reservation to the time they leave the restaurant, I

want them to think they've had one of the most wonderful experiences imaginable. A good restaurant gives you what you want, but a great restaurant gives it to you before you even ask for it."

Such magnanimity was foremost on everyone's mind, and there was a concerted effort to mitigate the perception on the public's part that The Four Seasons was an elitist haven for the rich and famous.

Of course, regulars liked nothing better than to perpetuate that feeling. "It's like a private men's club," Bill Blass told the style magazine *W*, "except that I'd much rather have lunch here than at my club." Oliver Stone, the hypermacho film director and conspiracy theorist, put it in his own parochial terms: "I like to come here: It reminds me of my high-school cafeteria. I know all the boys here." A postrecession *New Yorker* cartoon showed one menacing-looking lion saying to another menacing-looking lion, "I'm taking you to the Four Seasons. You'll enjoy the fear."

The media continued breathlessly to use The Four Seasons as a buzzword for privilege and power. Magazines and newspapers such as *W*, *Vogue*, the *New York Times*, the *Daily News*, and the *Post* dutifully printed the guest lists of the most dazzling parties of the week held at The Four Seasons, which, as a venue, bestowed a heightened cachet on the events.

So often was the restaurant mentioned in the gossip columns that the *New York Observer* listed it at number thirty-three out of the hundred most mentioned institutions in the media, well ahead of Paramount Pictures, Christie's auction house, *Harper's Bazaar*, and even the hottest restaurant of 1997, Balthazar, which came in at number seventy-one.

However suspect the "power lunch" idea at The Four Seasons had become during the recession, it sprang back when the economy picked up. Indeed, as the *Times* reported, some very busy executives would have two, and even three, business lunches each day with different clients at power tables at different restaurants.

Yet the management of The Four Seasons was working very hard to blunt that image, insisting that all people, not just the regulars in the Grill Room, were welcome and would be treated like honored guests.

Of course, the gossip and society pages gleefully reported the goings-on of celebrities at The Four Seasons with renewed buzz—the more risqué the item the better, as when four "young, beautiful women" stripped naked at lunch and jumped into the pool. When their cavorting was over, they were offered tablecloths for cover. Asked by a *Post* reporter how and why it happened, the restaurant's director of advertising and promotions, Regina McMenamin, merely shrugged, "spring fever."

➤ Who says our customers are not flexible? Bill Johnston, a good friend, attended our Halloween dinner featuring several vintages of Château Petrus. At the end of the dinner and after a lot of good wine, he called over the captain and said, "Bring me a couple more bottles of that '61!" The captain was incredulous and told him there were no more in the entire United States. Johnston didn't blink and countered, "OK, how about six Heinekens?"

— ALEX VON BIDDER

A more deliberate pool episode, dutifully reported with plenty of pictures, occurred when actresses Raquel Welch and Lauren Hutton started a catfight at their table that ended with a well-orchestrated tumble into the bubbling waters—all part of an episode of a short-lived TV series called *Central Park West*.

One of the most widely reported news events of 1997 occurred the day *Vogue*'s editor-in-chief, Anna Wintour, was lunching at The Four Seasons and was told that a staffer from her magazine had just arrived with a package for her. At the moment Wintour realized that the person approaching her table was not a *Vogue* employee (Wintour insisted that the impostor's lack of style tipped her off), the woman revealed herself as a member of the animal-rights organization PETA, then dumped a dead raccoon onto Wintour's lunch plate, shouting, "Anna wears fur hats!" and fled down the stairs. So notorious was the incident that Wintour complained that people on the street addressed her as "the raccoon lady" for weeks after. And, just to set the record straight, she insisted, "The last time I wore a hat was in high school—when berets were mandatory."

With Kovi and Margittai's final transfer of their partnership to von Bidder and Niccolini in October 1995, the two younger men took full control of the restaurant. Despite the heady feeling of the moment, von Bidder and Niccolini felt anxious about the awesome challenge they faced. With the old guard gone, how would the old-timers react to the new? Had the two younger men bought into a dinosaur whose best years lay in the past? Would they be able to attract a younger crowd of clientele who previously felt that The Four Seasons was forbidding? Was The Four Seasons ready to enter the new millennium in a fresh and exciting way?

Raquel Welch and Lauren Hutton rehearsing a scene from Central Park West *that called for the two legendary actresses to tumble into the restaurant's pool during a tussle.*

◄ A few of my girl-friends and I were having a relaxing lunch in the Pool Room. One of my friends dared me to take a skinny dip in the pool. I guess the bubbles from our champagne must have gone to my head because when I looked around the room and noticed that we were all alone, I said, "Why not?" As soon as the captain left the room, I slipped out of my sundress and started dancing on the edge of the pool. The maître d' returned. Seeing me in nothing but a thong, he dashed over and begged me to put my clothes back on. Before he realized what was happening, my roommate decided to join the fun and took off her skirt and blouse. The maître d' dashed over and pleaded with her to get dressed. That's when my other two friends quickly stripped down and joined me in the pool. Needless to say, it was a very memorable afternoon and a delicious lunch that I won't soon forget.

— ANONYMOUS

The night of the transfer, von Bidder and Niccolini called Bose, Klein, and their other top people to a meeting, explaining that the torch had been passed and the challenge undertaken to keep the flame of The Four Seasons bright. "I want each of you to tell us how we can do things better, right down to every detail you can think of," said von Bidder. "We have the chance to make a big difference without alienating anyone, so change must come slowly and subtly, but surely."

Von Bidder's invitation to speak brought out a competitiveness among the staff that was refreshing. If some feelings were hurt or if some tried to assume an importance that would have shifted the balance, von Bidder and Niccolini were careful to take it all in and to introduce changes that everyone could agree on as positive. Most important was the directive that the supposed exclusivity of the past was to be replaced with an openness and gregarious welcome to all who came up that grand staircase—yet it had to be done without seeming contrived, forced, or lacking in New York sophistication.

Not unexpectedly, the changing of the guard seemed to give Julian license to act with an even more self-assured irreverence toward his

▼ Scene: Scene: Post-premiere party for the movie *Patch Adams*. The chefs had worked very hard cooking up a feast for the star of the movie, Robin Williams. Von Bidder thought they would really like to meet Williams, so he asked the actor to go back to the kitchen with him. "I'd love to," he said, "but right now I want to spend some time with my wife and daughters. Please come back in fifteen minutes." Von Bidder timidly went back after half an hour. Before he could say anything, Robin Williams jumped up and declared, "You're late. Let's go meet the chefs." The clowning around in the kitchen made the chefs' night, and von Bidder was impressed by Williams' example of putting his family first.

regular customers. When investment banker Pete Peterson had the good-natured audacity to complain about the Grill Room's $9.50 baked potato, Julian sent a bushel to his office. "Julian is outrageous, out of control and smart," said Joni Evans. "He's savvy and wonderful. He and Alex just have wit. Great style like Tom and Paul, but they are like the bad boys on the block."

Von Bidder described Julian's behavior as diplomatically as possible: "We have a lot of CEOs who only hear yes-men all day long. Then they come here, and they don't get that." Nevertheless, Niccolini took his greatest pleasure in greeting newcomers to the restaurant. One day, an elderly couple approached him at the top of the stairs and handed him a faded letter. They explained to him that they had had their first wedding anniversary at The Four Seasons twenty-nine years before and had been treated rather poorly by a captain. "It spoiled our anniversary," said the man, "so we wrote to the management and complained. They were nice enough to send us back this letter"—which apologized for the captain's behavior and invited them to return for dinner at another time. "Well, today is our thirtieth wedding anniversary," the man said proudly, "and we were just wondering if you might still honor this invitation."

Julian gave them his grandest smile and said, "Honor this? Why, we are honored to have you. Please follow me," and guided them to a wonderful table by the pool, sent out a fabulous dinner, and chose all the wines for them.

Such moments gave the staff the most delight, but there was also great satisfaction in the way that The Four Seasons had again become a staging ground for meetings and grand events whose promoters sought to give added weight to their proceedings by holding them at the restaurant. Holding Philip Johnson's ninetieth birthday there made perfect sense, of course, but when bulldog editor Steve Brill launched his magazine *Brill's Content*—whose cover boy was independent prosecutor Kenneth Starr—the party was held at The Four Seasons, despite—or because of—the magazine's mission to stick in the eye of the powerful media people who regularly dined there.

The prospect of being present at such parties or even to sit next to New York's elite had long been part of the restaurant's appeal. Even the nonchalant pose of a *New Yorker* writer dropped when she wrote of the Pool Room, "What with the sound of water and the half-acre that seems to surround every table, it's almost impossible to eavesdrop. Which is too bad: at any given moment the net worth of the room probably exceeds the gross national product of Canada." There was always a good deal of nodding in the Grill Room, especially since three or four tables each day were occupied by editors and publishers from Conde Nast mag-

OPPOSITE PAGE
TOP » *The Four Seasons executive sous chef, Fred Mero, gently instructing a cook.*
LEFT » *Niccolini sampling wine at the dinner debut of the 1995 Bordeaux vintage.*

➤ The redhead sashayed to the captain's station and was escorted to my table. She wore a chic, discreet Valentino pantsuit, not the white sheath you had hoped for. But it was the hair that socked your eye like a Roy Jones Jr. jab. Not a blood red. Not a red red. More of a burnt-umber red, an orange red. It was the perfect dye job. Her colorist had transformed her, the sexiest blonde in the world, into the booth beside me. Julian Niccolini, the imperious manager who will occasionally condescend to act as a sommelier, poured her a glass of wine from a bottle chilling in a silver bucket. She sniffed, swirled. "A Chassagne-Montrachet, yes?" She sipped again. "A Romanée-Conti." Niccolini removed the napkin to reveal the label. It was indeed a Romanée-Conti, an '89. Niccolini, intimidated, skittered away. She giggled as we clinked glasses. "Not bad, was I," said Sharon Stone.

— ART COOPER,
Editor-in-Chief,
GQ magazine

azines such as *Vogue*, *Vanity Fair*, *The New Yorker*, and *GQ*. One newspaper estimated that Conde Nast executives—including its owner, multibillionaire Si Newhouse, who dutifully got out of his casual office clothes and into a jacket and tie to dine at The Four Seasons—accounted for more than a quarter of the restaurant's daytime revenues, a ridiculous miscalculation, since Conde Nast executives were on any given day outnumbered by people from a dozen other industries and arts.

There was no question that the restaurant's popularity and reputation rested on its own celebrity and that of those who dined there, which was evident when *Vogue* editor-in-chief Wintour invited *New Yorker* editor-in-chief Tina Brown to have lunch with the visiting Princess Diana, just weeks before Diana's tragic death—an event Brown wrote of in her own pages from the perspective of her table that day at The Four Seasons.

Softening the cherished image of privileged dining was not easy. In a review of the restaurant in *New York* magazine, Corby Kummer sniped, "Even if the Grill Room is a nicer place to visit these days, you still won't want to live there, unless your name is Newhouse or Astor or Bronfman."

Such outdated presumptions angered von Bidder and Niccolini, who, even then, were grooming managers Trideep Bose and Karen Klein to be The Four Seasons' next generation of caretakers. Since taking over the restaurant, they and the staff had worked hard to blunt such criticism by making a decision to bring in a younger crowd. Too many New York restaurants had faded into geriatric obscurity or closed entirely for failing to freshen the customer base. There was also a concerted effort to improve the quality of the food so that it would rank with the finest in the world.

Both requisites became increasingly important as the recession was replaced by a long, dizzyingly wonderful economic boom in America—and nowhere was this more evident than in New York, where every industry rebounded with renewed enthusiasm for both creativity and making piles of money.

In the mid-'90s, New York was the capital of the world. It was cleaner, better run, less corrupt, and, astoundingly, far safer than it had been in decades. In fact, 1998's crime rate was the lowest since 1964, and there was a palpable feeling among New Yorkers and out-of-town visitors that the city was again an enchanting place to stroll the boulevards, shop, go to the theater, and dine.

Museums were packed, real-estate prices soared, the Dow-Jones average went above 9,000, and tickets to a Knicks-Bulls game were being scalped for $1,200 a seat. Broadway shows were jammed, and von Bidder saw an opportunity to cash in on the boom by signing a contract in 1996 with Tele-Charge, the city's largest ticket-reservations company, which enabled him to offer theatergoers a chance to purchase tickets along with a pre- or post-theater table at The Four Seasons, all on one charge transaction.

The restaurant scene was booming, too, with scores of new entries of every stripe into a market that seemed quite able to absorb them. Most of the excitement was downtown, around Union Square and in Greenwich Village, SoHo, and TriBeCa, with chic trattorias, bistros, and boîtes opening on every corner. Restaurants with names such as Moomba, Lot 61, and Pravda were more like nightclubs than dining rooms, but they were full of young people on the make who didn't seem to mind decibel levels that could deafen a jackhammer worker. Their initial popularity was driven by hype, of course. A notice that a supermodel and her Hollywood boyfriend had been spotted at a new faux-French bistro on Duane Street gave the place a good fifteen minutes' of success before passing its transitory fame to another place a block away.

Yet such restaurants were not all dross: Superbly trained, brilliant young chefs were cooking downtown—David Bouley at Bouley Bakery, Nobu Matsuhisa at Nobu, Stephen Kalt at Spartina, Mario Batali at Babbo, Tom Colicchio at Gramercy Tavern, and Diane Forley at Verbena—and they were extremely serious about their food, the wines in the cellar, and the service for their patrons, who were generally younger and more adventurous eaters than those who ate uptown.

Nevertheless, there was no slackening of restaurant activity in midtown. After twenty-five years on East 65th Street, the swank, high-society restaurant Le Cirque relocated to the Villard Houses in the Palace Hotel on Madison Avenue and 50th Street, with a dazzling Adam Tihany circus decor that had to fit into the art-nouveau appointments of the landmarked interiors. The restaurant cost more than $6 million to build and had 3,000 requests for reservations the day it opened. Le Cirque's former chef, Daniel Boulud, took over the former Le Cirque premises and turned them into a testament to modern French cuisine; this time, the price tag on the restaurant was more than $10 million.

Then there was Patroon, named after New York's original Dutch land barons, which owner Ken Aretsky deliberately positioned to pull

➤ The kitchen at The Four Seasons is a hospitable place. I should know. I spent much of the night there when I covered MCA's 1997 post-Grammy bash.

Since so many party-goers filled the restaurant, I couldn't get to Bruce Springsteen, Diana Ross, and the other celebs I needed to interview. So I cut through the kitchen, using this culinary oasis to scribble notes, grab an hors d'oeuvre, and chat with the staff about what I'd seen and heard.

On one of my many jaunts into the Grill Room, I ran into shock-rocker Marilyn Manson. Although he stared at me with two different colored eyes and had a black line drawn down the middle of his ghostly white face, our time together was quite pedestrian. Then he mentioned that his girlfriend was pregnant. I had to pull out the tape recorder for that one. "I'm just joking," he said, laughing. Some joke.

By the end of the night, I had made so many kitchen pit stops that the staff and I were practically family. And I was at least three pounds heavier.

— K.C. BAKER,
The New York Daily News

customers away from "21" (where he'd previously worked) and The Four Seasons. Patroon was to be a 1990s version of those two older restaurants, with a steaks-and-chops menu overseen by Franck Deletrain, stolen away from—not surprisingly—The Four Seasons. "Right now, New York is a much better city than it's been for years," Aretsky told *Esquire*. "There's such a tremendous amount of wealth no longer confined to a small group that the power base is much larger, and that's who I'm going after."

Despite all that, Patroon started to lose steam after its first dazzling year, even as the numbers at The Four Seasons climbed. Banquet business especially soared during the economic boom of the late '90s, and $100,000 parties that took over the entire restaurant for lunch and dinner were not unusual.

A whole new crowd began to develop for parties as dazzling as any held in New York. MCA Music threw its Grammy awards party at the restaurant, with its attendant rock and rap singers such as Bruce Springsteen, Elvis Costello, and Marilyn Manson gazing upon that grand Philip Johnson interior for the first time.

With the appearance of such arrivistes at the top of the grand staircase, some accommodations to dress had to be made, but as one New York newspaper reported, The Four Seasons offered underdressed patrons the very best blue blazers in various sizes. Ties were no longer required.

Parties that would once have been sedate and genteel became imaginative and fun. One night, a dinner for the Irvington Institute for Immunological Research featured a theme of old TV shows, leading The Four Seasons kitchen to rename its classic menu items A Brady Bunch of Broccoli, McHale's Navy Beans, Bionic Woman Beefsteaks, Macaroni and Kojak Cheese, and Name That Tuna. On another occasion, the party was a country hoe-down, and ducks were set swimming in the pool. When lifestyle guru Martha Stewart threw a promotional party at The Four Seasons, she had lawn furniture and umbrellas trucked in to replace the restaurant's tables and chairs.

Newness, not mere novelty, guided von Bidder and Niccolini's efforts. As part of a grand renovation in 1997, they closed the restaurant for nineteen days, installed a new $2 million, state-of-the-art kitchen, and replaced the pool, which had sprung a few leaks over the years, using the same Carrara marble as the original and installing fiber-optic lighting that enabled them to change the color of the water. For Saint Patrick's Day, it was emerald green, and when orange-juice producer Tropicana threw a party there, the water was the color of its product.

New, subtle lighting gave both rooms a cheeriness that put people at ease, and every staff member was instructed to treat all customers with absolute delight that they had chosen to dine at the restaurant, echoing Karen Klein's dream that all customers leave the restaurant believing that they've had one of the most wonderful experiences imaginable.

Their efforts succeeded on every front. In a 1996 *Gourmet* magazine readers' poll of favorite restaurants, The Four Seasons came in fifteenth out of twenty on the New York City list, and was rated "tops for business" overall. That same year, *Where*, a magazine placed on hotel-room night tables, polled its readers, who put The Four Seasons among tourists' top ten favorite restaurants in New York. A year later, The Four Seasons took the Grand Prize on that same list, surpassing Le Cirque 2000, Tavern on the Green, and Sardi's. After citing the usual litany of dead-or-alive celebrities—Jackie Onassis, Elizabeth Taylor, and Henry Kissinger—who frequented the restau-

ABOVE » *At the television-themed party thrown by the Irvington Institute, each table took on the guise of a classic television show.* OPPOSITE PAGE » *The Through-the-Kitchen Party invitation was cleverly disguised as a TV dinner to fit the event's theme.*

rant, *Where's* editors gushed, "Is there a restaurant in all New York destined to be so memorable?"

Von Bidder and Niccolini's methods were working well at a time of increasing competition from all segments of the restaurant-going public. Since opening in 1959, the restaurant had received very good notices for its food, even though the reviews at times sounded more respectful of the institution than ecstatic over the cooking. Albin, who had long been content to oversee the kitchen with a strategic eye toward control, efficiency, and consistency, was now encouraged to let his imagination soar without betraying the original vision of The Four Seasons to do American cuisine uncommonly well.

New talent was brought into the kitchen, such as Fred Mero from Ecuador and Pecko Zantilaveevan from Thailand, who added their own sense of seasoning and style to specials of the evening.

When Albin and pastry chef Patrick Lemblé were asked to cook at the James Beard House (to which The Four Seasons had donated its portrait of the great man himself, which used to hang in the small

FROM LEFT » *The Four Seasons kitchen during the $2 million renovation.*

upstairs private dining room), they showed a tremendous range of creativity—sweet-potato gnocchi with civet of wild boar, oysters wrapped in tuna sashimi, skate wings with heirloom tomatoes and cumin vinaigrette, the famous duck with apples and red cabbage, and various desserts.

The annual Bordeaux dinners were more popular than ever. In 1996, the event sold out for an evening that featured the '93 vintage of the Premier Crus, with host Madame Maryvonne Pinault of Château Latour commenting on the wines. A dinner spotlighting the glorious '92 vintage of Barolo was as spectacular as any given at the restaurant, and people begged to be put on a waiting list that started to grow the day that the event was announced.

For a Halloween dinner at which guests came dressed as witches, samurai warriors, and even Richard Nixon, the wines featured were Château Petrus and its California property Dominus, with owner Christian Moueix at the helm. When Moueix confessed that he hadn't enough of the great '61 vintage of Petrus to bring to New York, Edgar Bronfman, Sr., found enough in his own cellar to serve 180 people that night.

Recognizing The Four Seasons' commitment to California wines as well as knowing where the big spenders were, Domaine-Chandon of Napa Valley celebrated its twenty-fifth anniversary at the restaurant in June 1998.

The seasonal dinners became more dedicated to fine cuisine, eschewing the nouvelle extravagances of the past. The winter dinner of January 30, 1996, began with seared tuna tartare with '94 Landmark "Overlook" Chardonnay, then moved on to grilled squab with rosemary, wild mushrooms, and polenta with '93 Steele "Dupratt" Zinfandel,

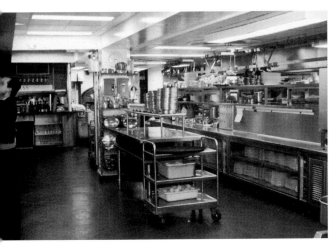 

braised short ribs of beef with parsnips puree with '92 Ridge York Creek Vineyard Petite Syrah, and chocolate hazelnut napoleon with Merryvale "Antiqua" Muscat.

When Niccolini announced that he would throw a party celebrating the great Tuscan wine Brunello di Montalcino, producers scrambled to get in on the evening, which ended up serving twenty-one different Brunellos to three hundred people, for whom Albin and his crew turned out a meal of oxtail terrine with salsa verde, black bass with a red-wine risotto, Hudson Valley foie gras with baked apple, filet of venison with sweet potato puree, and an almond semi-freddo. So lavish was the praise

LEFT» *A sneak peak inside the newly renovated Four Seasons kitchen.* RIGHT» *The Four Seasons chefs, from left to right: Pecko Zantilaveevan, Patrick Lemblé, Fred Mero, and Christian Albin.*

Niccolini with Taillevent owner Jean-Claude Vrinat.

for this tour de force that some guests asked why such dishes were not on the nightly dinner menu. Niccolini replied, "With the exception of the terrine, they all are."

Increasingly, The Four Seasons began inviting some of the world's acknowledged master chefs and some new young talents to hold dinners at the restaurant. One of its greatest coups was to coax Jean-Claude Vrinat, owner of Paris's great Taillevent, his chef Philippe Legendre, and patissier Giulles Bajolle to New York for celebratory dinners over two evenings (which sold out the day that they were announced) that would promote Taillevent's own label champagne. Vrinat had sworn never to leave Taillevent if the restaurant were open; for this trip to The Four Seasons, Taillevent was closed.

Because of such meals and because the day-to-day menu had taken on so many superb seasonal specials, The Four Seasons' culinary reputation rose beyond the respectful "classic good taste" that so many critics had previously noted. In fact, while never straying from the path of simple cooking in the American style, The Four Seasons menu had always evolved; it had just never paid any attention to culinary fads. For this reason, *Forbes* magazine continued to award the restaurant its highest accolade—four stars—and the Automobile Association of America repeatedly awarded the restaurant its highest, five diamonds.

In 1996, *Wine Spectator* magazine's readers' choice award for "the U.S. restaurant that delivers the best dining experience" went to The Four Seasons, especially for its "outstanding wine service," an honor replicated at the James Beard Foundation Restaurant Awards a year later, and followed a year after that by an outstanding service award.

For its celebration of the one hundred favorite foods, people, places, and things, *Saveur* magazine chose The Four Seasons, noting, "The food is expensive, seasonal, refreshingly simple, and alternately contemporary and traditional (foie gras with pineapple and pistachios and baked salmon in a potato crust with root vegetables; Caesar salad and aged double sirloin Bordelaise). The experience is unforgettable."

Bon Appetit pronounced that "the kitchen, under chef Christian Albin, has been getting better, producing food that is very much up-to-date while grounded in the classics," while the persnickety *Gayot* guide to New York restaurants gave The Four Seasons the same rating (sixteen out of twenty points) as it did to acknowledged culinary stars Le Bernardin, La Caravelle, Felidia, and Gramercy Tavern. Even Jane and Michael Stern, two indefatigable chroniclers of the best roadside eateries, barbecue pits, crab shacks, and taco stands of America, could not resist including one of the world's most elegant restaurants (wedged between write-ups of Eisenberg Sandwich Shop and Grabstein's Delicatessen) in their book, *Eat Your Way Across the U.S.A.*, sighing,

"Our favorite meal—utterly atypical of this kitchen, yet taste buds' siren call—is grilled calves' liver with onions and potatoes and creamed spinach on the side, followed by chocolate velvet cake. Accompanied, of course, by plenty of champagne."

But the most gratifying review was from Ruth Reichl of the *New York Times* in 1995. Reichl had recently been appointed restaurant critic after a long stint in the same job at the *Los Angeles Times*. At the beginning of her tenure in New York, she demonstrated a California slant on food that had taken more than one sacrosanct institution down a few pegs. Thus, her award of

Von Bidder and Niccolini celebrating their 1998 James Beard Award for Outstanding Service.

three stars (which the previous *Times* critic, Bryan Miller, had given in 1989) out of four was based primarily on the food, not the celebrity or landmark status of the restaurant. In her radio review of the food, she said, "The kitchen is at its best with unfussy food, like perhaps the most perfect duck in the city, beautifully presented broiled Dover sole and impeccable smoked salmon. The menus in the two rooms are similar at lunch, but at night the airy, romantic Pool Room gets the nod. Either way, a meal is an experience in pampering and privilege."

Another *Times* columnist, architecture critic Paul Goldberger, chimed in at a dinner given to celebrate the official landmarking of the restaurant, "Here did modern design achieve a kind of brilliant monumental interior that in the 1950's it had only barely begun to figure out how to do; here, also, did the art and business of making restaurants in this country change; here, of course, have more events of historic importance to New York taken place than there is room or time to list.

"Alex and Julian are not producing Four Seasons coffee bars on every corner, or Four Seasons branches in other cities. In an age of precious little authenticity, this restaurant is unique, a thing unto itself, a thing whose very existence seems to bespeak that rare commodity of authenticity, and whose identity is as closely tied to New York as the Brooklyn Bridge."

Von Bidder and Niccolini had what they'd long dreamed of. Now all they needed was a new lease to take The Four Seasons into the millennium. Their landlord hadn't changed, nor had the owners, but it had become increasingly clear that the landmark status that had taken so much time, effort, and money to achieve would pay off in the new negotiations. As a landmark, the interior of The Four Seasons could not be altered in any way (just as Le Cirque had discovered when it moved into the Villard Houses). The Lippold sculpture had to be maintained as an integral architectural fixture, and Seagram owned the famous Picasso tapestry. Since the interior was designed specifically to be a restaurant, there was no way to attract anyone but a restaurant client to the building.

The landlord's broker insisted that there had, in fact, been several restaurateurs who had approached him about the property, and there was no assurance that the space would be retained by Seagram, with von Bidder and Niccolini continuing as managing partners.

In 1997, there had been a huge battle for the lease on the World Trade Center's Windows on the World (which does not have landmark status), and the Joe Baum & Michael Whiteman Co. took control. Yet this same company had lost control of the grandest of New York nightclub-restaurants, the Rainbow Room, which they'd run for more than a decade. The new owners, the Cipriani family, which had put several branches of Venice's Harry's Bar in Manhattan, announced that major changes were under way to alter the Rainbow Room's extraordinary and unique art-deco beauty, despite media and public protest.

Nothing is ever sacred in New York, except perhaps The Four Seasons. After the usual tough negotiating, Seagram, von Bidder, and Niccolini signed a new lease with the landlord on November 11, 1998, guaranteeing at least seventeen more years of operation as The Four Seasons restaurant. When asked by the *Times* how far Seagram's largess extended toward Niccolini and von Bidder, Alex replied, "The words that come to mind are arts patron, not sugar daddy."

The joy of that moment had been sadly offset in that same year by the death of two men of immense importance to The Four Seasons.

➤ "I was enjoying a rare treat: dinner with my six-year-old son Josh. We were served ice water by the waiter as we sat down, and Joshua drank half a glass before we even ordered our food. Naturally, the waiter replenished our glasses as he took our order. Josh again drank some water and the waiter replenished his glass. The third time this happened, Josh said, "Dad, at this rate I will never be able to finish the glass!"

— GARY BUCKWALD,
Florist, Surroundings

Within months of each other, both Paul Kovi and Joe Baum passed away. Kovi, though retired, had never really been happy letting go of The Four Seasons. With Tom Margittai, he had been a great part of its evolution and of its critical middle period and had turned it into one of the most famous and profitable restaurants in the world. Margittai had been content to settle permanently in Santa Fe, New Mexico, but for Kovi the restaurant had been his life, and he missed seeing the regulars—those faces that were very happy to see his—and planning the wine dinners, and giving the place the warmth of his personality, which had never flagged. Yet he kept away from the restaurant for an entire year, but was finally coaxed back by von Bidder for a dinner at which the elder man told the younger how proud he was of what had

The 1999 Four Seasons management staff in the Grill Room.

*Four Seasons manager
Trideep Bose.*

been accomplished and maintained. It was Kovi's last visit to The Four Seasons. He died a few weeks later.

Not longer after, Joe Baum succumbed to cancer. Until the day he died, Baum was at work, planning new restaurants and consulting on others, still complaining that there was always something wrong with the consommé. His contribution to the earliest days of The Four Seasons—when it was little more than a fantasy for a restaurant that might have ended up being called "The Indoor-Outdoor Room" or "Season-o-Rama"—was incomparable, and he set as its goal the universal opinion that it was the greatest restaurant ever conceived and built. After forty years, as other multimillion-dollar restaurants, including some of his own, foundered and failed, Baum lived to see The Four Seasons become a testament to his vision.

Forty years; 160 seasons; hundreds of thousands of meals and oceans of wine. How many glasses had been broken? How many people jumped into the pool, with or without their clothes on? How many deals? Marriages? Divorces? Nominations made? How many acts of war and of conciliation? Spring fashion lines? Magazine covers? How much money had been earned and spent here? How much longer could it all go on?

For forty years, The Four Seasons has not just survived, but under successive owners, visionaries, bean counters, and personalities it is now thriving with all the vivacity of a hot new restaurant in SoHo. Business, like the New York economy itself, is booming, and von Bidder and Niccolini, working closely with Bose and Klein, feel that they have done the right thing both as caretakers of a great landmark institution and as partners in a business that made them comfortable and very much a part of New York social history. But just to make sure that the restaurant would continue to thrive in the face of any economic fluctuations, when the New York stock market got the jitters in autumn 1998, they dropped the fixed price in the Grill Room from $76 to $59, while the Pool Room pretheater dinner went for just $45.

So on a fine spring day in 1999, four decades into its existence and as embedded in New York's cityscape and social consciousness as the Statue of Liberty and the Empire State Building, the dining rooms of The Four Seasons were full and tingling with celebrity. Beverly Sills was dining with novelist Shirley Lord and TV newswoman Barbara Walters. ABC's Bob Iger was entertaining advertisers, as was Conde Nast's Steve Florio. Also in attendance were Primedia's CEO, Bill Reilly, *Parade* magazine's president, Carlo Vittorini, hotelier Leona

Helmsley, U.S. Ambassador to Hungary, Peter Tufo, and adman Jerry della Famina. Former mayor Ed Koch, now a TV judge, sat with his former archenemy, black activist and well-coiffed felon Al Sharpton, yakking it up about old times. There, too, was Philip Johnson, ninety-one years old, still master of all he surveyed.

It was not an atypical day in the Grill Room, and at night, as always, the Pool Room had most of the action, though far less celebrity. The reservations book was full, and had been so for more than a week in advance. Some had booked their tables months before, combining a dinner at The Four Seasons with a suite at the Pierre, two orchestra tickets to a revival of the musical *Cabaret*, brunch at the Palm Court in the Plaza Hotel, a visit to the Museum of Modern Art, and a horse-drawn carriage ride through Central Park.

As much as any other New York landmark, The Four Seasons continues to draw people for whom a visit to the city would not be complete without lunch in the Grill Room or dinner in the Pool Room.

So on this lovely, clear spring night, people arrived at The Four Seasons with great expectations. Many of them dined there regularly, every Saturday; others were there for the pretheater dinner, in by five-thirty, out by seven-thirty. But for most of the six hundred people who would dine there that night, it was a special occasion, perhaps a once-in-a-lifetime occasion when everything had to be perfect.

The weather cooperated. The sun was setting in a crystalline sky above the city's towers, and a full moon was on the rise over the East River. The doorman at The Four Seasons had changed into his pink jacket and the waiters into their pink sashes for spring, and the just-installed cherry-blossom trees in the Pool Room were in full silk bloom, and would be for the next three months.

The soft light of the city and the moon came through the metal curtains of the darkened Grill Room and was echoed in the small votive lights at the tables. Through the hallway, past the Picasso curtain, the Pool Room was filling fast after seven o'clock—there would be at least two seatings tonight—and the room already rang with the sound of people having a good time.

Trideep Bose received the parties at the top of the stairs and sent some off to the Pool Room, where Karen Klein greeted them warmly and assigned their tables. The new spring menu had, as always, taken full advantage of the season's offerings. There was shad and soft-shell crabs and spring peas and baby lamb.

For those who had never been to The Four Seasons, this would be a night to remember, for it seemed to sum up everything that made New York grand and wondrous: a setting like nowhere else in the world in a city unlike any other in the world. A place that, as the new restaurant critic for the *New York Post*, Steve Cuozzo, put it, "celebrates prosperity but not pretension. It is at once vast and intimate, cosmopolitan and cozy. And like the town it symbolizes, the Four Seasons has reinvented itself for a new day."

At one table, a famous jazz musician was finishing off the last spoonful of raspberry soufflé. At another, eight women were singing "Happy Birthday" to their friend as a waiter brought out The Four Seasons cotton-candy dessert.

Julian darted from one part of the room to another, directing the theatrics of the evening, joking with the regulars, gesturing flamboyantly as he guided an out-of-town couple, who seemed awed by the sight of the pool in the middle of the dining room, to their table. A captain was discussing the merits of an Italian sparkling wine with

Four Seasons co-owners Julian Niccolini and Alex von Bidder looking back on the restaurant's 40-year history.

a mathematician from California. A party of six Japanese businessmen were finishing their second round of drinks and then all ordered the same exact meal. And every man who passed by the table where an exquisitely beautiful model sat sipping a martini fell in love with her.

By ten-thirty, the dining rooms had begun to clear of guests, but other guests were arriving after the theater. A young couple, arm in arm, came slowly up the stairs, their eyes full of wonder at what they beheld. They walked toward the maître d's desk, where Julian was on the phone.

"May I help you?" he said as he hung up.

The man spoke with hesitancy. "Well, this is our first time in New York and we just came from the theater, and I'm sorry, but we don't have a reservation. But we've heard so much about this place, we just wondered if you might have a table for the two of us?"

Julian's eyes warmed with pleasure. "A table for two? Of course we do. We've been waiting just for you."

Acknowledgments

The first time I went to The Four Seasons, I walked out on the bill.

Some college friends and I, seeking a grand gesture at the end of the school year, decided to treat ourselves to drinks at The Four Seasons, never even considering ordering any food—any morsel of which would have wiped out our monthly meal allowance.

We climbed the stairs to the bar, where we ordered one round of drinks and subsequently found ourselves ignored by a waiter twice our age and grumpier than any of our fathers. Nothing could rouse him to return to our table, so, having finished, we got up and walked quickly down the stairs and out into the street, laughing hysterically that we'd put one over on The Four Seasons.

I suppose writing an authorized history of The Four Seasons may be my penance for that disgraceful exit. But in reality, it has been a joy to work with some of the true professionals of the restaurant business in piecing together what I believe is a remarkable story of an institution and the city in which it is set.

Originally I was approached by Alex von Bidder, currently manager and co-owner of The Four Seasons, to see if I'd be interested in such a project. I told Alex I would only undertake it if I could write the story as I believed it to have happened and make my own assessments and judgments about the good times and the bad. I am delighted to report that no one at The Four Seasons asked me to excise a single sentence from my manuscript, with the exception of two brief anecdotes about two current regular customers. "Authorized" though this book may be, it is, for better or worse, entirely mine, dependent on The Four Seasons only for correcting errors of fact and for the massive amounts of research material put freely at my disposal.

My first debt of gratitude, therefore, goes to Alex for opening doors every step of the way to those who might otherwise have remained silent. So, too, I thank Tom Margittai and Paul Kovi, co-owners of this remarkable institution, who took it from a foundering failure to an unparalleled success and who have guided it through recessions and recastings since the early 1970s.

Without the support of my editor, Erica Marcus, in maintaining the integrity of this book's contents, I would never have proceeded with it at all. And for her encouragement and advice, my agent Diane Cleaver has been an invaluable guide for more than a decade of my professional life. So many other people were so kind in providing extensive information and reminiscences about The Four Seasons and the restaurant business that I can do little more than thank them en masse. My sincere thanks to Joe Baum, Jerry Brody, George Lang, Stuart Levin, Philip Johnson, Julian Niccolini, Phyllis Lambert, Roger Martin, Philip Miles, Irena Chalmers, Fred Rufe, Edison Price, Ada Louise Huxtable, Alan Reyburn, Max Pine, George Lois, Lee Eisenberg, Marion Gorman, and Charles Pierce.

As always, thanks to my wife, Galina, who still puts up with a husband who sits at home all day writing.

Photo Credits

The authors gratefully acknowledge the use of photographs from the following sources. Every effort has been made to trace the proper copyright holders of the photographs used herein. If there are any omissions, we apologize, and we will be pleased to make the appropriate acknowledgments in future printings.

Julian Allen: page 97, page 156; Tom Allen of the Washington Post, courtesy of The Four Seasons: page 40 (top left); *Architectural Record,* November 1959, copyright © 1959 by McGraw-Hill, Inc. All rights reserved. Reproduced with the permission of the publisher: pages 50–51, page 145; Copyright © by Miles Austin Photography, courtesy of The Four Seasons: page 189; Courtesy of Joe Baum: page 8 (top), page 9, page 17; Camera Associates, courtesy of The Four Seasons: page v (third from top), page 30; Bela Cseh, courtesy of The Four Seasons: page 69 (left and right), page 98 (left and right), page 99 (right); Frank Donato, courtesy of The Four Seasons: page iv, page 39; S. Karin Epstein, courtesy of The Four Seasons: page 101, page 114 (top right), page 126; Dana Fineman/Sygma, courtesy of The Four Seasons: page 96; Courtesy of The Four Seasons: page x (top and bottom), page xi, page xiv, page 12, page 20 (top right), page 21, page 29, page 31, page 32, page 33, page 34 (top), page 37 (right), page 40 (bottom left), page 40 (bottom right), page 41, page 44, page 45, page 46, page 62 (top left), page 62 (bottom right), page 68, page 71, page 72 (top left), page 72 (bottom right), page 73, page 78, page 80, page 84 (bottom right), page 85, page 86, page 89, pages 90–91, page 93, page 95, page 99 (left), page 103, page 104, page 108, page 109, page 110, page 114 (bottom left), page 114 (bottom right), page 115, page 118, page 120, page 121, page 122, page 125, page 137, page 149, page 151, page 152, page 153, page 158, page 159, page 166 (top right and bottom left), page 168, page 170, page 171, page 172, page 176, page 180 (bottom left), page 181, page 191, page 194; Oberto Gili, courtesy of House & Garden. Copyright © 1984 by The Condé Nast Publications, Inc.: page 166 (top left), page 175; Copyright © by Henry Grossman, courtesy of The Four Seasons: page 185; Copyright © by Mary Hilliard, courtesy of The Four Seasons: page viii, page 180 (top right), page 183 (left and right), page 186 (left and right), page 187 (left and right); Impact Photos, courtesy of The Four Seasons: page 1, page 34 (bottom); Copyright © by Insights, courtesy of The Four Seasons: page 35, page 36 (left), page 62 (bottom left), page 70, page 184, page 200; Tim Kantor, courtesy of The Four Seasons: page 72 (top right); Copyright © by Matthew Klein: page v (second from top), page 84 (top); Copyright © 1993 by Mark Kozlowski: page 198; Copyright © by Roxanne Lowit, courtesy of The Four Seasons: page 180 (top left), page 180 (bottom right), page 192–193; M Magazine/Fairchild Publications: page 106; Jack Manning/NYT Pictures, courtesy of The Four Seasons: page xvii, page 20 (top left); Cyril Morris, courtesy of The Four Seasons: page 114 (top left); Al Naidoff, courtesy of The Four Seasons: page 92; The New York Post, April 25, 1989: page 131; NYT/Pictures: page 84 (bottom left); Edward Ozern, courtesy of The Four Seasons: page 64; Louis Reens, courtesy of The Four Seasons: page v (bottom), page 20 (bottom left and right), page 36 (right), page 37 (left); Courtesy of Restaurant Associates: page 8 (bottom), page 72 (bottom left); Copyright © Salou Design, Ltd., American Ballet Theater Dances at Dinner, Decoration and Flowers, photography by Bill Cunningham, courtesy of The Four Seasons: page 166; Paul Schumach, courtesy of The Four Seasons: page 67; Seagram Building 1956–58. Architects: Ludwig Mies van der Rohe and Philip Johnson. Photograph by Ezra Stoller, 1958. Lent by Joseph E. Seagram & Sons Inc.: page xviii, page 167; Copyright © by Mark Seliger: page 105; Ezra Stoller, 1958. Architects: Ludwig Mies van der Rohe and Philip Johnson. Lent by Joseph E. Seagram & Sons, Inc.: page 6; Copyright © by U.P.I/Bettman: page 5; Dan Wynn, courtesy of The Four Seasons: page vi, page v (top); Joel Yale, Life Magazine © Time Warner: page 40 (top right), page 53; Dudley-Anderson-Yutzy, courtesy of The Four Seasons: page xv, page 62 (top right).

PAGE NUMBERS IN ITALICS REFER TO PHOTOGRAPHS OR ILLUSTRATIONS

CONVERSION CHART
EQUIVALENT IMPERIAL AND METRIC MEASUREMENTS

American cooks use standard containers, the 8-ounce cup and a tablespoon that takes exactly 16 level fillings to fill that cup level. Measuring by cup makes it very difficult to give weight equivalents, as a cup of densely packed butter will weigh considerably more than a cup of flour. The easiest way therefore to deal with cup measurements in recipes is to take the amount by volume rather than by weight. Thus the equation reads:

1 cup = 240 ml = 8 fl. oz.   ½ cup = 120 ml = 4 fl. oz.

It is possible to buy a set of American cup measures in major stores around the world.

In the States, butter is often measured in sticks. One stick is the equivalent of 8 tablespoons. One tablespoon of butter is therefore the equivalent to ½ ounce/15 grams.

LIQUID MEASURES

Fluid ounces	U.S.	Imperial	Milliliters
	1 teaspoon	1 teaspoon	5
¼	2 teaspoons	1 dessert spoon	7
½	1 tablespoon	1 tablespoon	15
1	2 tablespoons	2 tablespoons	28
2	¼ cup	4 tablespoons	56
4	½ cup or ¼ pint		110
5		¼ pint or 1 gill	140
6	¾ cup		170
8	1 cup or ½ pint		225
9			250, ¼ liter
10	1¼ cups	½ pint	280
12	1½ cups	¾ pint	340
15	¾ pint		420
16	2 cups or 1 pint		450
18	2¼ cups		500, ½ liter
20	2½ cups	1 pint	560
24	3 cups or 1½ pints		675
25		1¼ pints	700
27	3½ cups		750
30	3¾ cups	1½ pints	840
32	4 cups or 2 pints or 1 quart		900
35		1¾ pints	980
36	4½ cups		1000, 1 liter
40	5 cups or 2½ pints	2 pints or 1 quart	1120
48	6 cups or 3 pints		1350
50		2½ pints	1400
60	7½ cups	3 pints	1680
64	8 cups or 4 pints or 2 quarts		1800
72	9 cups		2000, 2 liters

SOLID MEASURES

U.S. and Imperial Measures		Metric Measures	
ounces	pounds	grams	kilos
1		28	
2		56	
3 ½		100	
4	¼	112	
5		140	
6		168	
8	½	225	
9		250	¼
12	¾	340	
16	1	450	
18		500	½
20	1¼	560	
24	1½	675	
27		750	¾
28	1¾	780	
32	2	900	
36	2¼	1000	1
40	2½	1100	
48	3	1350	
54		1500	1½
64	4	1800	
72	4½	2000	2
80	5	2250	2¼
90		2500	2½
100	6	2800	2¾

OVEN TEMPERATURE EQUIVALENTS

Fahrenheit	Celsius	Gas Mark	Description
225	110	¼	Cool
250	130	½	
275	140	1	Very Slow
300	150	2	
325	170	3	Slow
350	180	4	Moderate
375	190	5	
400	200	6	Moderately Hot
425	220	7	Fairly Hot
450	230	8	Hot
475	240	9	Very Hot
500	250	10	Extremely Hot

LINEAR AND AREA MEASURES

1 inch	2.54 centimeters
1 foot	0.3048 meters
1 square inch	6.4516 square centimeters
1 square foot	929.03 square centimeters